Lofts
Living, working, and trading in a loft

Lofts
Living, working, and trading in a loft

h.f.ullmann

LOFTS
All Rights Reserved
Copyright © Atrium Group 2003
Text Copyright © Atrium Group 2003
Artwork and Commissioned Photography Copyright © Atrium Group 2003

Author
Arco Team

Editorial package:
Loft Publications, s.l.
Domènech 7-9, 2° 2ª
08012 Barcelona, Spain
Tel: + 34 93 218 30 99
Fax: + 34 93 237 00 60
e-mail: loft@loftpublications.com
www.loftpublications.com

Editor
Lola Gómez

Graphic design and typesetting
Mireia Casanovas Soley, Jaume Martínez Coscojuela, Emma Termes Parera

Text
Lola Gómez, Dieter Kramer (Kreuzberg. Berlín), Manel Bailo and Rosa Rull (idea for Loft Manual), Marçal Navarro, (realisation of Loft Manual)

Copy editor
Susana González Torras

Project co-ordinator
Silvia Gómez de Antonio

We have made every effort to contact the holders of the copyright for the images published in this book. In some cases we have not succeeded, and so we suggest that the owners of these copyrights contact the publishing company (loft@loftpublications.com).

Original title:
Lofts: Vivir, trabajar y comprar en un loft
ISBN: 978-3-8331-2569-0

© for the English edition: 2006/2007 Tandem Verlag GmbH
h.f.ullmann is an imprint of Tandem Verlag GmbH

Translation from Spanish into English:
Matthew Clarke in association with First Edition Translations Ltd., Cambridge UK
Editor: Jenny Knight in association with First Edition Translations Ltd., Cambridge UK
Typeset: The Write Idea in association with First Edition Translations Ltd., Cambridge UK

Printed in China

ISBN: 978-3-8331-4632-9

10 9 8 7 6 5 4 3 2 1
X IX VIII VII VI V IV III II I

All rights reserved. Any reproduction, either total or partial, of this work via any medium or process, including reprography, computer treatment and the distribution of copies for renting or public lending, is strictly forbidden, under the penalties established by law, unless the holders of the copyright grant their written consent.

Introduction		12
Origins. New York		18
Legacy. London		24
Kreuzberg. Berlin		32
Loft manual		94
Essentialist loft		128
Living in a loft		132
Luminous environment	Peter Tow Studios	134
Dualities	Dean/Wolf Architects	140
Visual freedom	Alexander Gorlin	146
Chelsea district	Kar-hwa Ho Architecture & Design, S. Sirefman	152
Intimacy	Kar-hwa Ho Architecture & Design	160
K-Loft in New York	George Ranalli	166
Potter's loft	Resolution: 4. Architecture	172
Monolithic structure	Resolution: 4. Architecture	178
Renaud Residence	Cha & Innerhofer	184
Spatial flexibility	Kar-hwa Ho Architecture & Design	190
New trends	Hardy Holzman Pfeiffer Associates	196
Apartment in Manhattan	Shelton, Mindel & Associates	204
Residence for artists	Abelow Connors Sherman Architects	210
Urban interface	Dean/Wolf Architects	216
An industrial touch	Alexander Jiménez	224
A blank canvas	Vicente Wolf	230
Play of light	Moneo Brock Studio	236
Rosenberg residence and studio	Belmont Freeman Architects	242
Minimalist continuity	Form Werkstatt	248
Versatility	Abelow Connors Sherman Architects	254
O'Malley residence	Carpenter/Grodzins Architects	260
Accessibility	Paul Guzzardo, Ray Simon	266
Number 1709 Studio	Paul Guzzardo, David Davis	272
Sophisticated innovation	Cecconi Simone Inc.	278

Private residence	Cecconi Simone Inc.	284
House and studio	Fernando Campana	292
Formal unity	Knott Architects	298
Translucent floors	Fraser Brown McKenna Architects	304
White and empty	Hugh Broughton Architects	308
New Concordia Wharf	Mark Guard Architects	312
Oliver's Wharf	McDowell + Benedetti Architects	318
London post office	Orefelt Associates	324
Home for a painter	Simon Conder Associates	330
FOA London	FOA. Foreign Office Architects	336
Conversion of a warehouse	Adam Caruso, Peter St. John	342
Wall Street lofts	Chroma AD. Alexis Briski + Raquel Sendra	346
Attics on Wardour Street	CZWG Architects	352
Lee House	Derek Wylie	356
Loft in Clerkenwell	Circus Architects	364
Unit 203	Buschow Henley & Partners	370
Chromatic treatment	AEM	376
Interior landscape	Florian Beigel Architects	382
Neutral space	Felicity Bell	388
No restrictions	Blockarchitecture: Graeme Williamson + Zoe Smith	394
Kopf loft	Buschow Henley	400
Light from all sides	Buschow Henley	404
Piper Building	Wells Mackereth Architects	410
Change in function	Project Orange: Christopher Ash, James Soane	416
Number 8C, French Place	Project Orange: Christopher Ash, James Soane	420
Spatial contrast	María Rodríguez-Carreño Villangómez	426
Leisure and business	Ramón Úbeda/Pepa Reverter	434
La Nau	Carol Iborra, Mila Aberasturi	442
Urban panorama	Antoni Arola	450
Vapor Llull	Cirici & Bassó, Inés Rodríguez, Alfonso de Luna,	
	Norman Cinamond, Carla Cirici	458

Apartment for an actress	Franc Fernández	464
Verticality	Pere Cortacans	470
Austerity or design	Joan Bach	476
Working from home	Helena Mateu Pomar	482
Efficient distribution of space	Joan Bach	488
Camden Lofts	Cecconi Simone Inc.	494
House in Igualada	Pep Zazurca i Codolà	500
Fitting out an attic	A-cero estudio de arquitectura y urbanismo SL	506
Interior garden	Alain Salomon	512
Visual connections	Christophe Pillet	520
Home and studio	Christophe Pillet	526
Cluster of lofts	Alain Salomon	532
Spaciousness	Patrizia Sbalchiero	538
House for a painter	Antonio Zanuso	546
House in San Giorgio	Studio Archea	552
Transparencies	Rüdiger Lainer	558
Ecological apartment	Lichtblau & Wagner	564
Loft in Bruges	Non Kitch Group	570
Old spinning mill	Ernst & Niklaus Architekten ETH/SIA	576
Sopanen/Sarlin Loft	Marja Sopanen + Olli Sarlin	584
Working in a loft		590
@radical.media	Rockwell Group	592
Connors Communications	Lee H. Skolnick Architecture + Design	598
Design studio in Tribeca	Parsons + Fernández-Casteleiro	604
Sunshine Interactive Network	Gates Merkulova Architects	608
Miller-Jones studio	LOT/EK	612
Stingel studio	Cha & Innerhofer	616
Three spaces in one	Tow Studios Architecture	622
WMA Engineers	Valerio Dewalt Train Architects	628
BBDO West	Beckson Design Associates	632

Rhino Entertainment	Beckson Design Associates	638
MTV Networks	Felderman + Keatinge Associates	644
Praxair Distribution, Inc.	Herbert Lewis Kruse Blunck Architecture	650
Meyocks & Priebe Advertising, Inc.	Herbert Lewis Kruse Blunck Architecture	656
German Design Center	Norman Foster & Partners	662
Nuremberg	Wirth	666
Michaelides & Bednash	Buschow Henley	670
Shepherd's Bush Studios	John McAslan & Partners	676
London Merchant Securities	John McAslan & Partners	680
Advertising agency	John McAslan & Partners	686
Derwent Valley Holding	John McAslan & Partners	692
Thames & Hudson	John McAslan & Partners	696
Williams Murray Banks	Pierre d'Avoine Architects	702
Metropolis Studios Ltd.	Powell-Tuck, Connor & Orefelt	706
Studio in Glasgow	Anderson Christie Architects	712
Labotron. Offices and workshops	Pep Zazurca i Codolà	718
Double You	Marc Viader i Oliva	724
Hispano 20	José Ángel Rodrigo García	730
Montardit SA	Josep Juvé & Núria Jolis	736
GCA	GCA Arquitectes Associats	742
Casadesús studio	Antoni Casadesús	748
B & B studio-home	Sergi Bastidas	754
Studio in Madrid	Enrique Bardají	762
Empty SA	Víctor López Cotelo	768
Salamanca neighborhood	Manuel Serrano, Marta Rodríguez Ariño	774
Cyclorama	Manuel Serrano, Marta Rodríguez Ariño	780
Architecture studio	José Miguel Usabiaga Bárcena	786
IU-EB headquarters	José Miguel Usabiaga Bárcena	794
Studio Naço offices	Studio Naço	802
Silos in Amsterdam	Die architectengroep	808
Architecture office	Jacob Zeilon & Partners	816

Trading in a loft		820
R 20th Century	Mike Solis + Nick Dine / Dinersan Inc.	822
Spazionavigli	RBA. Roberto Brambilla & Associates	830
Shin Choi in New York	Wormser + Associates	838
Knitwear	Bailo + Rull. ADP. Arquitectes Associats	844
Round Store	Pep Zazurca i Codolà	850
Joan Lao Mobiliario	Joan Lao	854
Esprit	Citterio & Dwan	860
Preu Bo	Joan Lao	866
Becara	Emilio Tárraga + Pascua Ortega	874
La Farinera del Clot	Josie Abascal	878
ArtQuitect	Francesca Ricós Martí	884
In Mat. ArtQuitect	José Luis López Ibáñez	890
Magna Pars	Luciano Maria Colombo	898
Progetto Lodovico	Luciano Maria Colombo	904
Nani Marquina showroom	Nani Marquina	910
1997 showcase	Estudi Metro	916
1996 showcase	Francesc Rifé & Associats	922
Two Italian showrooms	King-Miranda Associati	928
P.S.1 Museum	Frederick Fisher, David Ross, Joseph Coriaty	936
Dromokart	Florencia Costa Architecture	942
Talls Tallats	Eugeni Boldú, Orlando González	948
Bar Zoom	Pau Disseny Associats	956
Club Cabool	Lorens Holm, Ray Simon	962
Taxim Nightpark	Branson Coates	968
Paci Restaurant	Roger Ferris + Partners Llc.	974
Restaurante Porto Colom	B&B Estudio de arquitectura	980
Restaurante Thèatron	Philippe Starck	984
Belgo Centraal	Ron Arad, Alison Brooks	990
Belgo Zuid	FOA. Foreign Office Architects	996

Photograph courtesy of Ramón Úbeda and Pepa Reverter.

"Lofts were once

spaces, nothing more than mere spaces"

Marcus Field

Introduction

The *Oxford English Dictionary* defines "loft" as a relatively large, generally open space found on each floor in multistory industrial buildings and warehouses in the United States. It can also describe an attic or upper floor. These days, however, "loft" is applicable to any large rehabilitated space whose original structure has been adapted for domestic use.

In *Loft Living: Culture and Capital in Urban Change* (Rutgers University Press, 1989), Sharon Zukin writes:

"While loft buildings are constructed on a comparatively small scale, their proportions are generous. Usually they have five to ten stories, with 2,000–10,000 square feet [180 to 900 sq m] of space on each floor. Older loft buildings have only a freight elevator, but newer ones also have passenger elevators. Ceilings are high – 12–15 feet [3.5 to 4.5 m] – and are supported by either vaulted arches (in smaller buildings) or columns. Architectural detail is often classical, reflecting late-19th-century taste for the Italian Renaissance. Columns in loft buildings are frequently fluted, and the building façades are generally cast iron, which marks an important innovation of the time in the industrialization of construction technique. In contrast to the construction materials used in modern buildings, those used in loft buildings are more solid (brick and iron) and more valuable (often oak flooring and even copper window sills). Because loft spaces are indeed "lofty," they offer the potential for drama in everyday life. Lofts are good for exhibiting large works of art, using professional stoves and refrigerators, luxuriating in mammoth whirlpool baths, and experimenting with an avant-garde *mise en scène* or décor. In short, lofts present a perfect setting for gracious late-20th-century living."

Loft: illegal space

In the early days of the loft movement, which emerged in SoHo in the 1950s, occupying industrial buildings for residential purposes was illegal, and so, right from the start, the movement constituted, above all else, a new – and clandestine – way of living.

The first inhabitants of lofts were students and artists with few financial resources but a great need for space. Their defense of an architectural style considered obsolete by the industry, turned them into activists, who soon came to represent a lifestyle in which art formed an integral part of everyday life. The spatial characteristics of the loft anticipated the open planning that would be championed by the modern movement. Monsieur Hulot, the film character, summed it up as follows: "Oh, c'est si practique, tout communique" (Oh, it's so practical, everything joins up.) (*Mon Oncle*, 1958, Jacques Tati).

This book gathers together over 150 loft projects from all over the world. The opening section describes the origins of the loft as a feature of urban development in the heart of cities such as New York, London, and Berlin. A longer section takes a look inside lofts that were meticulously designed in the last decade of the 20th century as an ideal space for living, working, or trading.

By recycling old and abandoned commercial spaces and converting them into shops, studios, or business premises, the inhabitants of lofts show their deep respect for the history and architecture of their cities.

"Don't give up, the occupation continues!"

Nancy Robbins was born in Michigan, USA, and studied at the Rhode Island School of Design. In 1986 she opened a furniture shop in Barcelona, where she currently lives and works as a designer and interior decorator. She has won several awards and her designs have been marketed by a number of companies since 1988. She has given lectures in Spanish universities and in Korea and has exhibited in Spain and Italy.

Here there's always something to decide tomorrow

The elevator is big and full of dents and messages
from passengers put out by its slowness
and the work that has brought them here.

They have all left their marks.

I'm drawn to living inside this world stripped of any embellishment that hides its use.

I like the contrast between the noise of the daytime activity
and the silence of the nights and weekends
when everything is abandoned.

I feel freer with so much space.

The enormous distance between one place and another,
the four-meter- [13-foot] high ceiling,
the line of windows looking out on the confusion of antennas
and chimneys
and badly kept roofs
... this is a loft.

With so much space it's easy to forget that people outside exist,
one can do without curtains and leave the windows open.
"They" can see you, but what the hell,
you feel as if the space wraps itself around you and protects you.

We have the notion that we can change everything.
Maybe we don't often do it,
but just knowing that the possibility exists
is exciting.

Images courtesy of Tsutomu Kurokawa, furniture designer for the Japanese company Out. DESIGN CO. LTD. " Photographs: Kozo Takayama.

We notice the changes in light over the course of the year.
Probably what we're thinking now will not be what we think tomorrow.
I suppose that tomorrow we'll feel different…
Tomorrow what was right here will be better there.

We hang up a wrought-iron candelabra,
inherited from some tacky workshop where it shone
daubed with gold paint
which was long ago eaten up by rust
until an inimitable patina remained.
The height of the ceiling means that we can light the candles over the dining-table
and as there's no need for electricity we can move them from place to place.

Now the chairs, so many chairs, serve as rests for folders,
books and piles of magazines,
like a cluster of side-tables
that turn into chairs when required.

In the summer heat we can free the bed from the walls,
a bed "without head or feet,"
a volume floating in space… a couch,
an ideal place for a picnic, for reading, for breathing.

And when the cold arrives we put the bed back in a more sheltered and intimate spot.

I don't know what we'll do with the ping-pong table.
Sometimes it serves its intended purpose,
but at other times it ends up as a catch-all.
I don't know, I don't know… should it go or should it stay?
It could also be used as a banqueting table…
It's a good thing it can be folded up and we can decide tomorrow,

Here there's always something to decide tomorrow,

Nancy Robbins, Barcelona, August 2000

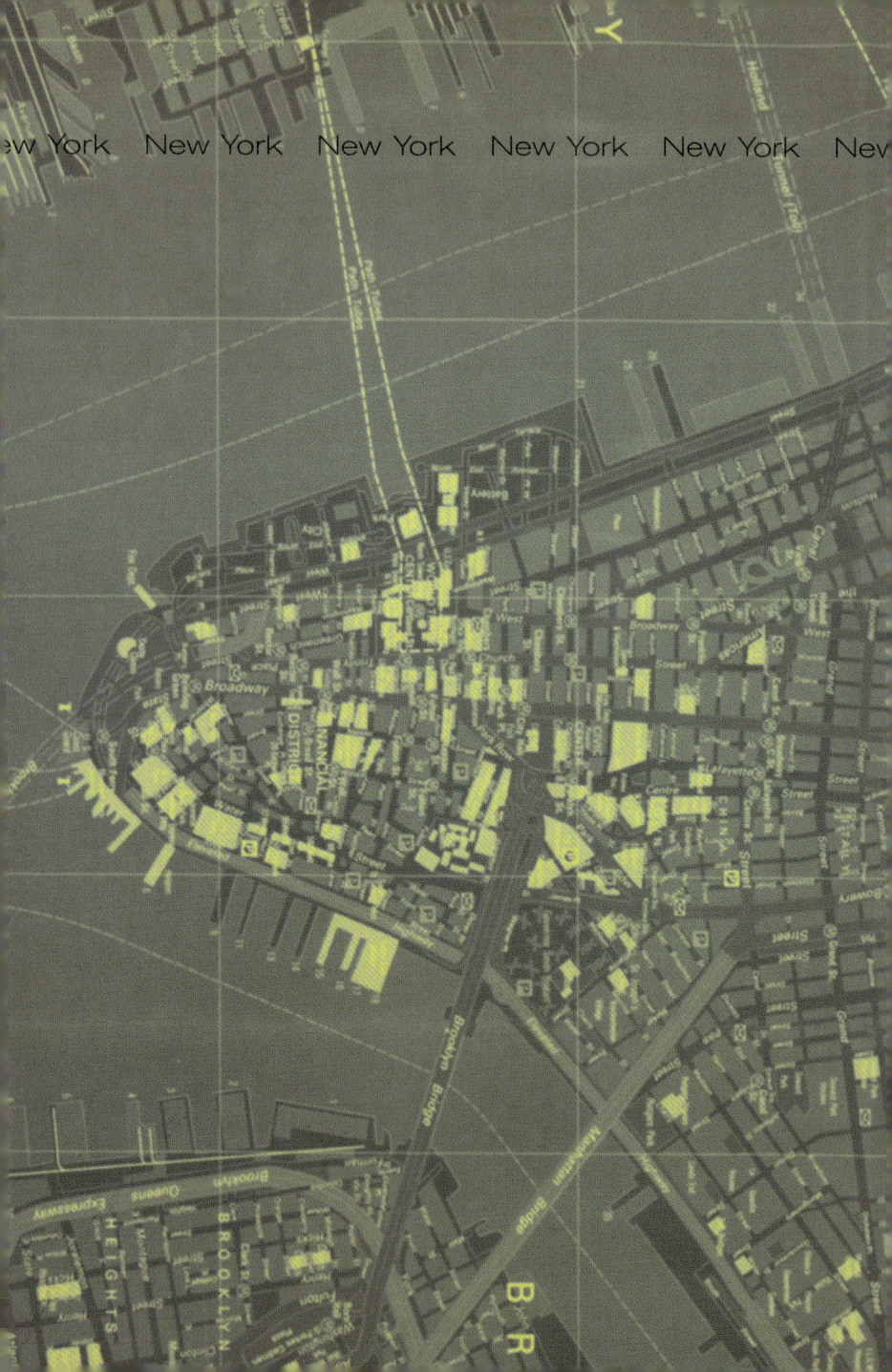

Origins

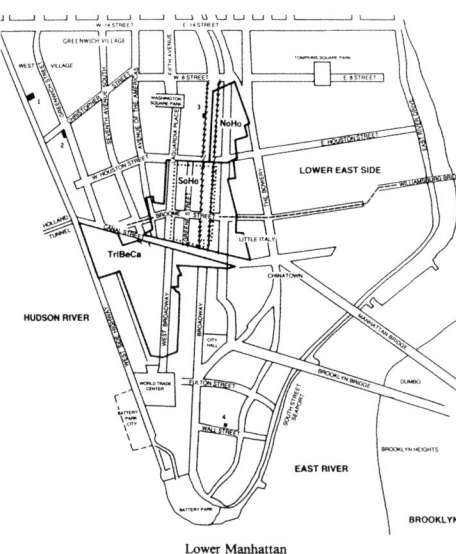

Lower Manhattan

The loft is an American creation, dating back to the 1940s and originating in Manhattan, alongside the skyscrapers and commercial buildings of the Wall Street district.

The loft lifestyle constitutes one of the major trends in urban development over the last 50 years. The conversion of warehouses and factories into middle-class residences has not only reversed the migration to the suburbs and brought about a regeneration of deteriorating city centers, it has also, even more importantly, given rise to a new consciousness.

Most of New York's loft buildings were put up in the late 19th and early 20th centuries to serve the needs of light manufacturing industries: weaving, printing, upholstery, laundering, and varnish-making. The SoHo district in particular contains the highest concentration of wrought-iron warehouses and factories in the United States.

Despite the eclectic ornamentation of the façades of this type of building, the interiors are all quite similar: long spaces with big windows, a structure largely made of wrought iron, and a distinctive style of architectural decoration. Tribeca

© Jordi Miralles

and the west side of Chelsea are also studded with loft buildings, due to their proximity to the quays on the Hudson river.

In the 1930s and 1940s New York's manufacturing industries moved to larger complexes outside the city, deserting the loft buildings and leaving them to waste. The once-prosperous financial district of SoHo fell into decline, cut off from the new centers in Wall Street and Greenwich Village. However it soon attracted artists in search of large spaces at low rents.

By the end of 1940 the Abstract Impressionist painter Barnett Newman was already happily settled in his SoHo loft. The infrastructures of these first lofts barely covered basic living requirements. This scene gradually created a style and an aesthetic which seeped into the underground culture of the 1950s. The obvious privations of the loft lifestyle – the lack of heating and running water – quickly became incorporated into the image of the enterprising bohemian artist. From the practical point of view, the sheer size of these lofts was ideally suited to the large-scale works being produced by the Abstract Expressionists. These spaces also became a stage for other types of work – by, for example, the activist painters of the Klondike group, who worked out of Manhattan lofts in the 1950s, and Andy Warhol, who was at the height of his career in the 1960s, in the most famous creative loft of all – the silver-painted Factory, at 231, East 47th Street.

While lofts were successfully providing a setting for the work of Abstract Expressionists, they also witnessed the birth of a new radical aesthetic forged by the subsequent generation of avant-garde artists, such as Robert Rauschenberg, Jasper Johns, John Cage, and other bit-players eager to sign up for the show which the movement had now become. The lofts were breeding grounds for the avant-garde dance of Merce Cunningham and Judson Church and the ground-breaking "Fluxhouse Number 2" project, dreamed up by the artists of the Fluxus movement, which sprung out of a group of communal lofts.

Lofts also provided a setting for the new era of minimalist sculpture, as they could provide sufficient space to satisfy the demands of its creation and exhibition. Sculptors such as Donald Judd,

Carl André, Dan Flavin, Robert Morris, and Sol LeWitt all enthusiastically embraced industrial production methods, thereby distancing themselves from the myth of the individual artist's handmade creation so beloved by the first- and second-generation Abstract Expressionists.

Abstract Expressionism and Pop Art are both essentially American creations that emerged in the heart of the nation's industrial sector and went on to establish New York's supremacy over Paris as the art capital of the Western world.

The first wave of SoHo artists soon attracted art dealers, who created galleries that were a variation on the theme of artistic lofts. In the 1970s, however, the galleries gave way to other types of businesses, such as restaurants and shops. By the 1990s, SoHo had become the hotspot for the latest creations in fashion, art, and interior design. The area has gone up in the world, thanks to a marketing process that still continues today.

Aside from its cultural aspects, SoHo has provided a crucial example of urban renewal at a time when both the theory and practice of city planning were being questioned. In 1964 and 1971 the city of New York, using SoHo as a model for urban restructuring, passed by-laws permitting the occupation of lofts for residential use in specific areas, including the Tribeca and SoHo neighborhoods in Manhattan. Artists had to put plates on their doors with the initials AIR (artist in residence) to facilitate access to firemen in cases of emergency. These plates have now become extremely valuable collectors' items.

The official permission to occupy lofts brought an end to the clandestine, improvised lifestyle of the early pioneers, and a more controlled renovation process gave rise to imaginative architectural transformations over the course of the 1980s and into the 1990s.

London London London London London London London Lon

Legacy

London is currently the hub of loft development in Europe. The changes inflicted on the economy by Margaret Thatcher, coupled with the financial boom and subsequent recession in the 1980s, resulted in the abandonment of a large number of buildings formerly used for light industry. In the early 1990s these began to attract the attention of developers and builders.

Although the first owners of the New York lofts were mainly creative artists, they had been quick to see the commercial possibilities of their bohemian image and environment. So a loft became not only a center for artistic production, but also an enticing space in which, according to their builders' advertising brochures, their buyer could find freedom of expression and emotional fulfillment.

After the huge success of lofts in the United States, it was only a matter of time before they

Views and plans of the Factory project (Shepherdess Walk, Hackney, London), refurbished by Buschow Henley & Partners in 1999 © Nick Kane/Arcaid.

would break into the European market as well. Tony Goddard was the first architect to create a loft building in London when he converted a former Victorian tea warehouse on Oliver's Wharf, on the banks of the Thames, into 23 open-plan, spacious, but modestly equipped apartments. "It was the first building in London to be transformed in this way," remembers Goddard, "and we weren't very sure how it was going to be accepted. We put a small ad in *The Times*, aimed at potential buyers, and we received thousands of replies."

Despite the great welcome for the loft phenomenon in Europe, it was obvious that the market for lofts was not as large as it was in the United States. In the 1970s and 1980s living in a loft was considered, in both London and Paris, an eccentricity exclusive to rich, arty types, like film directors and collectors of modern art. It constituted a

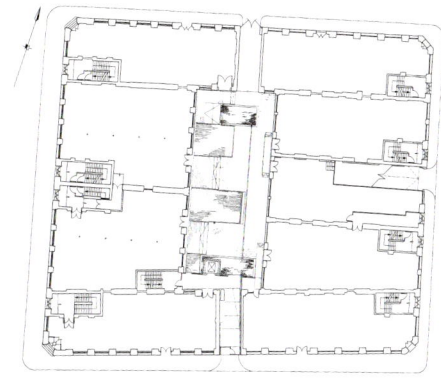

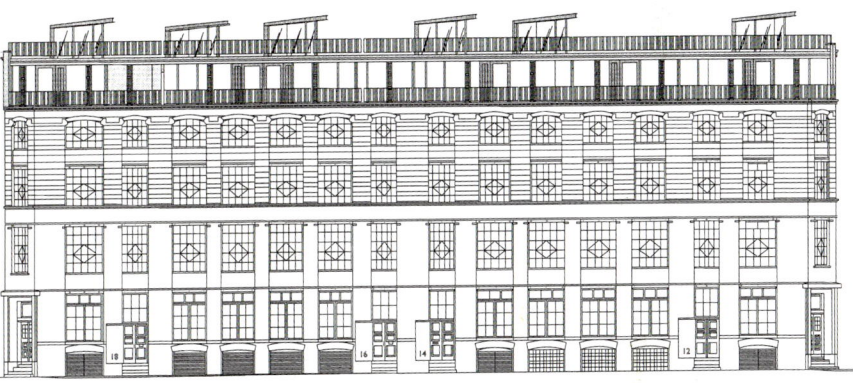

personal choice rather than a mass movement. At the same time, developers eager to obtain a quick profit converted old warehouses in the London docklands into extremely expensive, single-space apartments, far removed from the original conception of the loft and, often resulting in, resounding failures.

It was George Zozlowski and the Kentish Group PLC who were the first to accurately assess the loft market with their plans for the conversion of the old Bryant & May factory in Bow, in the East End of London (a project that was subsequently developed by London Buildings). Presented as a "New York-style loft in East London," this project offered apartments equipped with the basic essentials – although a great deal more refined than their original New York models – that elicited an extremely positive public response. Thus encouraged, London Buildings went on to convert other industrial buildings into loft spaces for residential use.

Manhattan Loft Corporation (MLC), currently the most important building company operating in this field in the United Kingdom, has transformed several of London's former industrial sites in areas such as Summers Street, Shoreditch, Clerkenwell, and Wardour Street, in Soho. Harry Handelsman, the company's president, explains: "When we first developed the loft concept in 1992, it was something relatively new in London. A number of explanations were required to make it more accessible. We had to promote our lofts in a way that emphasized how each buyer could create his or her own space. The message was simple: if you want to

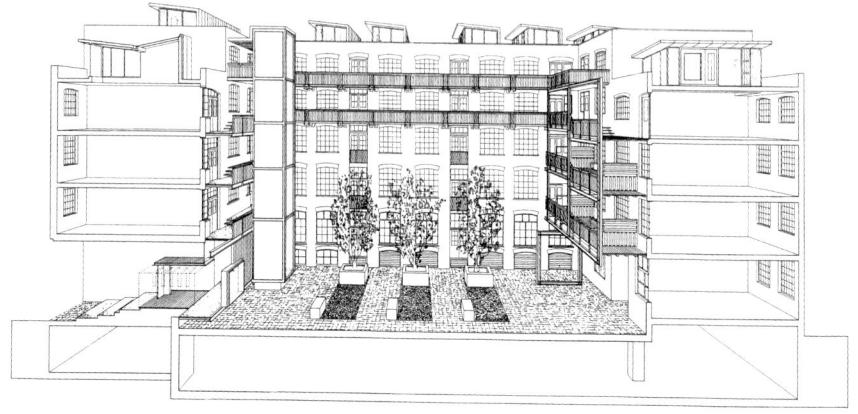

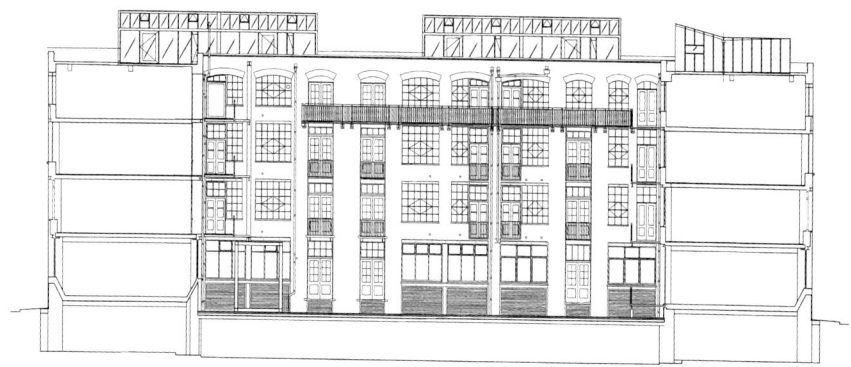

create your own identity, we can do it for you." Referring to his first brochure, he adds: "We were selling a lifestyle, and I'm very glad to have been a part of it."

One of MLC's projects in London's Shoreditch is called the Factory, reminiscent of Andy Warhol's famous New York loft and beacon for the loft movement. This reference to the artistic events of that era is underlined in the advertising brochure: "The artistic legacy lives on, with over 10,000 artists living in the square mile [3 sq km] of Shoreditch, creating one of the most authentic loft environments on this side of the Atlantic."

MLC has recently begun to develop loft projects in other European cities, such as Paris, Cologne, and Berlin. Meanwhile, London has implemented policies that have led to whole areas being given over to the development of new lofts. The United Kingdom has firmly established itself as the epicenter of this field, with conversions and buildings to be found not only in London, but also in Leeds, Bradford, and Manchester.

erlin Berlin Berlin Berlin Berlin Berlin Berlin Berlin

Berlin Berlin Berlin Berlin Berlin Berlin Berlin Berlin

Kreuzberg

Dieter Kramer, an artist and photographer born in Minden (Westphalia) in 1943, specializes in the photography of urban landscapes. With the help of his postcard collection, which he has published in several series since 1971, Kramer presents a survey of the construction and development of the Kreuzberg neighborhood, the heart of Berlin's loft movement, based on his own personal experiences.

©Dieter Kramer

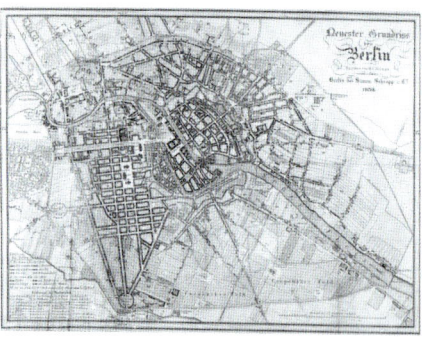

The photograph above shows the city as seen from the southeast corner of the map. On the right, the river Spree; in the center, the historic part of the city.

The red building is the Lindström factory, an industrial complex typical of the district. The warehouses across the river, in what used to be the city's east zone, are no longer used for their original purposes and have been converted into lofts with an asking price of around 2,500 Euros per sq m. (10.76 square feet).

I moved into one of these buildings in 1982 to set up a studio for putting on exhibitions. The rent of the lofts was 1.90 Euros per sq m., or 0.60 Euros in the case of the basement storage spaces. In 1991 I reduced my space and moved into a 2,152-square-foot (200-sq m) loft, where I still live. The rent is 5 Euros per sq m.

The map shows the historic Berlin of 1832. For some 500 years the central circle was a small city with little significance in the Brandenburg region.

After the rise of Prussia in the 18th century, Berlin became the residence of the new royal family in the reign of the first of the three kings called Frederick, although it was still eclipsed by other German cities. This era saw the construction of Friedrichstadt, the junction between the long Unter den Linden boulevard and the equally long Friedrichstrasse. In the 19th century this area became the center of the city.

The southeast was still countryside, but it later became one of the most densely populated parts of the city: the district of Kreuzberg.

This is my loft.

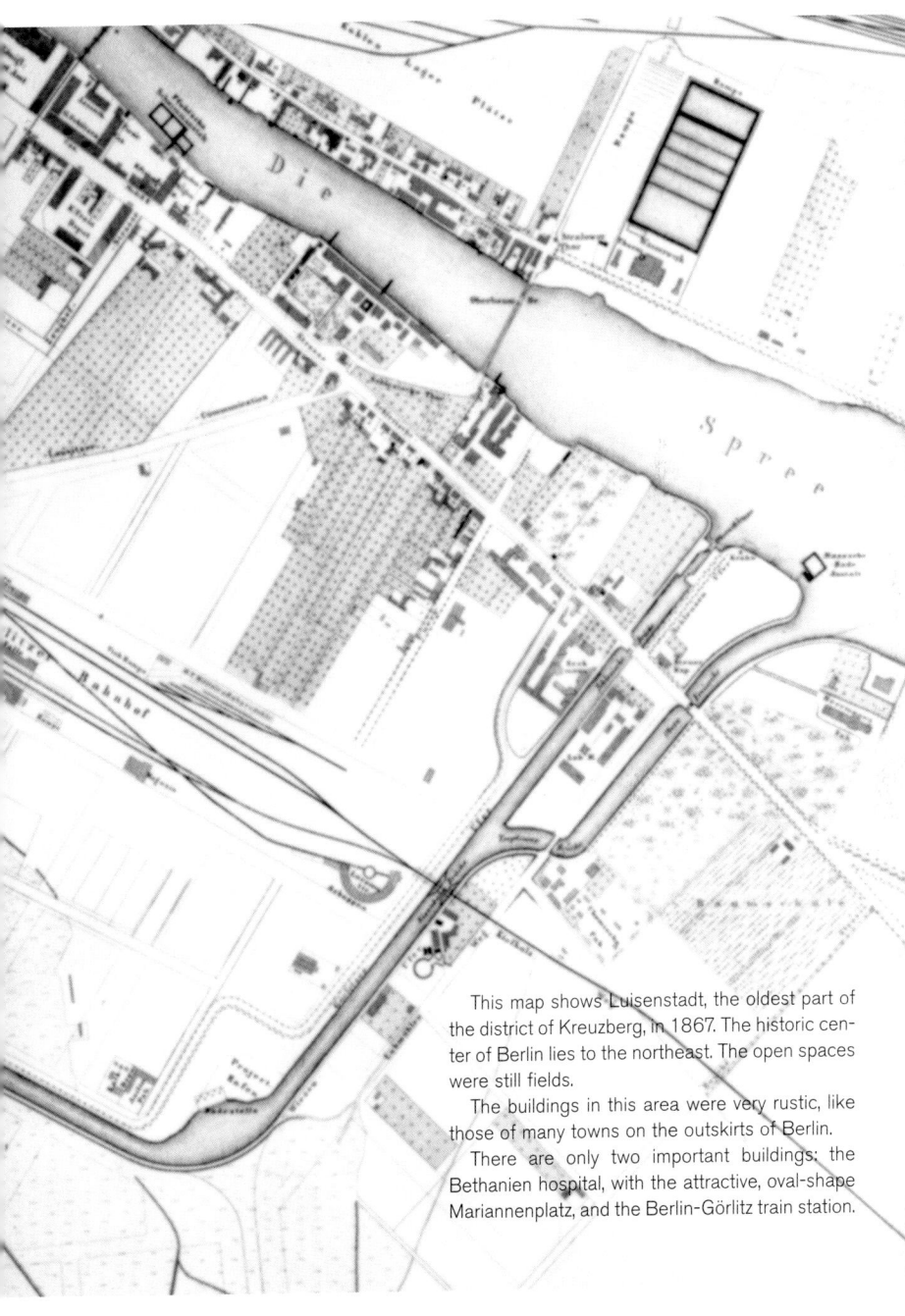

This map shows Luisenstadt, the oldest part of the district of Kreuzberg, in 1867. The historic center of Berlin lies to the northeast. The open spaces were still fields.

The buildings in this area were very rustic, like those of many towns on the outskirts of Berlin.

There are only two important buildings: the Bethanien hospital, with the attractive, oval-shape Mariannenplatz, and the Berlin-Görlitz train station.

In the next generation, the population of the city of Berlin shot up, from 750,000 inhabitants in 1870 to one million in 1880. Thirty years later, the population had already reached two million.

After the war against France in 1870–1871 (which Germany won), the French had to pay five million Reichsmarks in gold as compensation to Bismarck's new Reich. This represented a windfall

Luisendstadt in 1900.

for the German economy and new banks and businesses were created. The immediate consequence of this economic boom in Berlin was a gradual influx of thousands of people leaving the countryside in the hope of finding a better life in the city. A similar phenomenon could be observed in a number of other cities of Germany and Central Europe in the late 19th century.

Sarotti chocolate factory, 1893.

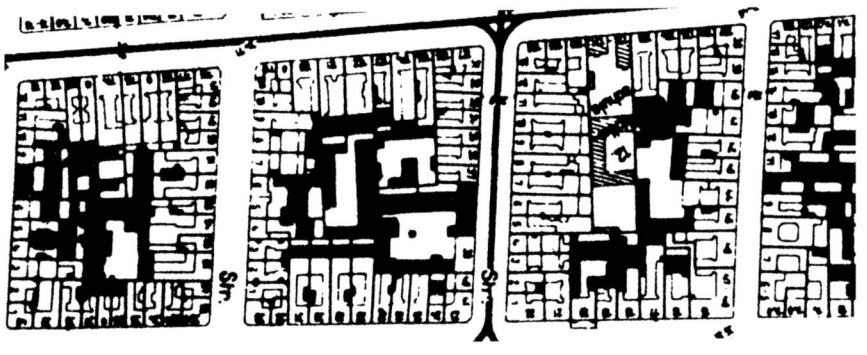

The plans show how the outer sides of each block were designed for residential use, while the interior was occupied by workshops.

The building regulations were very strict and all the houses were virtually the same height. The outer faces of the blocks were used for private construction and speculation increased the price of floor space so much that, as far as the fire regulations permitted, buildings started to be put up in the space inside the blocks. These areas housed communal infrastructure: schools, hospitals, water works, electricity plants, and so on. The chimneys in the photo give an idea of the noise and pollution of the time, problems that were not alleviated until the mid-20th century.

View of the textile mills in 1860, as seen from Oberbaumbrücke.

View from the same spot in 1930.

The banks of the river Spree have been exploited by the inhabitants of Berlin throughout the city's history. First there were the timber merchants who used them to store coal, building materials, and so on. Then, in the first half of the 19th century, the textile industry established itself in this area. By 1900 the banks of the river were lined with industrial buildings that stored or manufactured all the products required by a big city.

Later, when the river Spree came to mark the frontier between East and West Berlin in this part of the city, all the buildings on the right-hand (north) side were knocked down by the East German army to prevent any escape from the "workers' paradise" that the communist authorities claimed to have created.

In the 1960s many companies were forced to close down and many of the industrial buildings were abandoned.

After the economic blockade of 1948 and 1949, the allied governments on the western side ordered that stocks of meat, corn, coal, and so on, sufficient to supply the city for several months in the case of an emergency, should be stored. Many of the empty factories were used for this purpose; one of these was this beautiful loft building in Pfuelstrasse, which was filled with grain.

In the early 1980s the Senate emptied the

buildings and sold them. This particular one was purchased by the building company A. Kuthe GmbH for 306,775 Euros (the price of a 1,300 square-foot/120 sq m. loft these days) and its subsequent fate fills one of the darkest chapters in the history of such buildings.

Kuthe rented the lofts at a modest price, so the tenants put a lot of time and money into doing up their homes. However, shortly afterward, it raised the rents so high that most of the tenants had no option but to leave, unable to enjoy the fruits of their labor.

Ritterhof, at 11 Ritterstrasse.

From 1890 to 1914 Berlin enjoyed its golden age. Urban development, technical innovations, and cultural progress reached unparalleled heights in every sphere.

The exportation center of Ritterstrasse, until then on the outskirts, had been incorporated into the city. Many head offices of German industries and businesses were in the vicinity: the big banks on Behrenstrasse, all the major newspapers on the Kochstrasse, the garment industry around Hansvogteiplatz, the government on the nearby Wilhelmstrasse, hundreds of hotels, and so on. It was probably the most prosperous neighborhood in the city, along with the Friedrichstrasse; for this reason, the allied bombardments destroyed almost 95% of this area.

Luisenstadt in 1954, after the ruins had been cleared away.

Siemens, in the Charlottenburg neighborhood, seen from Markgrafenstrasse.

The same complex seen from Charlottenstrasse.

The most dynamic company with roots in Kreuzberg is Siemens. The engineer Werner von Siemens started to produce telegraph installations in 1847 with his partner Halske, and the two were soon inventing and manufacturing a wide range of electrical goods. In 1872 Siemens built a big factory in Charlottenburg, but the company expanded so quickly that it was soon obliged to build an industrial estate, Siemensstadt, to the north of Charlottenburg. Like most Berlin companies, Siemens moved to southern Germany after World War II, the blockade, and the construction of the Wall.

Siemensstadt.

In 1862 James Hobrecht conceived a general plan for Berlin that was as far-reaching as that of Cerdà for the city of Barcelona. The identical height of the residential buildings and the width of the streets and sidewalks produced an effect of openness and cleanliness. Landlords were also given more control over the spaces inside the blocks they owned.

This is illustrated by the images of the complex belonging to the Bechstein piano company. It first put up the factory and later added housing blocks and industrial premises alongside. Bechstein remained on this spot for almost a hundred years, but recently moved to the nearby Moritzplatz.

Two views of the Bechstein complex, before and after expansion.

The area surrounding the Bechstein factory.

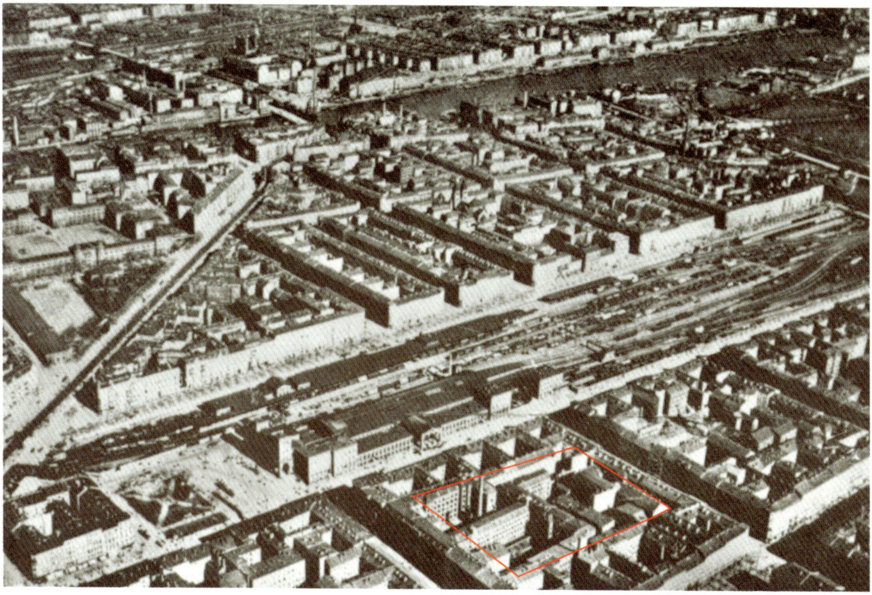

Hobrecht's plan for the city allowed for wide sidewalks whose paving stones defined three functions. The area closest to the buildings was reserved for children's games, the central one for passing pedestrians, and the outer one for municipal installations. The entrances to buildings were also marked out by the use of different materials.

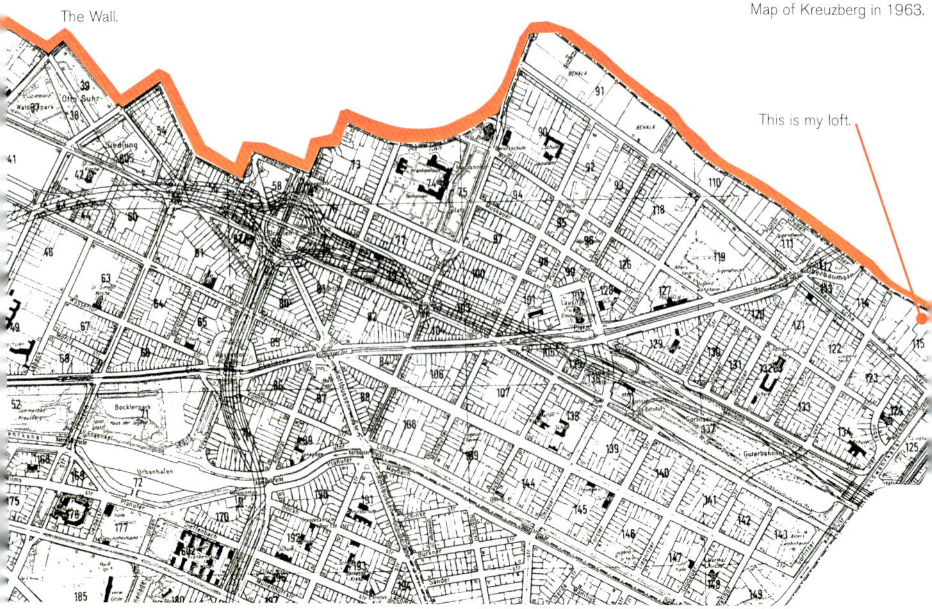

The Wall.

Map of Kreuzberg in 1963.

This is my loft.

In World War I most of Kreuzberg's companies went on manufacturing, although the end product was different: spare parts for weapons. However, defeat brought a long, deep depression that led to the closure of many businesses and, subsequently, unemployment. In these circumstances, many families experienced great poverty.

In World War II a large part of the district was destroyed in the bombardments. On February 3, 1945 the industrial zone was attacked by fire bombs; in just that one night, 2,500 people died, 700 disappeared, and 120,000 lost their homes. It took ten years to remove the millions of tons of ruins and repair anything that was still usable. In the late 1950s small shanty towns sprung up in the areas that had been left bare.

In 1961, however, disaster struck: the construction of the Wall. Kreuzberg was definitively relegated to the outskirts of the city and continued its decline.

At that time it was common practice for students to rent a room in the house of a widow. In those days there were many such women in Berlin, living in apartments too big for a single tenant.

When I began my studies in the Berlin Art Academy in 1968, I set about looking for an apartment with a studio, and I found one in the district of Kreuzberg, in the southeast part of the neighborhood – an area that was supposedly due for demolition. It was only in old, run-down neighborhoods like these that a student could find his or her own apartment, consisting of one room, a kitchen, and a bathroom which, in most cases, had to be shared with several neighbors living on the same staircase. But the most important thing was that I had found a flat just for me, and with a small studio as well. The two together worked out cheaper in Kreuzberg than a sublet room in any other part of the city.

Almost all the buildings of this type had stores on the first floor; there were one or two bakeries on every street, as well as grocery stores that sold milk, butter, newspapers, and cigarettes. When I moved to Kreuzberg, 90% of these stores were empty, so I rented one that was in my building when I outgrew my studio.

Years later, my photographic studio also became too small. On the other side of the street there was a small 1,075-square-foot (100-sq m) loft; I asked the owner if he was interested in renting it to me. There was no water or electricity, just unadorned, empty space. We agreed a price and it was there that I started my professional career.

In the 1960s large suburban estates were put up all over Germany, even in East Germany, and the old neighborhoods were abandoned.

This process accelerated with the arrival of foreign workers, most of them Turks. Before the Wall was put up, the flow of cheap manual labor ran in an east–west direction. One of the consequences of the Wall was the interruption of this traffic, and so Berlin's industries had to turn to countries like Turkey to obtain the manpower they required.

In 1925 the district of Kreuzberg had 380,000 inhabitants; in 1952 there were merely 200,000. In 1986 only 100,000 Germans lived there (mainly young people). The neighborhood's traditional community had almost all left, making room for around 40,000 Turks who moved there at the same time.

The inhabitants of the old neighborhoods enjoyed an atmosphere of familiarity and respect; however, the majority of the buildings were in poor condition. In contrast, the suburban estates

offered what most people wanted: adequate sanitation, central heating, light, and good ventilation.

The spaces inside blocks were often invaded by a strange mixture of sheds, debris, and small loft buildings.

Most of these buildings were repaired after the war, but they were in an appalling state and required a thorough overhaul.

Some of these sheds were used to store materials and old objects that could be reused as required for any number of purposes.

64

Land was in short supply in West Berlin, which also lacked houses in good condition. Entire blocks were knocked down in the old districts in the 1960s and 1970s and completely new complexes were put up in their place, free from the restrictions of the traditional street layout.

They were built in accordance with the principles used in the new suburban estates, that is in line with the concept of a city without factories or inner courtyards.

Demolition of some of the buildings in the neighborhood.

Renewal of the city.

One of the many loft buildings that were knocked down.

Spaces that benefited from new building work.

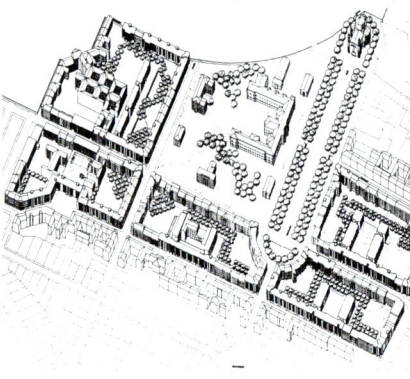

Ground plan of the Prakma complex

In 1973 it was agreed that industrial buildings that had lost their original use should not be demolished. The Prakma factory was the first to be saved. However, the company commissioned to restore the building eventually knocked it down in 1979, despite long negotiations to avoid this outcome.

This illegal demolition provoked a flood of protests, to such an extent that from then on most empty industrial buildings managed to escape the wrecking ball.

In all, around 70% of these buildings were knocked down, the remaining 30% being modernized after the 1973 agreement. Preserving the city's layout was considered the key to progress.

71

Around 1980 the failure of the urban renewal programs became apparent. Most of the empty houses due for demolition were being occupied by young people. The unexpected slowness of the process and the lack of financial resources to complete the project caused the authorities to

change their strategy. This period brought new hope to the neighborhood; its inhabitants organized street parties that briefly united the young Germans who had recently arrived with the Turkish majority, who had taken up residence some years previously and were well established.

The inhabitants of around 50 lofts joined forces under the slogans "New life in old factories" and "The new Kreuzberg mix" in order to fight against the imminent demolition of many empty buildings in the area.

It was obviously difficult to unite such a diverse range of individuals and groups under the same banner. The task was further complicated by the fact that many of them were residing in the area illegally. It was common to see graffiti on the walls proclaim-

ing "Legal, illegal, what does it matter?" Anyway, this collective, known as the loft people, did succeed in provoking a public debate, particularly after the demolition of the Prakma building, which caused so much outrage. The loft people met every second Sunday of the month in a different loft to have breakfast and discuss their common problems, which were always the same: contracts, heating, and the fear of demolition. In this way a clear sense of unity was developed, which helped their cause.

"Don't give up, the occupation continues!"

In the 1980s more than 7,000 apartments in the renovated areas of Kreuzberg were still vacant, as were many lofts. Nevertheless, there was a great lack of the cheap housing that was particularly being sought by young people. So the squatters' movement came into being.

Battles with the police did not deter young people from occupying buildings that had been empty for years and would have stayed that way until they were "renewed" (demolished).

The first blocks to be squatted in were on Cuvrystrasse. Several buildings were provisionally restored and, after long negotiations between the owners and squatters, a solution satisfactory to both sides was finally reached.

"It is better to squat and restore than to own and destroy."
"New life in old factories."

The F. W. Müller complex occupied number 23 on Cuvrystrasse.

Inner courtyard of the F. W. Müller factory at the beginning of the 20th century.

In 1980, just before it was occupied by squatters.

Some of the smaller buildings were squatted in without any opposition and were thus saved from demolition. Their previous owners' old machinery and tools were surprisingly often found abandoned in these lofts.

In early 1979 a thoughtful urban renewal program that provided support for the loft people was unveiled at the International Building Fair. Many were allowed to buy their homes at very low prices, giving them legal status.

Number 48, Mariannenstrasse was full of old tools.

The painter Frank Suplie's loft in Muskauerstrasse.

This art student kept the press left behind in an old printer's workshop and gave it a new use.

The pioneers of this period were artists – painters and sculptors who needed space and were not worried about the lack of fittings and heating or the broken elevators. They were joined by craftspeople keen to experiment with new types of furnishing and architectural models.

A third group arrived a little later: the students. Getting hold of a sufficiently large apartment was a very expensive affair, but a loft measuring 2,000 to 3,000 square feet (180-270 sq m) or even more could easily house a good number of people.

Although the occupation of factory lofts was illegal, despite the fact that the businesses that were once there had long since moved to classier neighborhoods, many of their owners were glad that the buildings were not being left empty and were willing to give the new inhabitants (admittedly spurious) contracts for industrial activities, allowing some loft people to move into a position of semilegality.

Exterior of a building on Liberdastrasse.

One of the communal breakfasts that used to be organized on Liberdastrasse.

Most tenants of lofts had very little spending capacity, so their furniture, if they had any, usually came from the street or was recycled from materials that had been found in wrecked buildings.

These lofts were light years away from the ones that are being designed nowadays, in which it is not unusual to find sculptures and paintings by famous artists and even antiques. The idea then was simply to have the space and freedom to try out things that couldn't be done in a normal apartment.

The charm of these lofts was the poverty of the furnishings, the wealth of the ideas, and the luxury afforded by the open space.

Number 11, Ritterstrasse.

Here I am, 20 years ago.

This artist and painter, who lived in 188, Oranienstrasse, published a children's comic in the 1970s.

Number 38, Naunynstrasse, where Rainer Graff still has his loft on the fifth floor. He was one of the leaders of the loft people.

These days it is fashionable to live in a loft and even the pioneers of the movement have to pay the market price. A great deal of money has been invested in these buildings over the last 20 years, so their price is no longer very different from that of an apartment in a better part of the city.

In the early 1980s the rents were extremely low: 1 or 1.50 Euros per sq m (10 square feet) was the norm. Now, in 2001, 5 Euros per sq m is considered very cheap, 8 Euros reasonable, but the normal price is 10.50 Euros per sq m.

Despite the oasis of calm evoked by Rainer's carefully tended garden, the loft people experienced serious problems: semilegal contracts and precarious infrastructure. One of the major drawbacks was the lack of heating; Rainer, like many others, built small cubbyholes inside his loft.

Note the two oil drums in Rainer's kitchen; they are used for heating, although it has never been possible to heat the entire loft in this way.

In winter Rainer heats this cubbyhole as a refuge from the cold.

In the 1980s, and even more so in the 1990s, living in a loft had ceased to be an adventure. The tenants of these buildings negotiated long-term contracts and put time and money into creating their own space. All types of cultural phenomena were seen: dance and theater pieces were per-

formed, workshops in esoteric practices were held, and many of the Turkish-owned lofts were adapted for use as mosques.

The loft is a space where virtually any type of activity is possible. All that is needed is a bit of imagination.

Loft manual

This manual for interpreting and realizing a loft is an exercise in both construction and reconstruction. In terms of interpretation and construction, it seeks to take apart the concepts that are not at first apparent in the lofts presented in the following sections, and then put them together and create a specific example.

In terms of reconstruction, this manual invites readers to create their own bright space using all the pieces they obtain, as in a jigsaw puzzle, in combination with their own personal criteria.

Loft manual

We will not go into the original meaning of the term "loft" here, or even the original meaning of "loft" as an applied concept; we will not discuss industrial buildings or factories; nor will we go back to the days of the artists and advertising people.

These days a loft is simply a quantitative, disproportionate, and almost always evocative way of conceiving the spatial idea of what must be everyday surroundings. In other words, home. In other words, workplace. In yet other words, leisure area.

Both quantitative and evocative, because there is an intention to suggest the idea of exterior – understood here as distance going to the limit – on the basis of the cult of space as quantity, thereby compensating for the density in which we move.

Disproportionate, because as lofts arise out of a process of spatial recycling – and therefore are not designed to measure – they succeed each other in their reutilization of excesses (cubic feet/m^3) and defects (number of openings), keys to understanding the genesis of their transformation.

Recycle means to use a material repeatedly in cycles of production, use, and recovery. The loft is the result of a process of spatial recycling, a recovery of a pre-existing space for uses that had not been previously anticipated, which guides its characteristics – both qualities and defects – toward other objectives, and in which a transformation is necessary for its reuse; a transformation involving dismounting, selecting, adapting, and completing – producing conglomerations of interventions.

This introduction seeks to serve as a manual for the interpretation/realization of lofts, on the basis of an overall reading of the interventions with various measurements (+/-) which affect a series of quantitatively measurable concepts, without entering into specific projects.

The idea is to deconstruct the lofts presented in the book so as to be able to reconstruct our own.

Theatrical loft

More is more loft

Loft or apartment?

Spiritual loft

Authentic loft

Essentialist loft

Conversion chart:
1 meter = 39.37 inches
1 m^2 = 10.76 square feet
1 m^3 = 35.31 cubic feet

Position = Density of the immediate surroundings
Lofts do not cease to be elements that form part of a bigger scheme
thought of as a unified whole. Lofts are located both above and below,
both inside and outside.
We can measure the pressure exercised on each loft by its outer
surroundings; it is the level of occupation of its environment that calibrates
its quality. So, we will find lofts ranging from those with surroundings that
are all air/vacuum to others that are mass/fullness.

Surface area = Extent in square feet/m².

Form = Level of spatial concentration
Every loft is defined by its perimeter, which cuts it off from the environment –
whether built or otherwise – of which it forms a part. We can establish a
relationship between the form of the perimeter and the qualities of the
demarcated space – from circular perimeters traced with a single line, creating
unified spaces (maximum concentration), to tentacular perimeters, without any
form, which give rise to successions of spaces (minimum concentration).

Vacuum = Level of volumetric disproportion
Volume (cubic feet/m³.), not so much in itself but in terms of excess, is a
factor common to all lofts.
Excess generates disproportion, which can be measured by establishing a
relationship between the minimum volume needed to satisfy an
established function and the volume finally used.
The disproportion will mean that the layout of a loft is configured more as
a series of functional corners within a whole than as a series of enclosed,
self-contained spaces.

Trajectory = Speed of displacement
The successive interventions in a loft, which are already derived from an
initially predetermined form – deconstruction, reconstruction,
implementation of program, furniture, objects – give rise to a scheme for
the positioning of masses that measures the resistance of the space to be
passed through linearly. Concentration is rushed and dispersion is immobile.

Pores = Level of exterior penetration
We can establish a relationship between the number of faces that demarcate a
volume (3, 4, 5, etc.) and the number of openings onto the exterior.
This is a determining precondition for the progress of the intervention, as it is
involved in the definition of the spaces as they are perceptively communicated,
because it often has to compensate for the disproportion of the number of
openings against that of the programmatic spaces to be defined.

Recycling = Reuse *versus* intervention
The loft as a result of a process of transformation.
We can distinguish types of loft on the basis of the capacity of the
intervention to reuse all the raw materials (100% recycling), or of having
gradually respected, assembled, fused, or masked them (0% recycling).

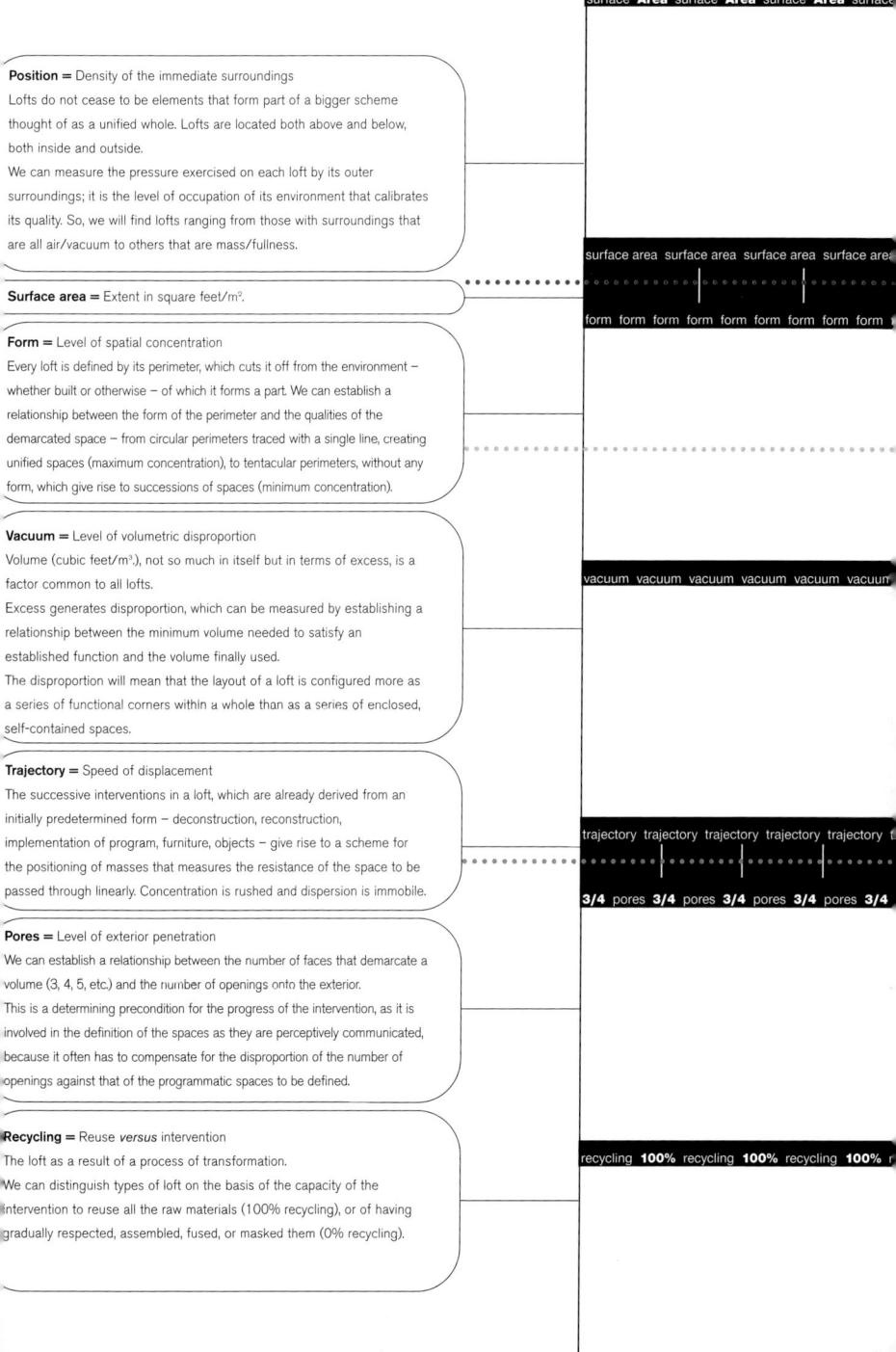

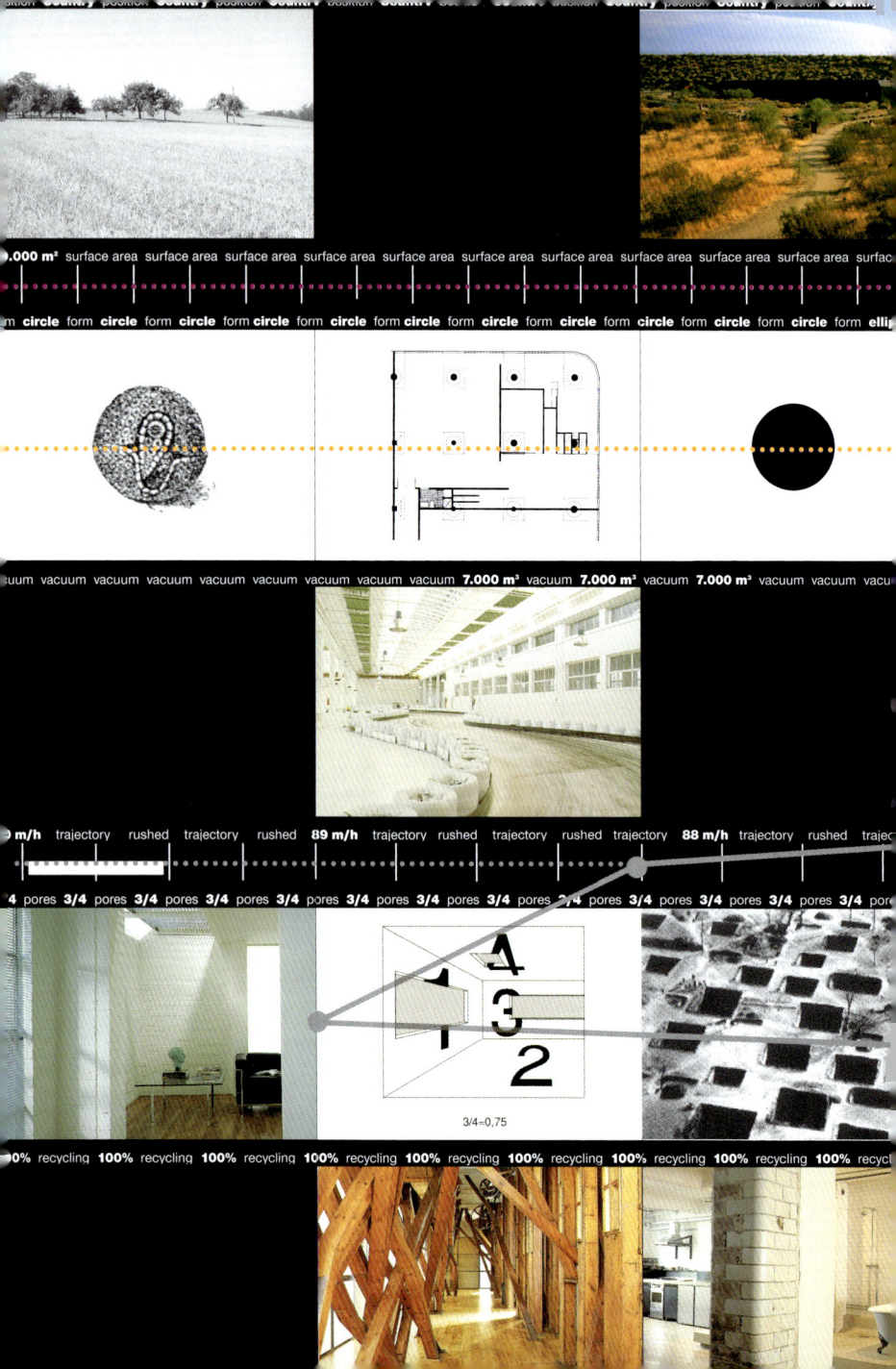

country position **country** position **country** position **country** position **country** position **country** position **country** position **country** po

face area surface area surface area surface area surface area surface area surface area surface area surface area surface area surface area surface area surfac

ellipse form **ellipse** form **ellipse** form **ellipse** form **ellipse** form **square** form **square** form **square** form **square** form **square** form **squ**

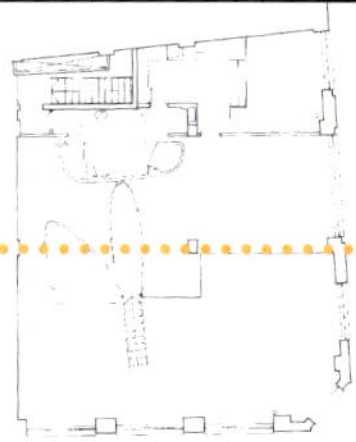

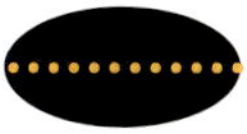

cuum vacuum vacuum vacuum vacuum vacuum vacuum vacuum vacuum vacuum vacuum vacuum vacuum vacuum vacuum vacuum v

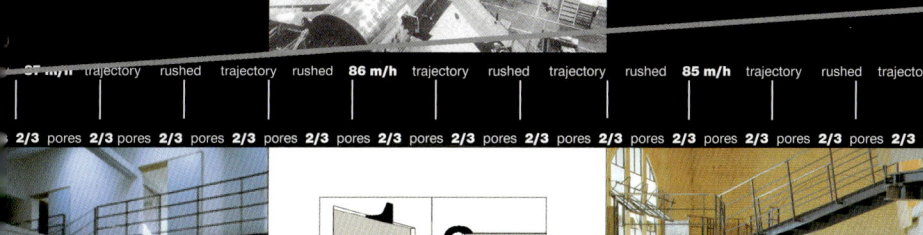

m/h trajectory rushed trajectory rushed **86 m/h** trajectory rushed trajectory rushed **85 m/h** trajectory rushed trajector

2/3 pores **2/3** pores **2/3** pores **2/3** pores **2/3** pores **2/3** pores **2/3** pores **2/3** pores **2/3** pores **2/3** pores **2/3** p

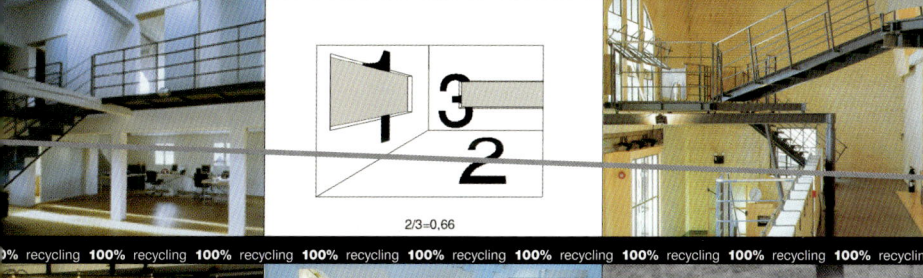

2/3=0,66

% recycling **100%** recycling **100%** recycling **100%** recycling **100%** recycling **100%** recycling **100%** recycling **100%** recycling **100%** recyclin

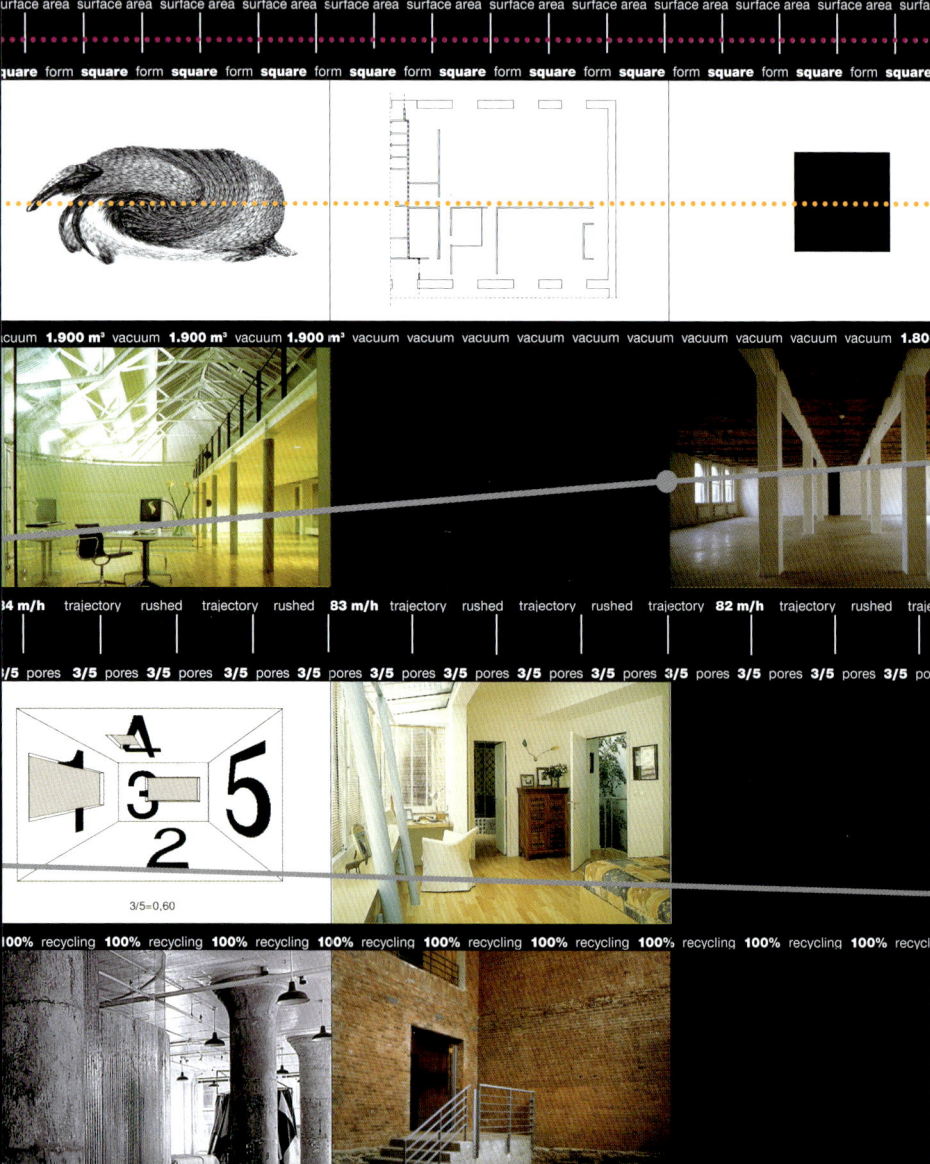

Country position Country position Country position Country position Country position Country position Country position Country pos

surface area surface area surface area surface area surface area surface area surface area surface area surface area surface area surface area surface area surface
● | | | | | | | |
square form square form square form square form square form square form square form square form form form form a form form form

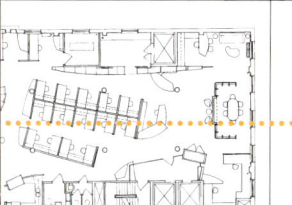 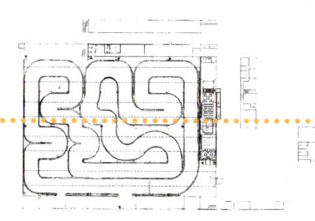 

vacuum **1.800 m³** vacuum **1.800 m³** vacuum **1.782 m³** vacuum **1.782 m³** vacuum **1.782 m³** vacuum **1.600 m³** vacuum **1.600 m³** vacuum

 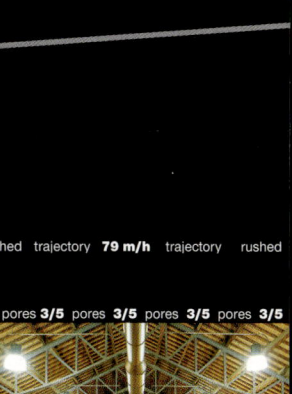

/h trajectory rushed trajectory rushed trajectory **80 m/h** trajectory rushed trajectory rushed trajectory **79 m/h** trajectory rushed

pores **3/5** pores **3/5** pores **3/5** pores **3/5** pores **3/5** pores **3/5** pores **3/5** pores **3/5** pores **3/5** pores **3/5** pores **3/5** pores **3/5**

% recycling **90%** recycling **90%** recycling **90%** recycling **90%** recycling **90%** recycling **90%** recycling **90%** recycling **90%** recycling **90%** recy

surface area surface area surface area surface area surface area surface area surface area surface area surface area surface area surface area surface area surfa

form square form square form square form square form square form square form square form square form square form square form square

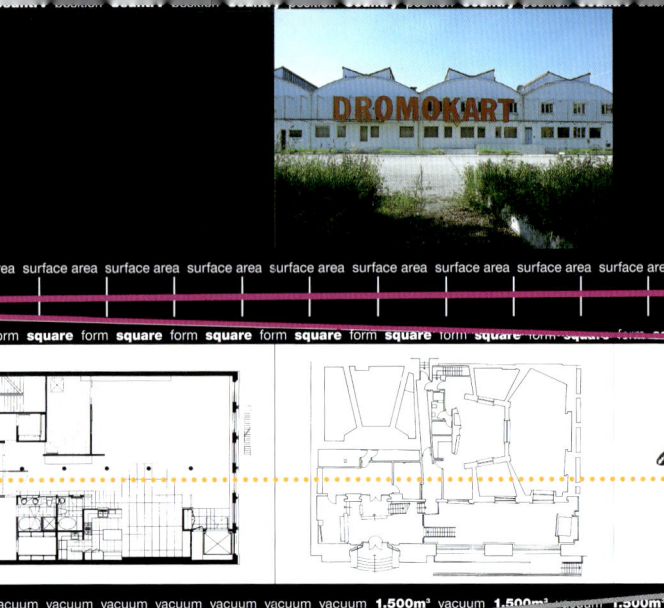

vacuum vacuum vacuum vacuum vacuum vacuum vacuum vacuum **1.500m³** vacuum **1.500m³** vacuum **1.500m³** vacuum **1.50**

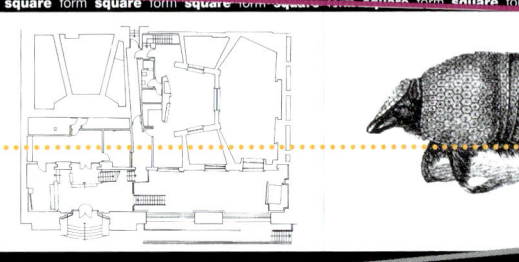

m/h trajectory rushed trajectory rushed trajectory **77 m/h** trajectory rushed trajectory rushed trajectory **76 m/h** trajectory fast trajectory fast

page **184**   page **394**   page **160**

/4 pores **2/4** pores **2/4** pores **2/4** pores **2/4** pores **2/4** pores **2/4** pores **2/4** pores **2/4** pores **2/4** pores **2/4** pores **2/4** por

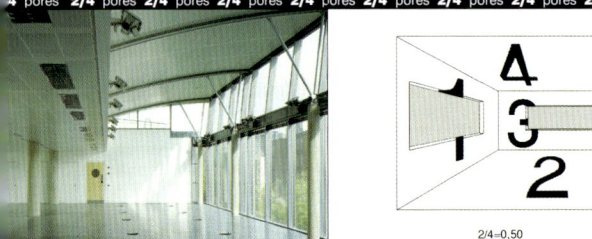

2/4=0,50

% recycling **90%** recycling **90%** recycling **90%** recycling **90%** recycling **90%** recycling **90%** recycling **90%** recycling **90%** re

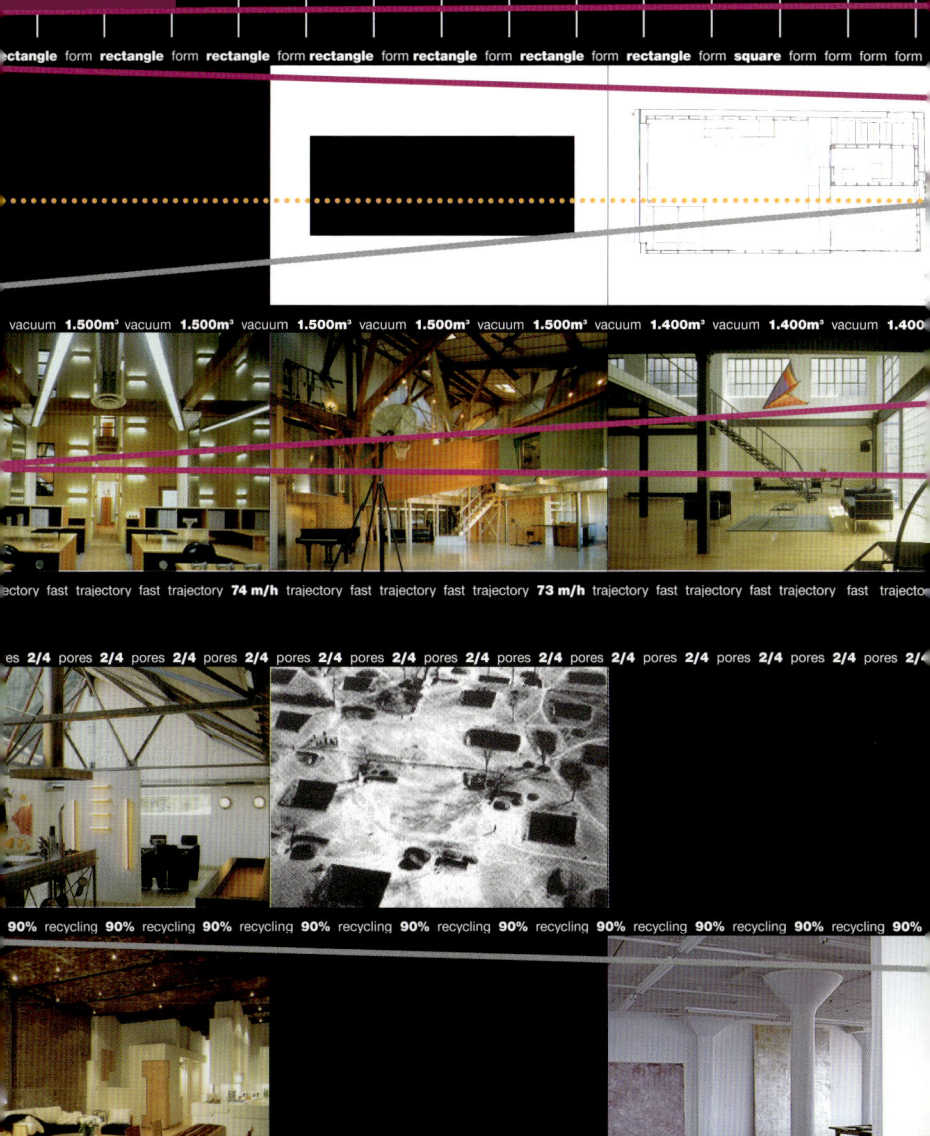

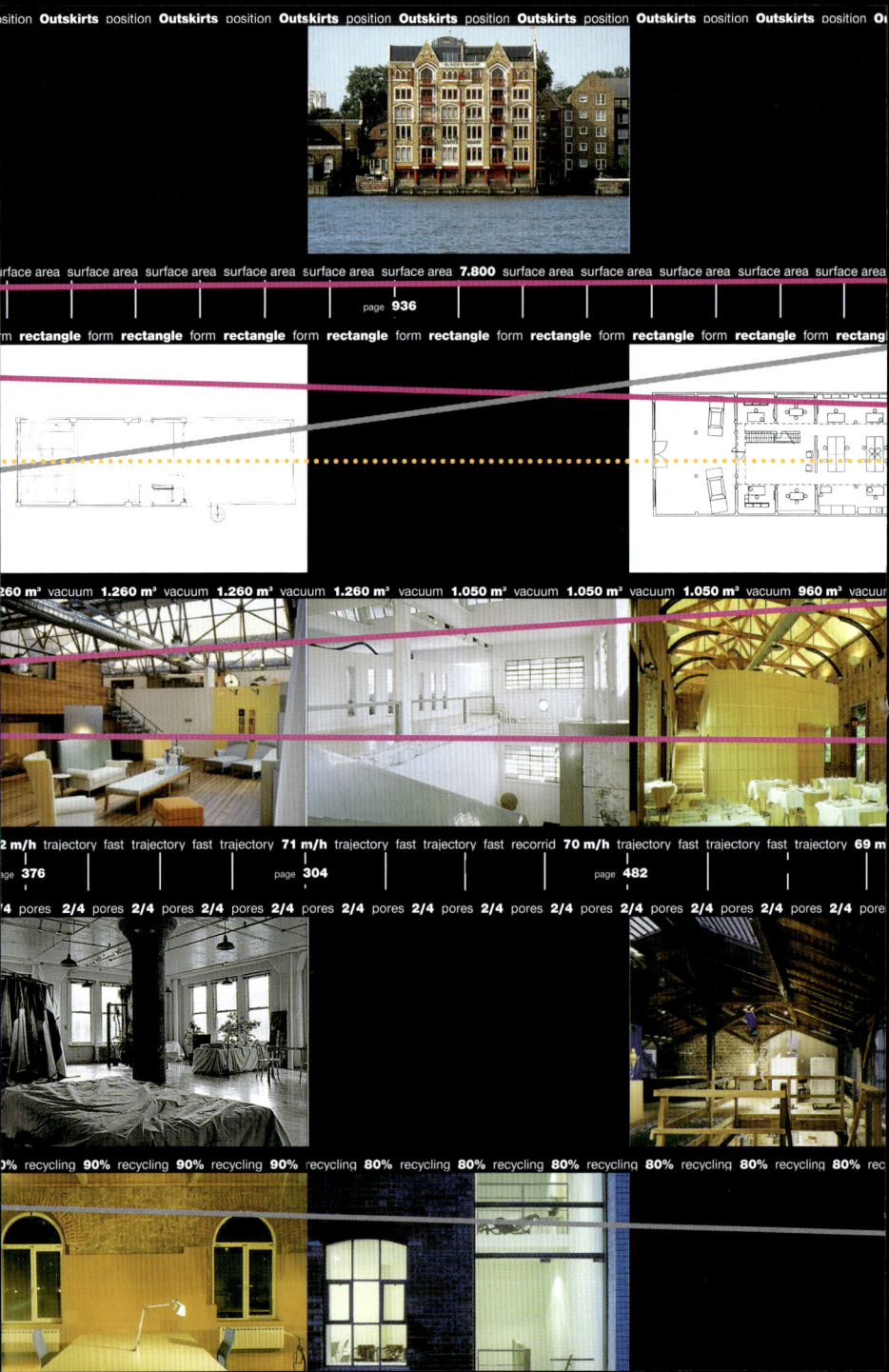

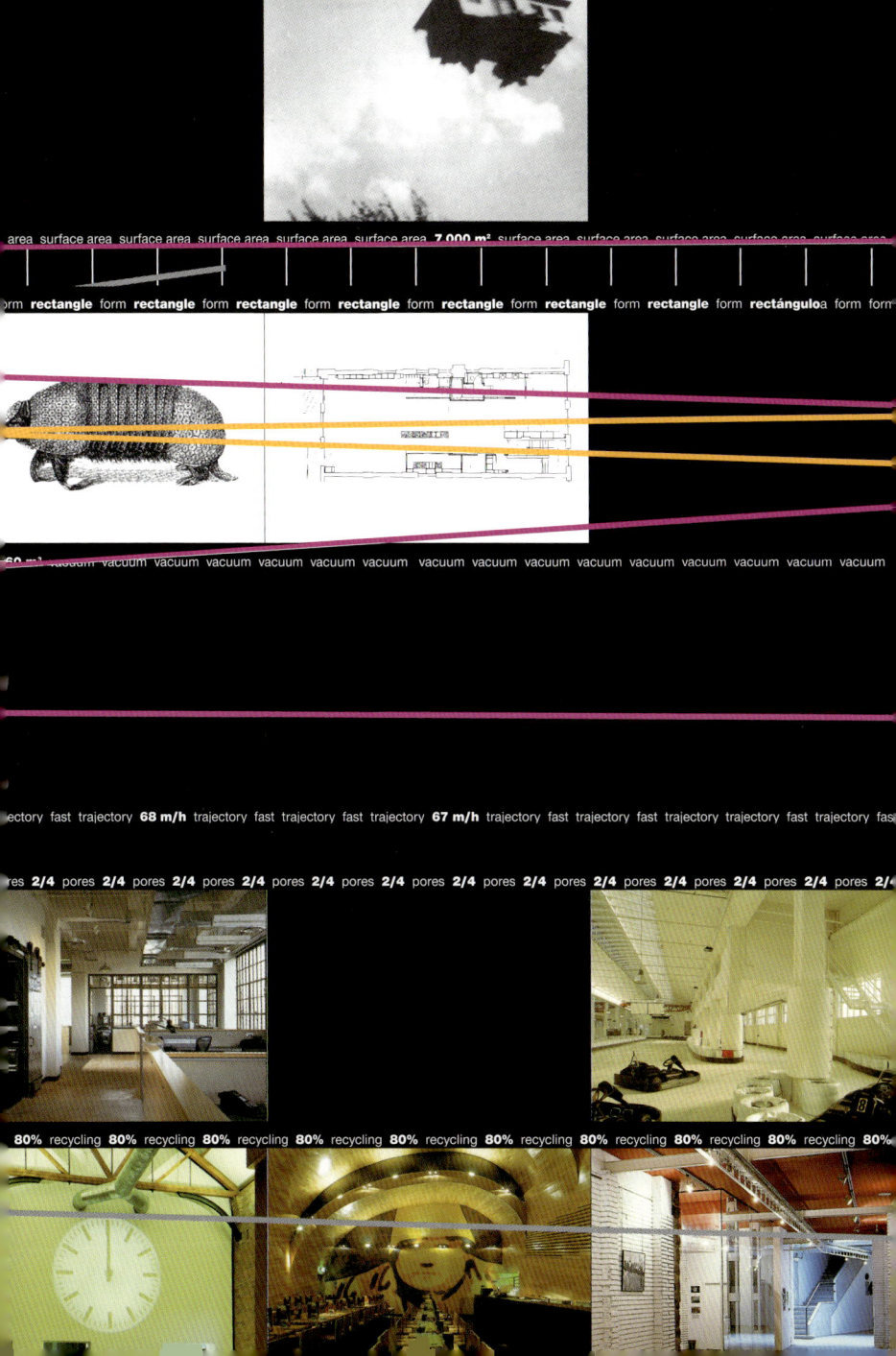

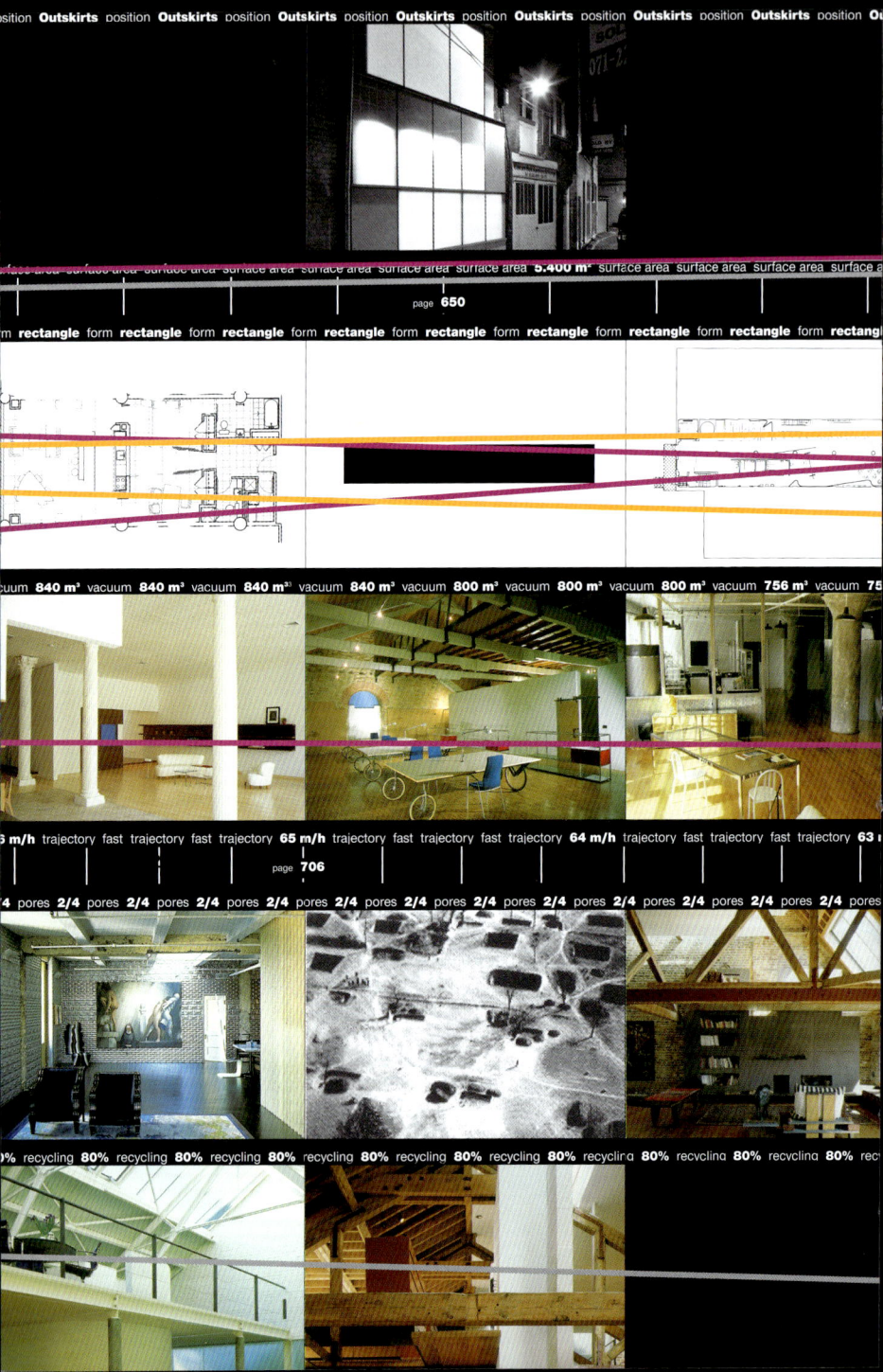

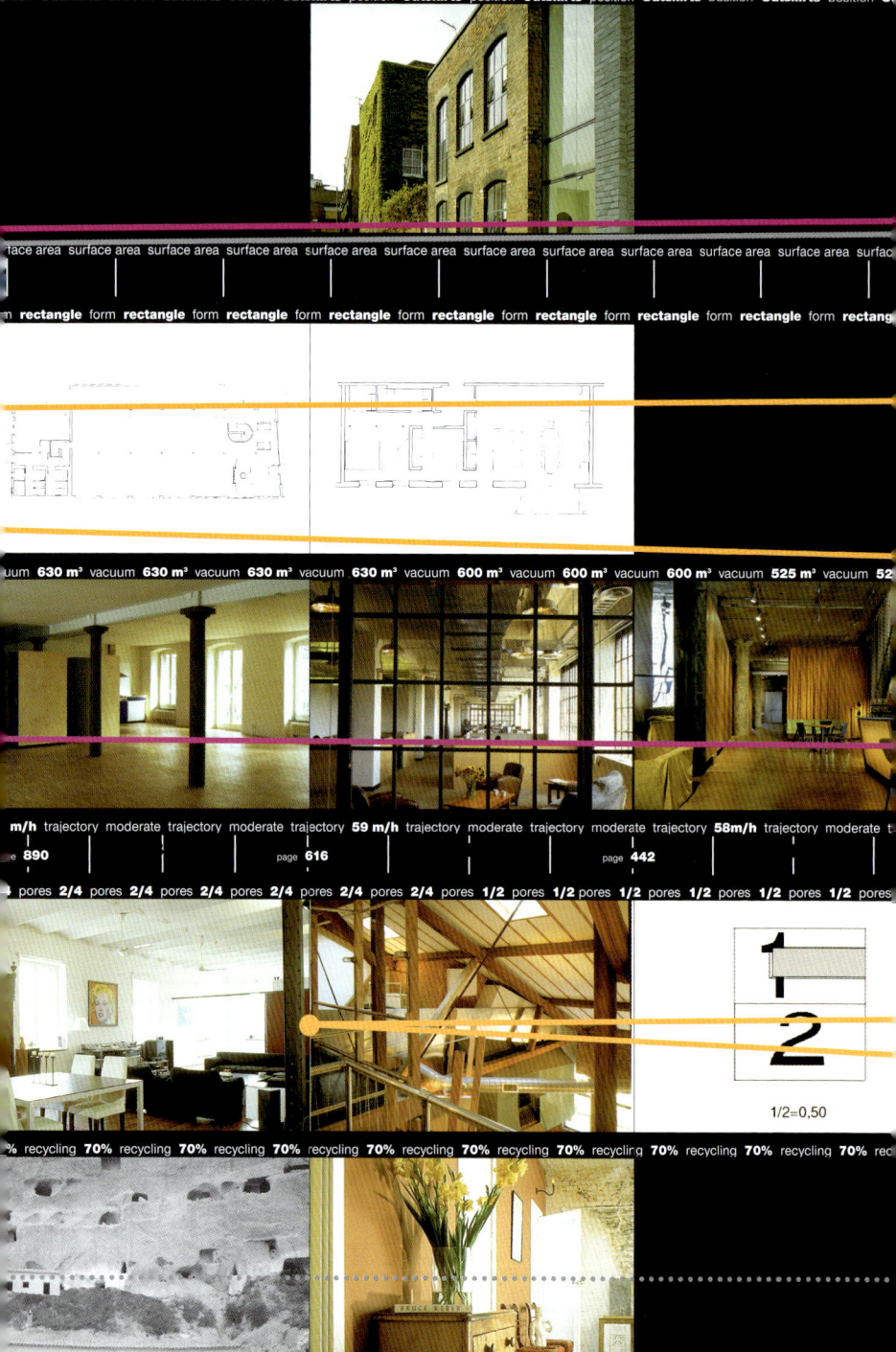

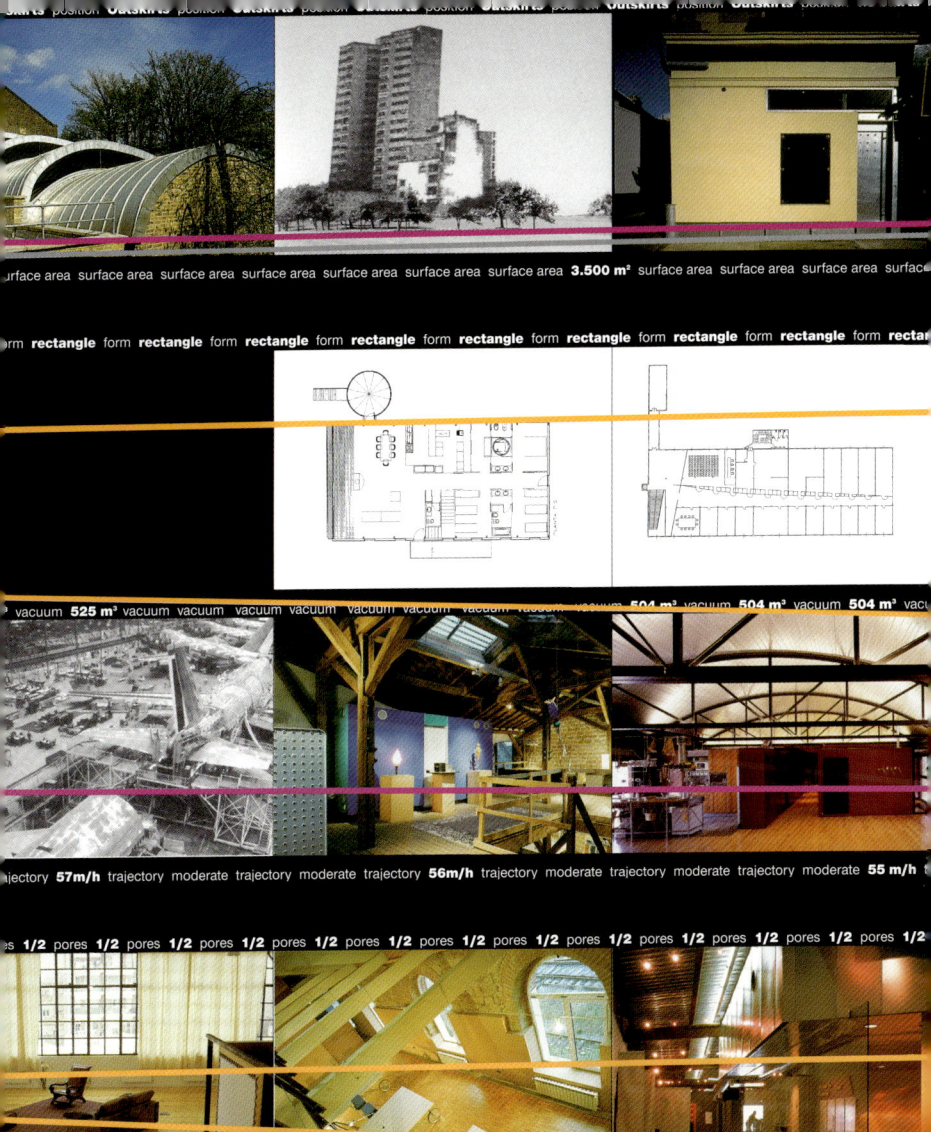

...irts position **Outskirts** position **Outskirts** position **Outskirts** position **Outskirts** position **Outskirts** position **Outskirts**

...urface area surface area surface area surface area surface area surface area surface area **3.500 m²** surface area surface area surface area surfac...

...rm **rectangle** form **rectangle** form **rectangle** form **rectangle** form **rectangle** form **rectangle** form **rectangle** form **rectangle** form **rectan...

... vacuum **525 m³** vacuum vacuum vacuum vacuum vacuum vacuum vacuum **504 m³** vacuum **504 m³** vacuum **504 m³** vacu...

...jectory **57m/h** trajectory moderate trajectory moderate trajectory **56m/h** trajectory moderate trajectory moderate trajectory moderate **55 m/h** t...

...es **1/2** pores **1/2** pores **1/2** pores **1/2** pores **1/2** pores **1/2** pores **1/2** pores **1/2** pores **1/2** pores **1/2** pores **1/2** pores **1/2**

70% recycling **70%** recycling **70%** recycling **70%** recycling **70%** recycling **70%** recycling **70%** recycling **70%** recycling **70%** recycling **70%**

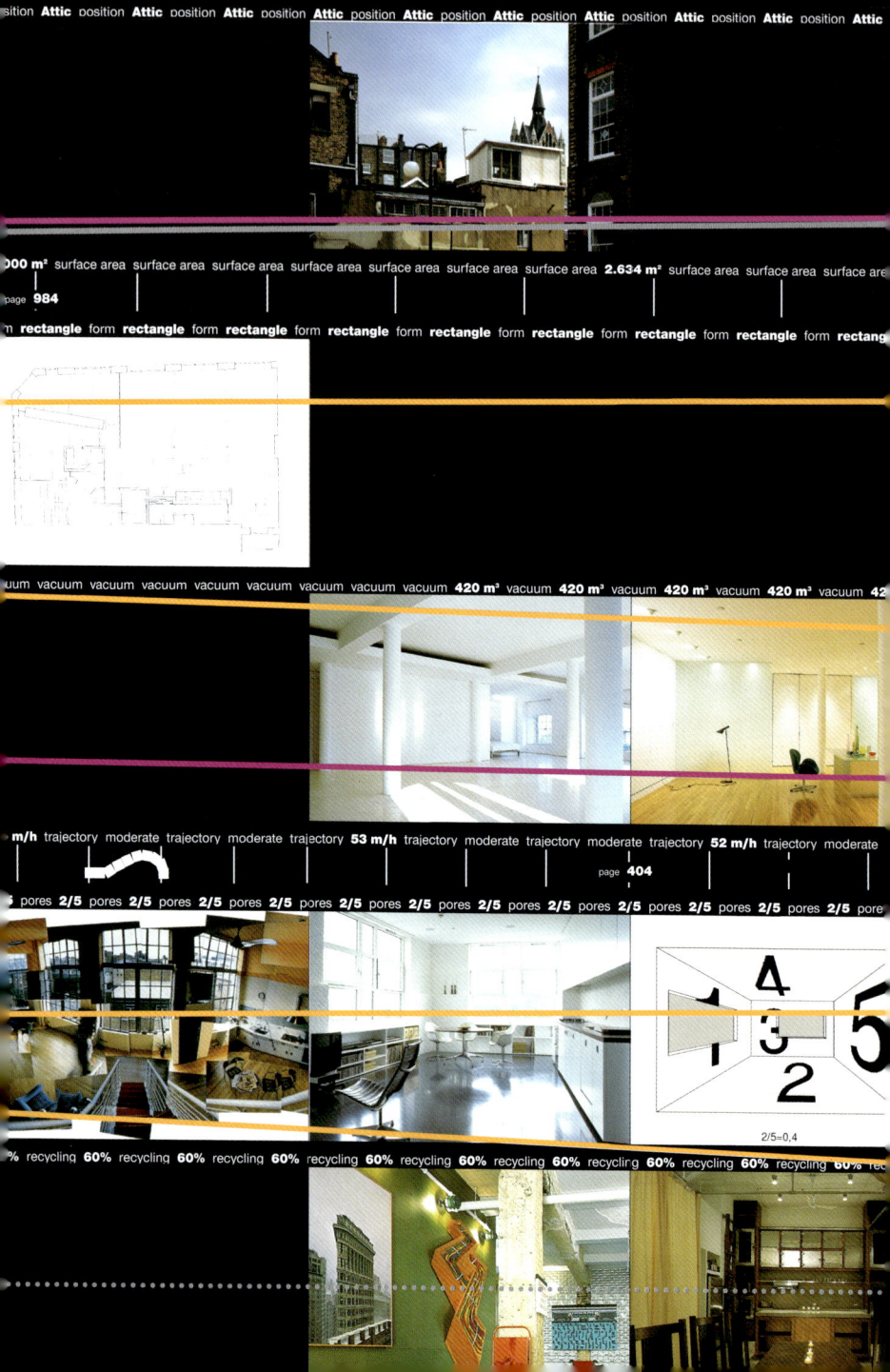

Attic position Attic position Attic position Attic position Attic position Attic position Attic position Attic

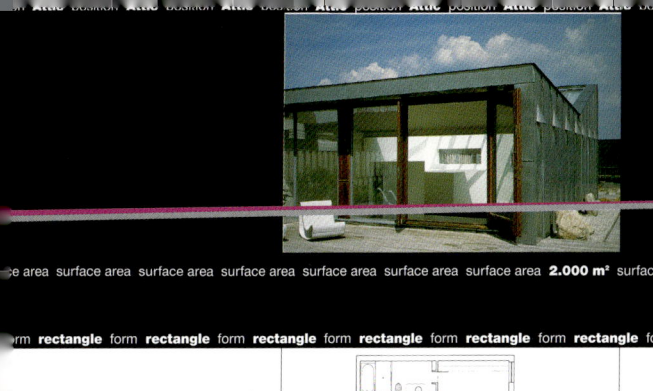

surface area surface area surface area surface area surface area surface area surface area **2.000 m²** surface area surface area surface area surface area

form **rectangle** form **rectangle** form **rectangle** form **rectangle** form **rectangle** form **rectangle** form **rectangle** form **rectangle** form recta

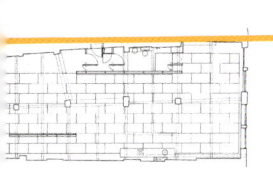 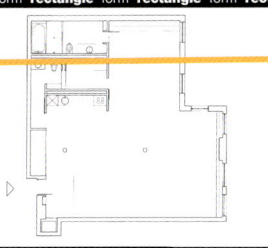 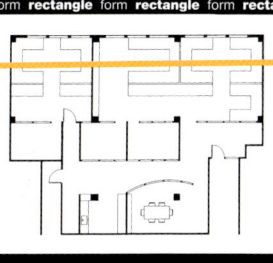

vacuum **420 m³** vacuum **420 m³** vacuum **420 m³** vacuum **420 m³** vacuum **420 m³** vacuum vacuum vacuum vacuum vacuum vacu

trajectory **51 m/h** trajectory moderate trajectory moderate trajectory moderate trajectory **50 m/h** trajectory moderate trajectory moderate trajectory **49 m/**

res **2/5** pores **2/5** pores **1/3** pores **1/3** pores **1/3** pores **1/3** pores **1/3** pores **1/3** pores **1/3** pores **1/3** pores **1/3** pores **1/**

60% recycling **60%** recycling **60%** recycling **60%** recycling **60%** recycling **60%** recycling **60%** recycling **60%** recycling **60%** recycling **60%**

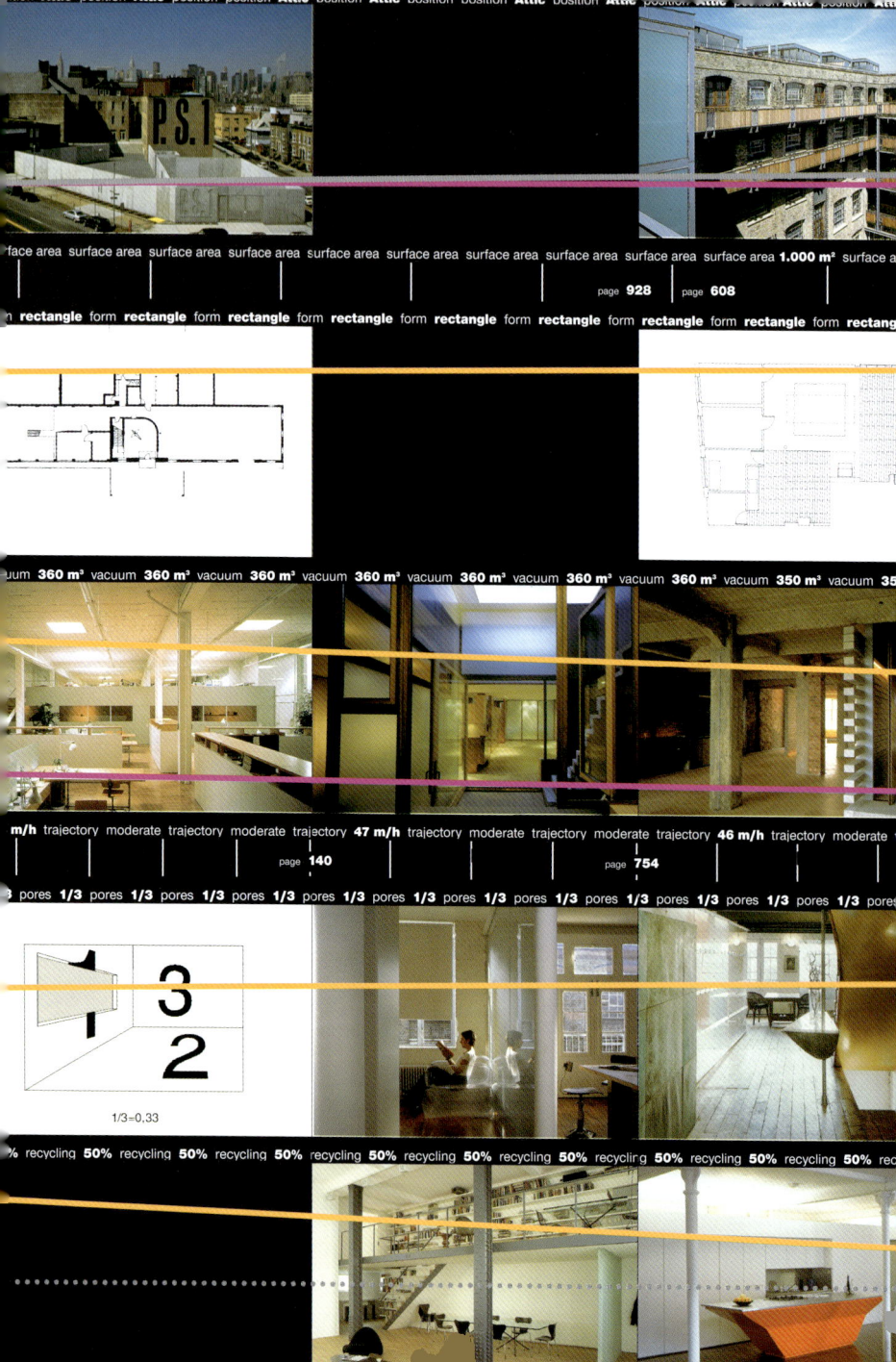

Attic position Attic position Attic position Attic position Attic position Attic position Attic position Attic position Att

surface area surface area surface area surface area surface area surface area surface area surface area surface area surface area surface

form **rectangle** form **rectangle** form **rectangle** form **rectangle** form **rectangle** form **rectangle** form **rectangle** form **rectangle** form **rectangle** form recta

vacuum **350 m³** vacuum **320 m³** vacuum **320 m³** vacuum **320 m³** vacuum **320 m³** vacuum **302 m³** vacuum **302 m³** vacuum **302 m³** vacuu

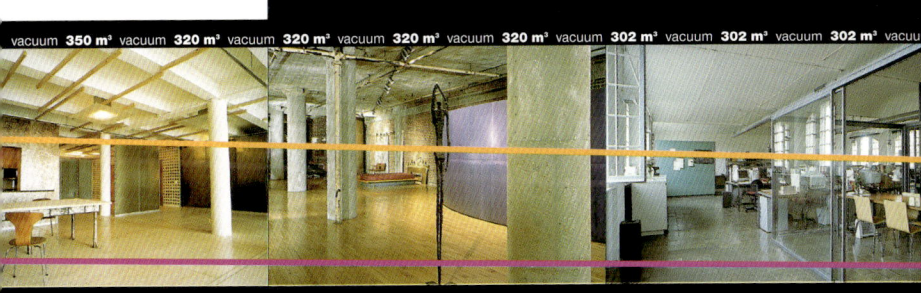

trajectory **45 m/h** trajectory cruising trajectory cruising trajectory **44 m/h** trajectory cruising trajectory cruising trajectory **43 m/h** trajectory cruisi

es **1/3** pores **1/3** pores **1/3** pores **1/3** pores **1/3** pores **1/3** pores **1/3** pores **1/3** pores **1/3** pores **1/3** pores **1/3** pores **1/3**

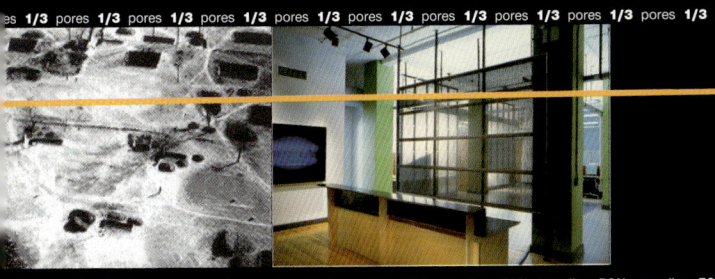

50% recycling **50%** recycling **50%** recycling **50%** recycling **50%** recycling **50%** recycling **50%** recycling **50%** recycling **50%** recycling **50%**

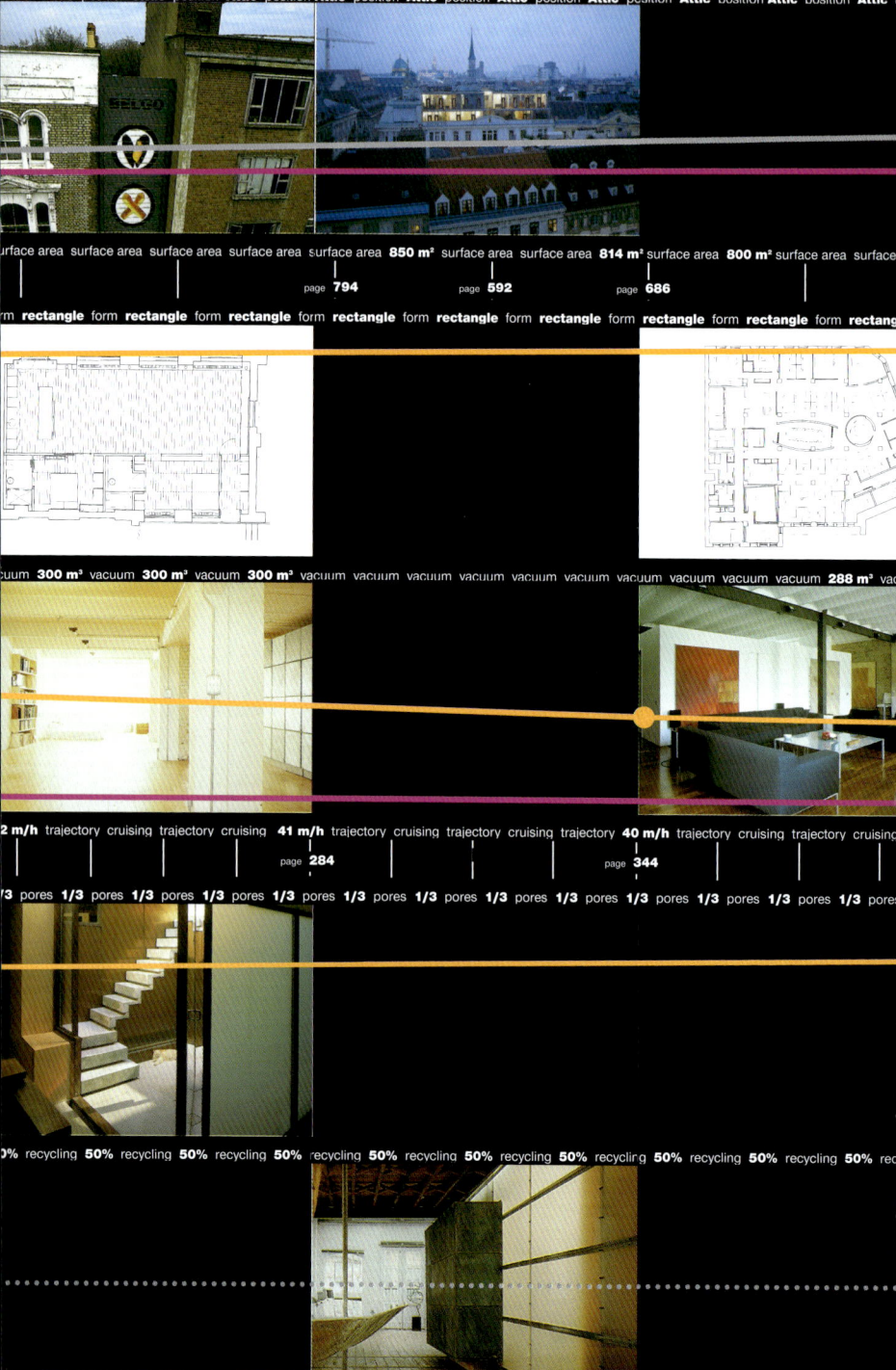

Attic position **Attic** position **Attic** position **Attic** position **Attic** position **Attic** position **Attic** position **Attic** position **Attic** position **Attic** posit

surface area surface area surface area surface area surface area surface area surface area surface area surface area surface area surface area **700**

rm **rectangle** form **rectangle** form **rectangle** form **rectangle** form **rectangle** form **rectangle** form **rectangle** form **rectangle** form **rectan**

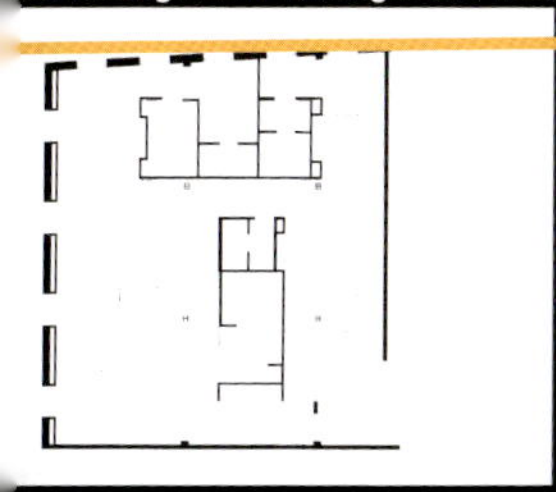

288 m³ vacuum **288 m³** vacuum vacuum vacuum vacuum vacuum vacuum vacuum vacuum vacuum **252 m³** vacuum **252 m²** vacuum **252 m**

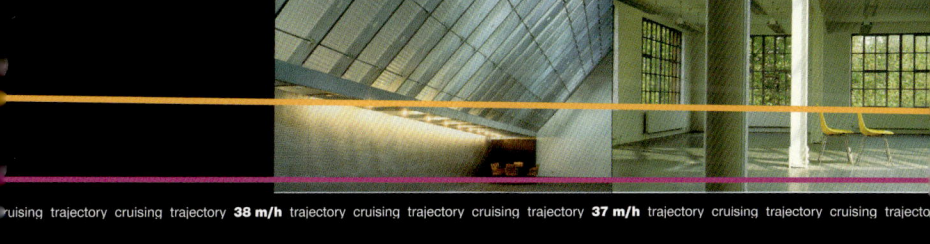

uising trajectory cruising trajectory **38 m/h** trajectory cruising trajectory cruising trajectory **37 m/h** trajectory cruising trajectory cruising trajecto

es **1/3** pores **1/3** pores **1/3** pores **1/3** pores **1/3** pores **1/3** pores **1/3** pores **1/3** pores **1/3** pores **1/3** pores **1/3** pores **1/3**

40% recycling **40%** recycling **40%** recycling **40%** recycling **40%** recycling **40%** recycling **40%** recycling **40%** recycling **40%** recycling **40%**

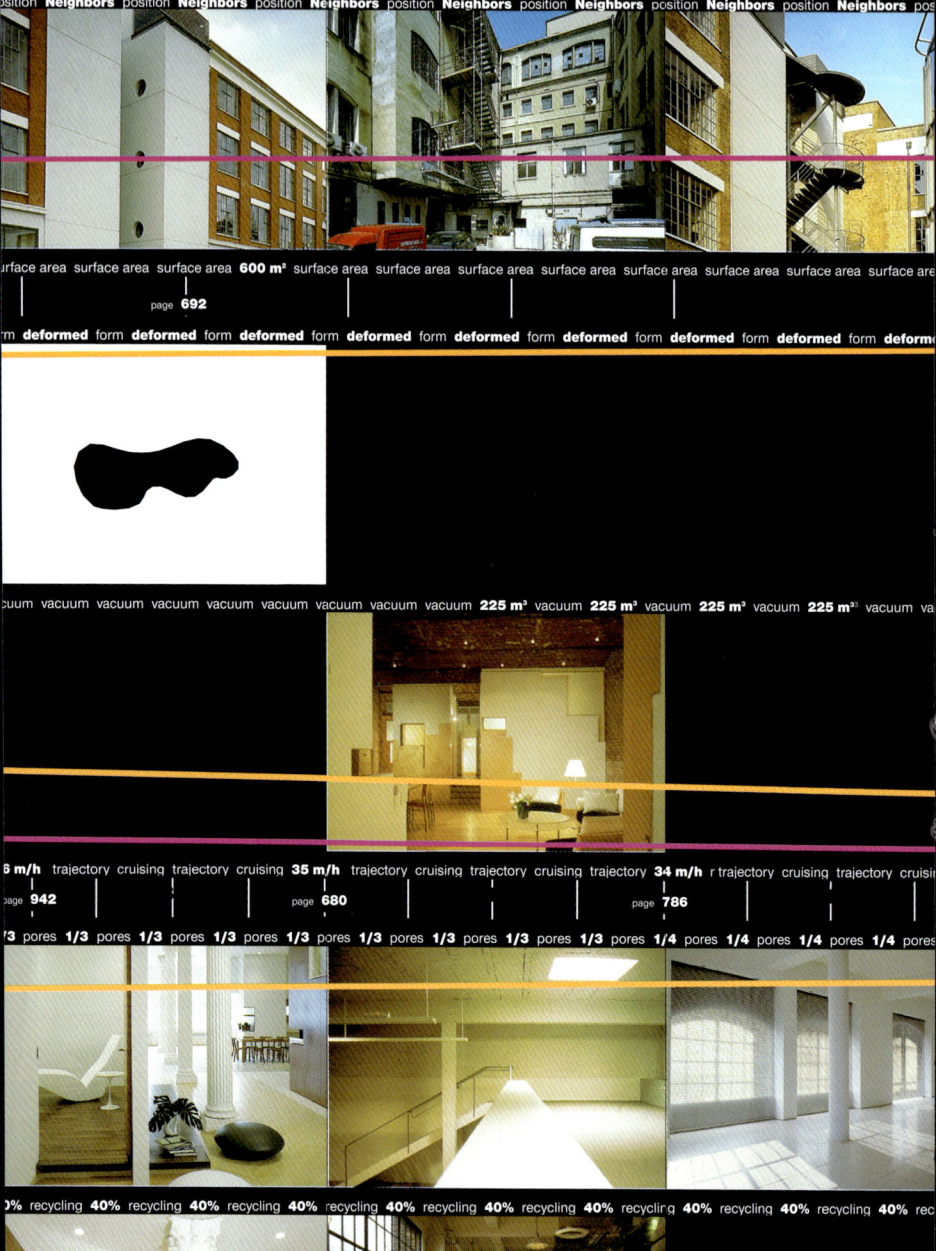

Neighbors position Neighbors position Neighbors position Neighbors position Neighbors position Neighbors position Neighbors positi

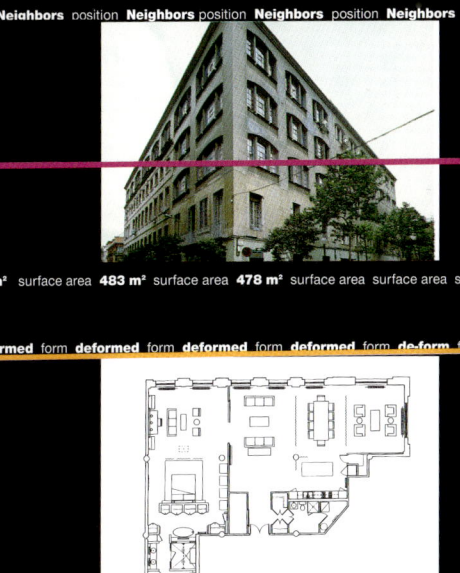

area surface area **500 m²** surface area **483 m²** surface area **478 m²** surface area surface area surface area surface area surface area surface a

rm **deformed** form **deformed** form **deformed** form **deformed** form **deformed** form **de-form** form **deformed** form **deformed** form **deformed** form **deform**

vacuum vacuum vacuum vacuum vacuum vacuum vacuum vacuum vacuum vacuum vacuum vacuum vacuum **210 m³** vacuum **210 m³** vacu

cruising trajectory cruising trajectory **32 m/h** trajectory cruising trajectory cruising **31 m/h** trajectory cruising trajectory cruising trajectory tra

s **1/4** pores **1/4** pores **1/4** pores **1/4** pores **1/4** pores **1/4** pores **1/4** poros **1/4** pores **1/4** poros **1/4** pores **1/4** pores **1/4** pores **1/4** p

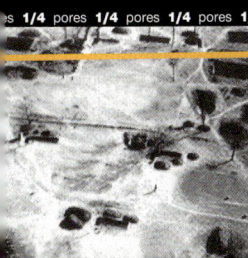 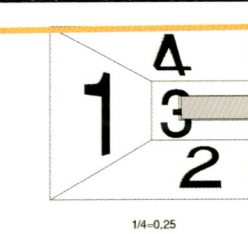 

1/4=0.25

40% recycling **40%** recycling **40%** recycling **40%** recycling **40%** recycling **40%** recycling **40%** recycling **40%** recycling **40%** recycling **40%**

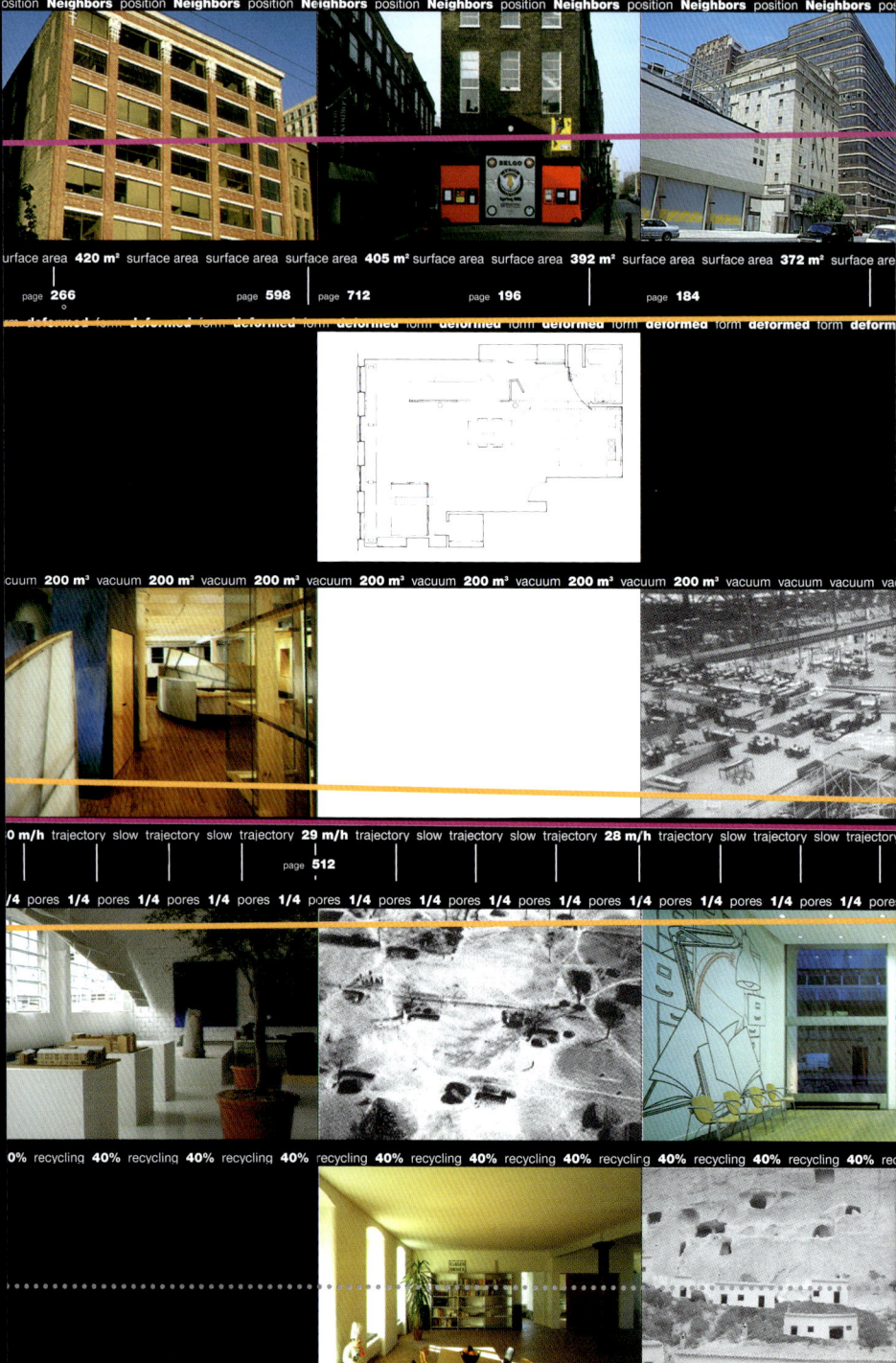

Neighbors position **Neighbors** position **Neighbors** position **Neighbors** position **Neighbors** position **Neighbors** position **Neighbors** position

area surface area surface area surface area surface area surface area surface area surface area surface area surface area surface area surface area

deformed form **deformed** form **deformed** form **deformed** form **deformed** form **deformed** form **deformed** form **deformed** form **deformed** form **deform**

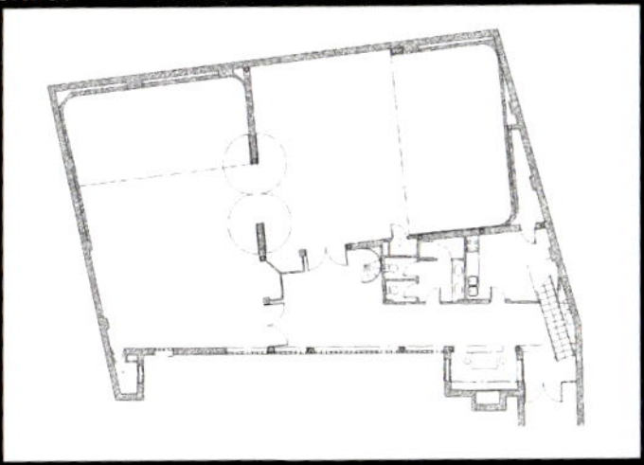

vacuum vacuum vacuum vacuum vacuum vacuum vacuum vacuum vacuum vacuum vacuum vacuum vacuum vacuum vacuum vacuum vacuum

ry slow trajectory slow trajectory slow **26 m/h** trajectory slow trajectory slow trajectory slow **25 m/h** trajectory slow trajectory slow trajectory sl

es **1/4** pores **1/4** pores **1/4** pores **1/4** pores **1/4** pores **1/4** pores **1/4** pores **1/4** pores **1/4** pores **1/4** pores **1/4** poros **1/4** p

40% recycling **40%** recycling **40%** recycling **30%** recycling **30%** recycling **30%** recycling **30%** recycling **30%** recycling **30%** recycling **30%** r

Neighbors position **Neighbors** position **Neighbors** position **Neighbors** position **Neighbors** position **Neighbors** position **Neighbors** position

0 m² surface area **190 m²** surface area **180 m²** surface area **160 m²** surface area **150 m²** surface area **135 m²** surface area **125 m²** surface area

form **deformed** form **deformed** form **deformed** form **deformed** form **deformed** form **deformed** form **deformed** form **deformed** form **deform**

vacuum **150 m³** vacuum vacuum vacuum vacuum vacuum vacuum vacuum vacuum **140 m³** vacuum **140 m³** vacuum **140 m³** vacuum **140 m³** va

1/4 pores **1/4** pores **1/4** pores **1/4** pores **1/4** pores **1/4** pores **1/4** pores **1/4** pores **1/4** pores **1/4** pores **1/4** pores **1/4**

30% recycling **30%** recycling **30%** recycling **30%** recycling **30%** recycling **30%** recycling **30%** recycling **30%** recycling **30%** r

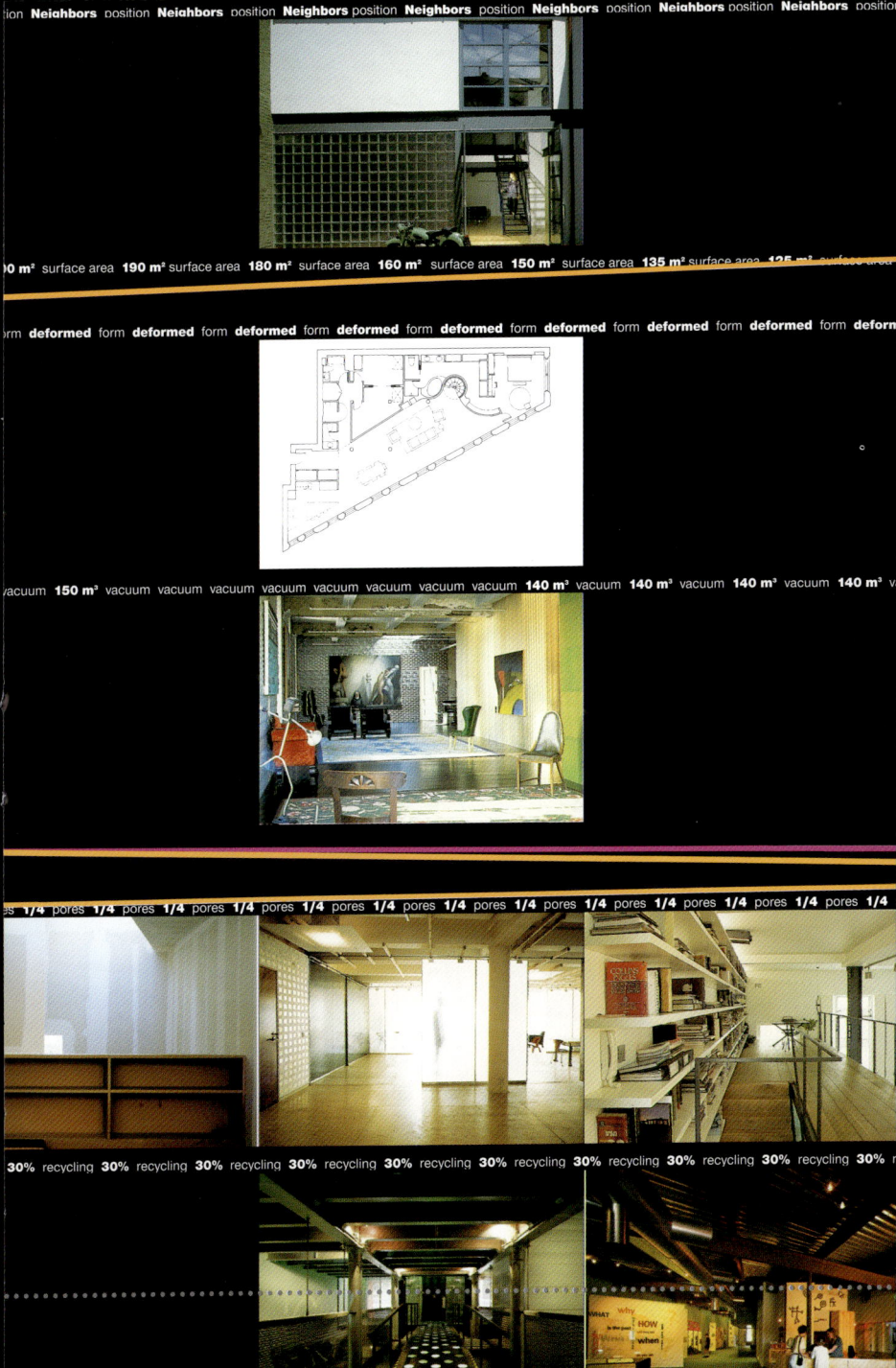

area surface area surface area surface area surface area surface area surface area surface area surface area surface area surface area surface area surface are

rm **deformed** form **deformed** form **deformed** form **deformed** form **deformed** form **deformed** form **deformed** form **deformed** form **deformed** form **deformed** form **defor**

acuum vacuum vacuum vacuum vacuum vacuum vacuum vacuum vacuum vacuum vacuum vacuum vacuum vacuum vacuum vacuum vacuum

ectory immobile trajectory immobile trajectory **14 m/h** trajectory immobile trajectory immobile trajectory **13 m/h** trajectory immobile trajectory

s **1/5** pores **1/5** pores **1/5** pores **1/5** pores **1/5** pores **1/5** pores **1/5** pores **1/5** pores **1/5** pores **1/5** pores **1/5** pores **1/5** pores **1/**

1/5=0,20

0% recycling **30%** recycling **30%** recycling **30%** recycling **20%** recycling **20%** recycling **20%** recycling **20%** recycling **20%** recycling **20%**

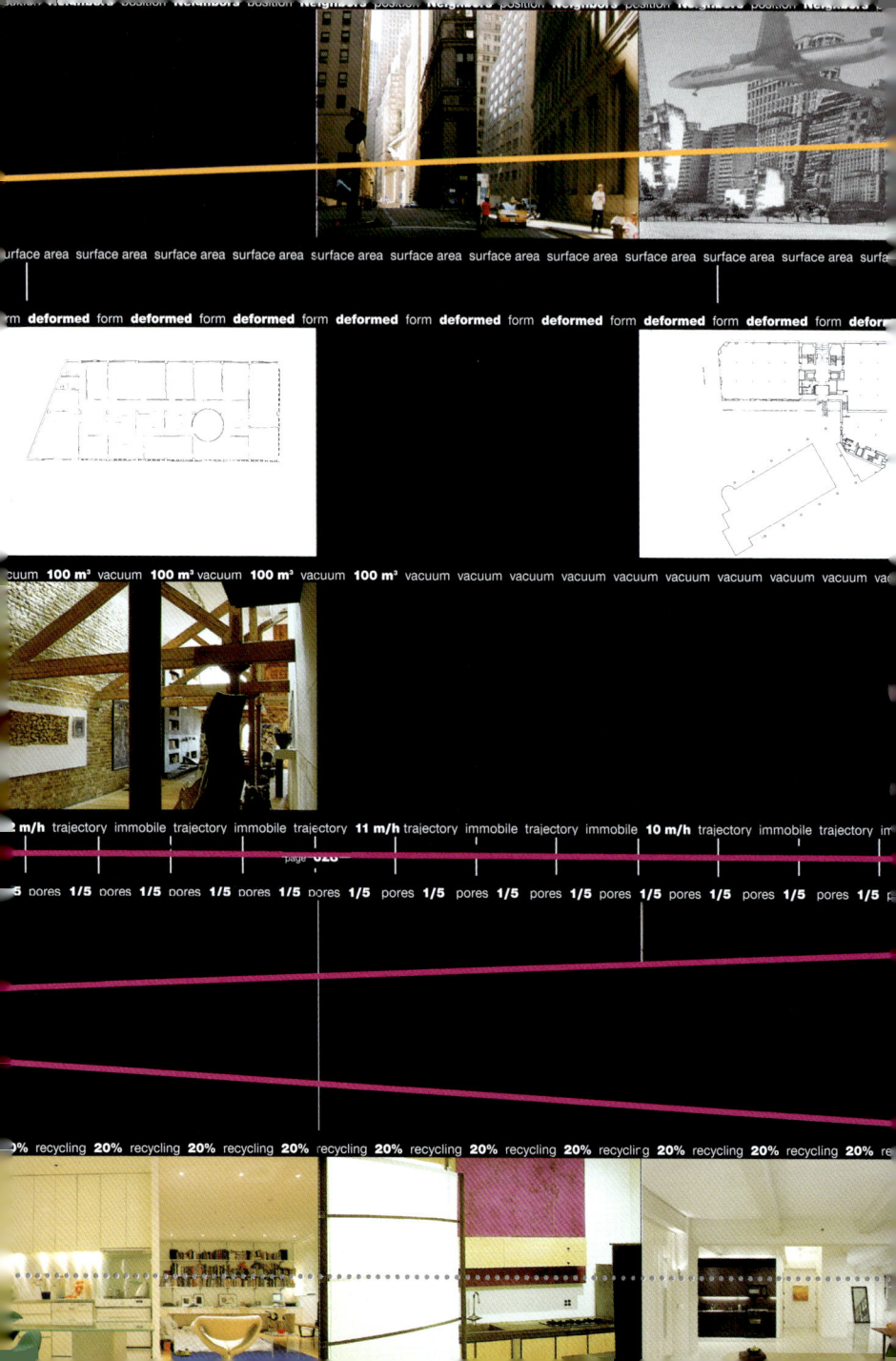

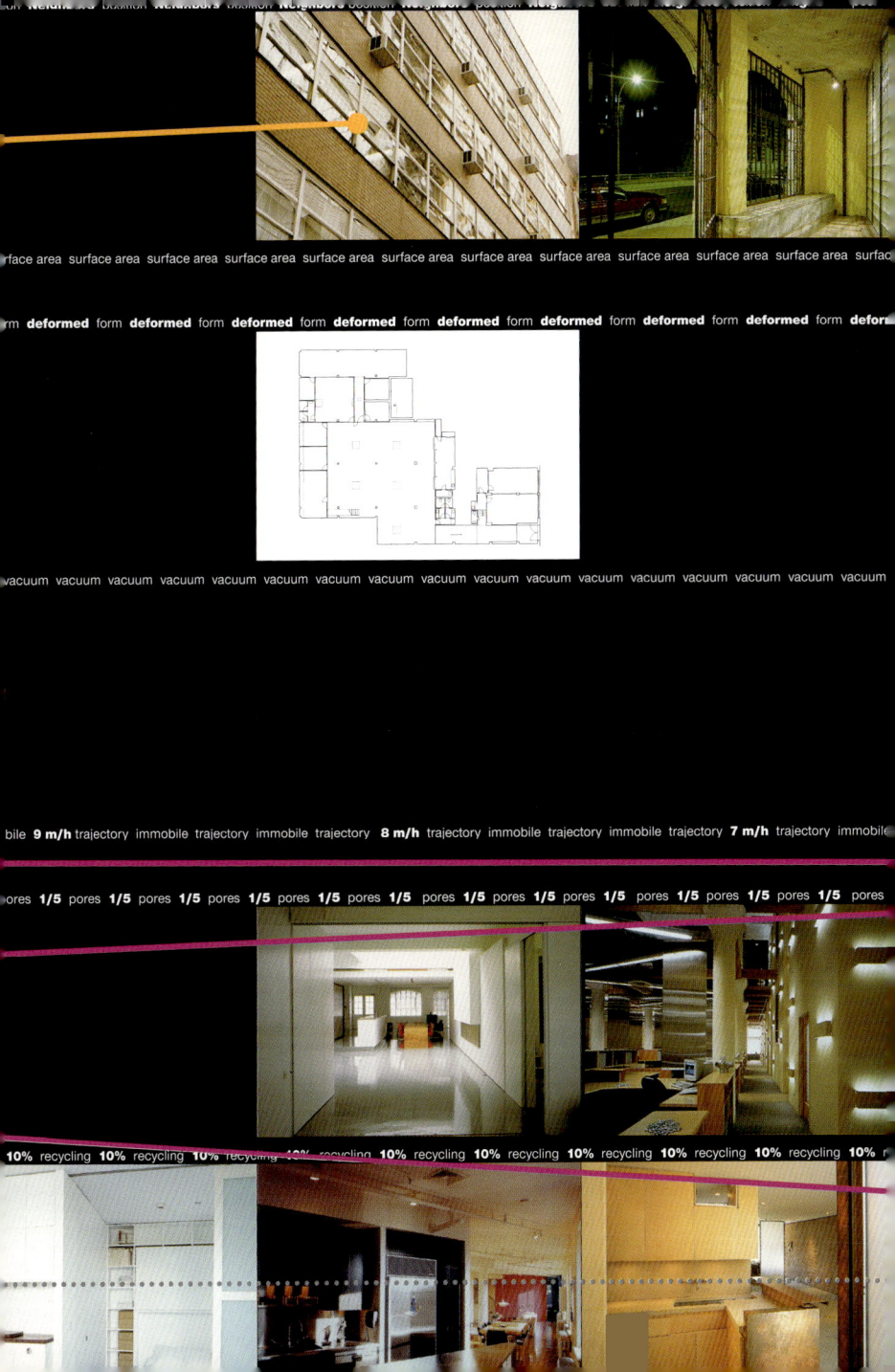

surface area surface area surface area surface area surface area surface area surface area surface area surface area surface area surface area surfa

form **formless** form **formless** form **formless** form **formless** form **formless** form **formless** form **formless** form **formless** form **formless** form

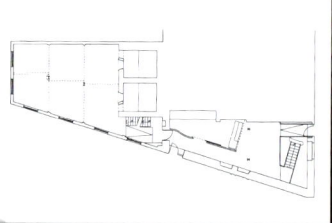

vacuum vacuum vacuum vacuum vacuum vacuum vacuum vacuum vacuum vacuum vacuum vacuum vacuum vacuum vacuum vacuum vacuum va

m/h trajectory immobile trajectory immobile trajectory **5 m/h** trajectory immobile trajectory immobile trajectory **4 m/h** trajectory immobile trajec

page **172** page **364**

1/5 pores **1/5** pores **1/5** pores **1/5** pores **1/5** pores **1/5** pores **1/5** pores **1/5** pores **1/5** pores **1/5** pores **1/5** pores **1/5** pores **1/5** pores **1/5**

% recycling **10%** recycling **10%** recycling **10%** recycling **10%** recycling **10%** recycling **10%** recycling **10%** recycling **10%** recycling **10%** rec

eraround position **Underaround** position **Underground** position **Underground** position **Underaround** position **Underaround** position **Undera**

face area surface area surface area surface area surface area surface area surface area surface area surface area **20 m²** surface area surface area

ss form **formless** form **formless** form **formless** form **formless** form **formless** form **formless** form **formless** form **formless** form **formless**

60 m³ vacuum **60 m³** vacuum **60 m³** vacuum vacuum vacuum vacuum vacuum vacuum vacuum vacuum vacuum vacuum vacuum vacuum vacuu

3 m/h trajectory immobile trajectory immobile trajectory **2 m/h** trajectory immobile trajectory immobile trajectory **1 m/h** trajectory immobile traj

ores **1/5** pores **1/5** pores **1/5** pores **1/5** pores **1/5** pores **1/5** pores **1/5** pores **1/5** pores **1/5** pores **1/5** pores **1/5** pores **1**

0% recycling **10%** recycling **10%** recycling **10%** recycling **10%** recycling **10%** recycling **10%** recycling **10%** recycling **10%** recycling **10%** rec

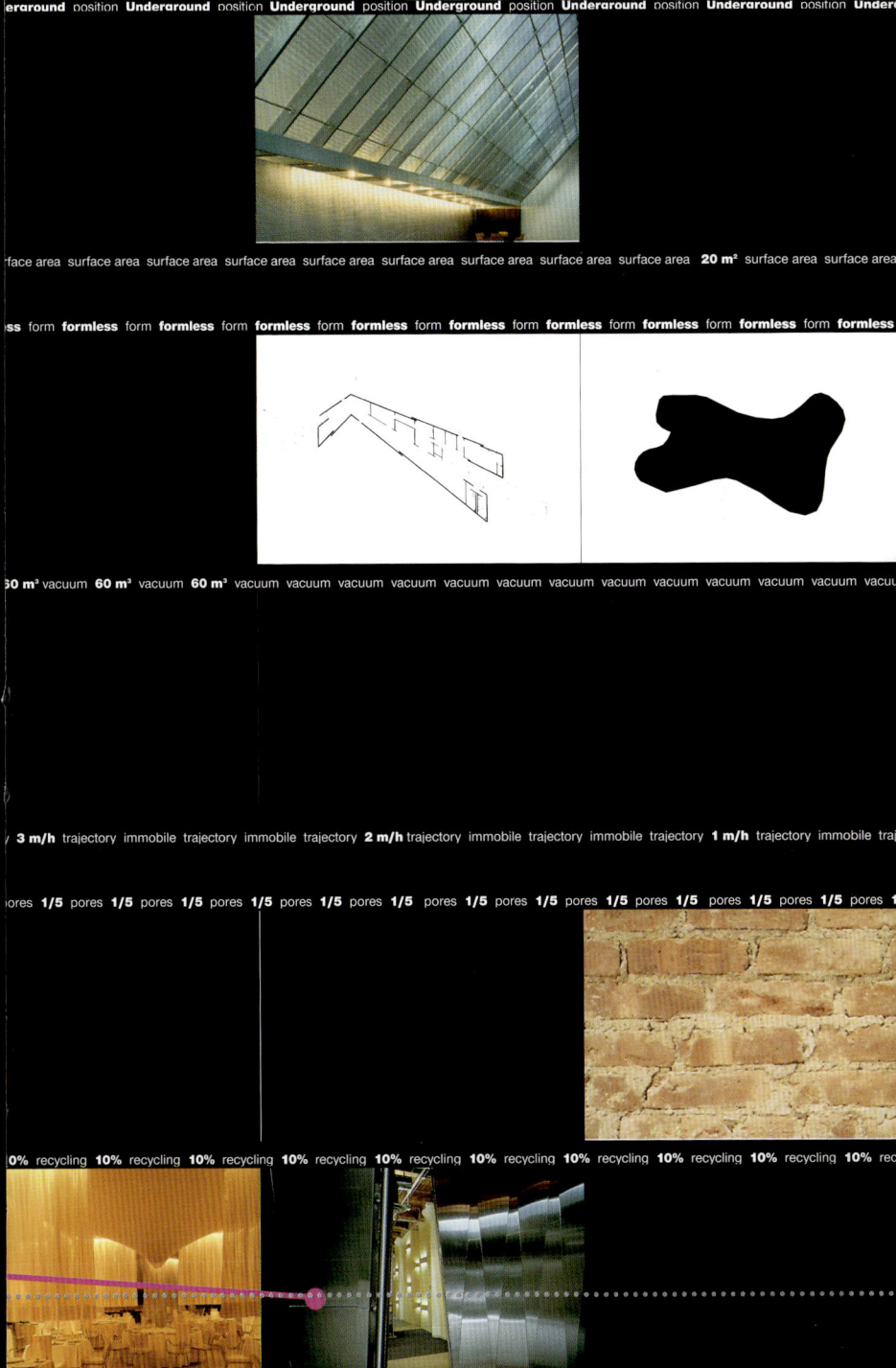

Essentialist loft

The exercise proposed in the manual has given rise to a classification of lofts, corresponding to personality types; here we present the essentialist loft.

"Essentialist" in this context denotes a loft that has been freed of any impurities.

The essentialist loft is also the result of a spatial recycling process, not merely in functional but also in qualitative terms.

Ridding a loft of impurities basically involves elimination and selection, always on the basis of criteria established from the outset and followed throughout the design and construction phases.

The essentialist loft can be situated on any story; in this case we have chosen an attic. It is big, but not too big, and it has a tightly controlled aesthetic style. It has a large amount of bare space, as the personality type in question is very coherent and only keeps what is essential.

In the essentialist loft there is a little of everything – building work, furniture, objects – but it is all selected with consummate care. It is possible to move about quickly and without any hindrance. There is usually a lot of light, and it is guaranteed that many of the loft's initial elements are retained and suitably adapted during recycling.

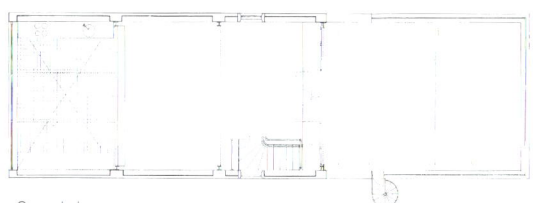

Ground plan

living
in a *loft*

"A house, even more than a landscape, is a psychological state"

Gaston Bachelard, *The poetics of space*

Luminous environment | Peter Tow Studios

Manhattan's West Side, on the banks of the river Hudson, is the setting for this loft overlooking the mouth of the Holland tunnel, which connects Manhattan island with New Jersey. The loft also has some wonderful views of the famous skyscrapers in this neighborhood, although the conversion aimed to provide a restful haven from the hubbub of the city down below. The industrial style of the exterior contrasts with the interior, which has been deliberately designed to be stark and luminous.

The original concrete floor has been covered by maple wood throughout the apartment – except in the entrance, where limestone has been used to mark the way to the kitchen. A frosted glass wall runs from north to south to separate the bedrooms from the rest of the space, thereby providing privacy without blocking the light. The contrast between the loft's sharply defined look and the roughness of concrete and the texture of the original brick walls emphasizes the refinement of the design, without ever straying from the loft aesthetic. All the closets and shelves are made of lacquered maple wood.

This loft is more or less square in shape and is lined with windows on three sides. The dining area is in the middle of the living room and constitutes the symbolic heart of the space. The bathrooms are simple and white; the kitchen is in the northeast corner, where it intersects with the translucent glass panel. The use of maple wood and stainless steel in the kitchen is both functional and elegant. The whole is tasteful and subtle.

Architects: Peter Tow Studios
Location: New York, United States
Photographs: Björg Amarsdoottir

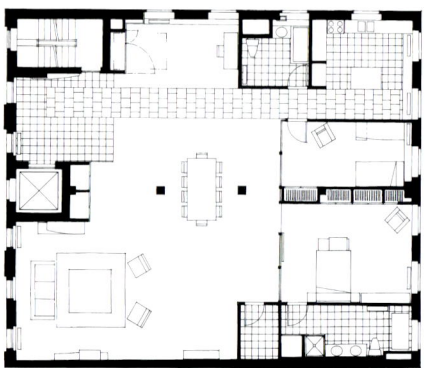

Ground plan

The central island in the kitchen has a black granite top that provides a clean position for the preparation of delicious meals, especially pasta.

A sliding panel in this wall works as a *shoji*-type screen, controlling the extent to which the room opens onto the rest of the loft.

Dualities | Dean/Wolf Architects

Prior to conversion, the main defining characteristic of this loft in New York's Tribeca neighborhood was the light that poured in through the windows on the southern façade. The two rooms in the back, however, were small and dark, and the irregular layout was awkward.

The first problem faced by the architects was these two small rooms, which blocked the flow of light into the apartment. They were demolished, creating a single flexible space that could be adapted to a wide range of circumstances. Minimalist furnishings serve to enhance the spaciousness of the new layout.

The loft's open space was adapted to accommodate the requirements of working and living in the same space. The strategy underlying the design saw the loft as a collage of operations, a system of mobile components, and a series of connections that not only increase the space but also give a sense of freedom.

The wall/office duality marks both the boundary and the visual link between the working area and the dining room. A screen made of natural fibers hides the disorder of the office while also leading the eye to the dining area. Other dualities are the bedroom/table and the bathroom/staircase.

Architects: Dean/Wolf Architects
Location: New York, United States
Photographs: Dean/Wolf Architects

143

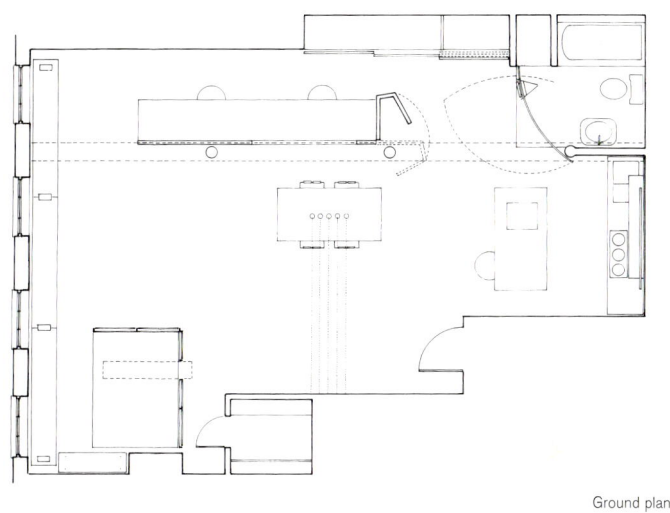

Ground plan.

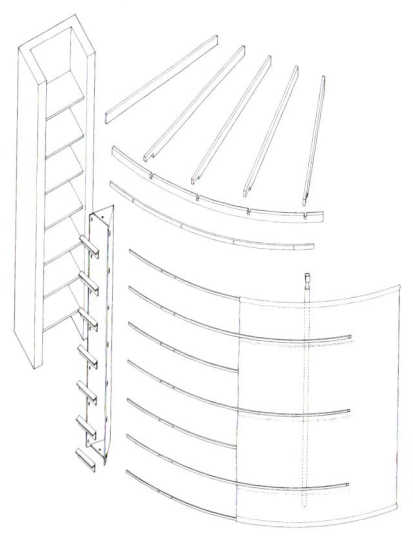

The three dualities that have been created are office/wall, bedroom/table, and bathroom/staircase.

Visual freedom | Alexander Gorlin

This loft on Hudson Street, in New York's Tribeca neighborhood, was designed in 1994 by the architect Alexander Gorlin, who skillfully organized the space to endow the entire area alongside the façade with visual continuity and freedom. The loft's triangular shape reflects the sheer diversity of forms within the apartment itself, where every constructed element, whether it is a staircase, a wall, or a simple closet, has been allowed to take on a strong identity of its own.

An organic circular wall marks off the spiral staircase that leads to the roof garden and also serves as a skylight that permits the sunlight to penetrate the interior.

The west-facing façade receives a lot of sunlight, which is reflected by the stainless steel of the fittings in the kitchen tucked into one of the corners of the triangle. The kitchen's central working space, also clad in stainless steel, echoes the apartment's triangular shape.

At the other end of the apartment, the curved wall shielding the spiral staircase also serves to separate the shared living space from the more private bedrooms. This succession of spaces contains the library, the main bedroom, the hall, and a fully fitted bathroom, with a tub that fits into the contours of the wall that separates it from the communal areas.

The result is a dynamic space with a richness of color and form, bathed in the natural light that pours through its long façade.

Architect: Alexander Gorlin
Location: New York, United States
Photographs: Peter Aaron/Esto

In one of the corners of the loft, a free-standing circular wall sets off the perimeter wall, which runs uninterrupted along the entire front of the apartment.

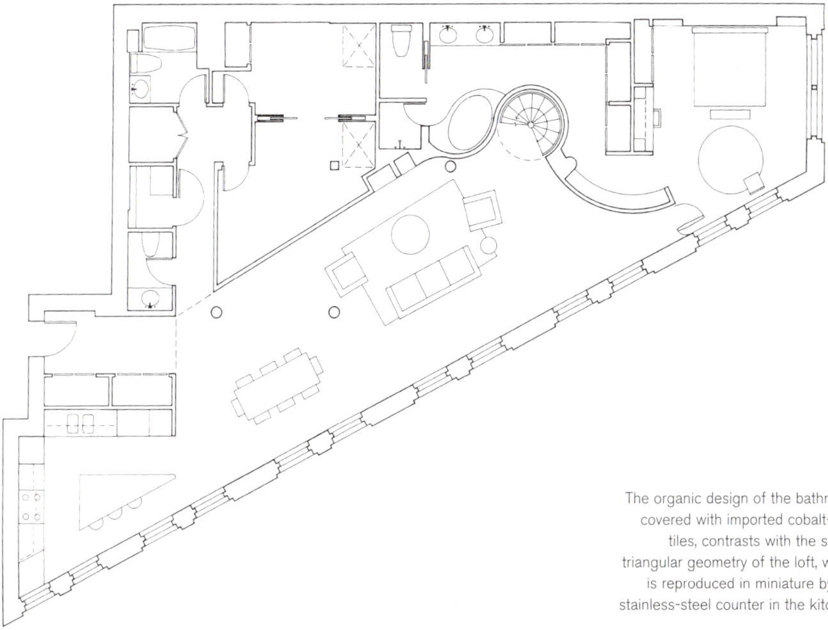

The organic design of the bathroom, covered with imported cobalt-blue tiles, contrasts with the sharp, triangular geometry of the loft, which is reproduced in miniature by the stainless-steel counter in the kitchen.

Chelsea district | Kar-hwa Ho Architecture Design, S. Sirefman

This loft in New York's Chelsea district has a total surface area of 2,300 square feet (214 sq m). The design and layout of this new home was entrusted to the team of the architect Kar-hwa Ho, working in conjunction with Susanna Sirefman. Their main objective was to capture as much sunlight as possible from the exterior. They tried to connect and define the various spaces according to their functions so that, although there was a spatial continuity and a visible connection between them, they also worked independently from each other. It was considered vital to make a clear distinction between the private areas, like the bedrooms, and the public ones, like the living room, dining room, and kitchen. It was also proposed that each separate area should be distinguished from the next by its design elements, although the overall effect should be one of complete calm and restfulness.

These ideas were brought to life by installing translucent windows to distribute light evenly in the interior. The lack of natural light in the interior of the apartment was compensated for by a bold and effective lighting system. The distribution of the furniture helped to define each space, and the relationship between the different areas was often defined by a mobile element, which also provided greater flexibility. A couple of distinctive finishing touches were added to the hall: zigzag chairs designed by Rietveld and a mirror by Gray.

A generally neutral chromatic range sets off each of the elements introduced into the space and, in combination with the apartment's dark floor, helps to unify the loft.

Architects: Kar-hwa Ho Architecture & Design, S. Sirefman
Location: New York, United States
Photographs: Björg/Photography

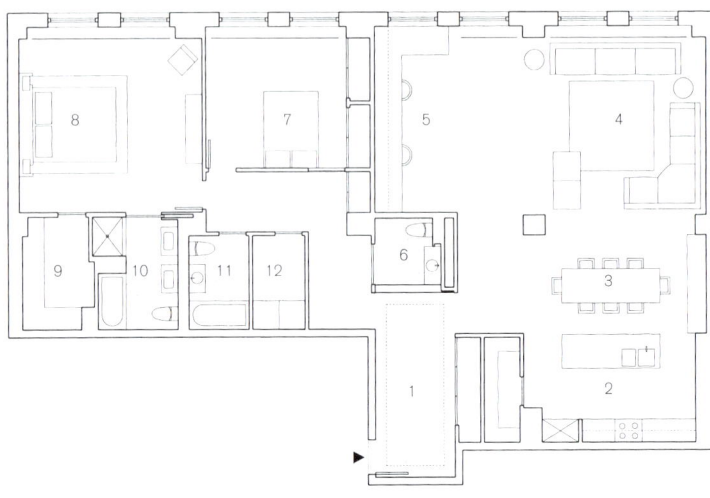

1. Hall
2. Kitchen
3. Dining room
4. Living room
5. Studios
6. Bathroom
7. Bedroom
8. Bedroom
9. Dressing room
10. Bathroom
11. Bathroom
12. Pantry

The architect designed low maple-wood closets with glass fronts and castors for the dining room.

The glass on each filing cabinet has been finished with a print in a different texture.

The desktop is made of translucent glass and is supported by the maple-wood table, which has legs tipped with stainless steel.

Intimacy

Kar-hwa Ho
Architecture & Design

This 1,205-square-foot (112 sq m) loft, refurbished by the architect Kar-hwa Ho, is set in a former garment factory in New York's Chelsea neighborhood.

The project focused on intimacy and contemplation of the interior space, as the views out of the windows are uninteresting! The strategy used was to enhance the luminosity effect in order to convey a sense of calmness and equilibrium.

The apartment's architectural features are unobtrusive, to allow both the furniture and the other objects to stand out and set off the space around them. The use of indirect light also mitigates any disorder resulting from the bustle of everyday life.

Spatial depth is achieved by using a series of transparent barriers incorporating translucent materials and frosted glass united by a range of very pale colors. Because the apartment's layout is designed for a single occupant, the spaces allocated for particular activities are allowed to flow into each other. The fact that the bathroom and toilet have no windows is compensated for by the use of luminous elements like mirrors, treated glass, and limestone, as well as by indirect lighting that adds a touch of glamour and comfort to these areas.

The details of the design maintain the same overall spirit, contributing to the brightness and fluidity characteristic of this loft.

Architects: Kar-hwa Ho Architecture & Design
Location: New York, United States
Photographs: Björg/Photography

1. Hall
2. Closet
3. Dining room/lounge
4. Kitchen
5. Bathroom
6. Dressing room
7. Bedroom/study
8. Library
9. Bathroom

K-Loft in New York | George Ranalli

This project involved refurbishing a space of around 2,150 square feet (200 sq m) in New York's Chelsea neighborhood for a couple of artists and their son. The building, once a garment factory, is 90 years old and is typical of the lower Manhattan architecture of that period, with long, narrow corridors, structural walls made of brick, and a series of small vaults framed by wrought iron.

The conversion emphasized the original structure by leaving bare both the brick walls and the metal girders running across the vaulted ceiling. The new materials that have been introduced create contoured areas that mark out the various functions of the home. White plaster walls rise up to the ceiling and link up with the brick walls, creating miniature versions of the juxtapositions that occur in the original space.

Wooden panels echo both the planked floor and the soaring white walls to create a complex interplay of lines and perspectives.

The only windows are situated at either end of the loft. Ranalli has dreamed up a succession of large spaces (exhibition areas, living room, bedrooms) separated in between by two small service areas (bathroom, kitchen, dressing room).

The K-Loft offers a wealth of connections between forms and materials, the new and the old, the perimeter and its contents.

Architect: George Ranalli
Location: New York, United States
Photographs: Paul Warchol

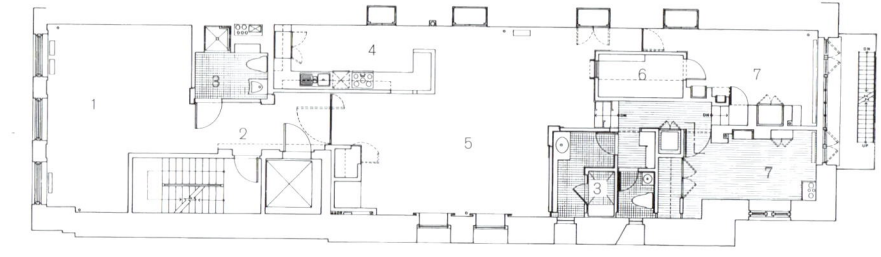

1. Gallery
2. Hall
3. Bathroom
4. Kitchen
5. Living room
6. Storeroom
7. Bedroom

The doors and closets are made of laminated ash, which is also used for the trim. Wooden panels with irregular edges provide a quirky contrast to the dominant linearity, in a manner reminiscent of Scarpa and Steven Holt.

Potter's loft

Resolution: 4. Architecture

The renovation of this loft, situated in New York's Chelsea district, reflects the ordered lifestyle of its owner. The loft comprises one long, open space leading to the central kitchen, with the bathroom and bedroom tucked away in the back. Each space is marked out by the different types of materials used: concrete panels on the ceiling set off the living room while the adjacent dining area is distinguished by its array of overhead lights and the stone block used as a fireplace. The kitchen closets and equipment are located in the center and along one side of the main area.

Both the kitchen and the dining area are lit by 20 or so strips of light, each connected to individual dimmer switches so that the lighting can be adjusted to suit any occasion.

The entrance is on one side of the loft, and the made-to-measure sliding metal door leads onto the building's staircase. In contrast, the pivoting door of the bedroom not only provides intimacy, but also lets in light and subtly changes the layout of the space according to its position. The outer windows offer a view of the street while adjustable roller blinds both protect privacy and make the sunlight pouring in from outside more diffuse.

This interplay of different textures and visual planes is the fruit of a painstaking search for the most suitable definition for each area, and its relationship to the whole.

Architects: Resolution: 4. Architecture
Location: New York, United States
Photographs: Eduard Hueber

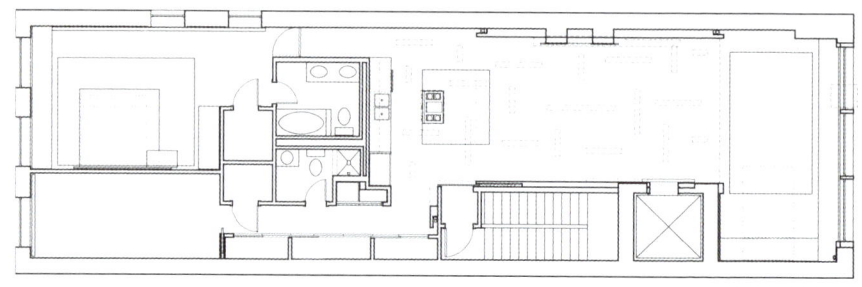

Concrete slabs on the ceiling mark out the living room, while an intense shower of light identifies the dining area.

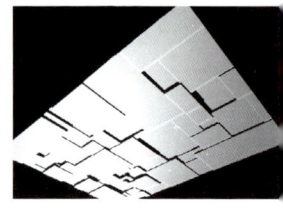

Monolithic structure

Resolution: 4. Architecture

This 1,700-square-foot (158 sq m) apartment in New York's financial district occupies the fourth floor of a former industrial building. The Resolution: 4 team, headed by the architects Joseph Tanney and Robert Luntz, was originally commissioned to renovate the kitchen area, but they came up with a proposal to overhaul the entire apartment and bring it closer to the classic loft aesthetic.

The long, narrow building, so typical of a New York loft, is divided into two by the elevator shaft and stairwell. The conversion project took advantage of this division by using it to differentiate the private spaces from the more public ones. One side was therefore given over to new, enlarged areas with two bathrooms, storage closets, and the bedroom – which has a specially designed folding bed that remains hidden behind a wooden screen when it is not in use. The other side of this screen (which also serves as a headrest for the extended bed) constitutes the rear wall of the kitchen. This monolithic but adaptable structure sets the tone for the whole apartment, with one space leading to another, from the bedroom through the kitchen on to the living room and, finally, the studio (which doubles as a guest room) situated in the front of the apartment.

Architects: Resolution: 4. Architecture
Location: New York, United States
Photographs: Eduard Hueber

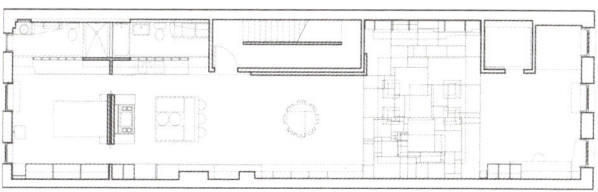

The walls have been painted white, and the dividing walls between the bathrooms are made of insulated Durock panels. These have also been used to cover the ceiling, in a series of layers that provide an effect of relief and texture.

Sliding polycarbonate panels help to distribute the light evenly by allowing it to penetrate into the back of the apartment.

Renaud Residence | Cha & Innerhofer

The 4,000-square-foot (372 sq m) loft provides a refuge from the bustle of New York's SoHo district; the young banker who lives here can use it both to unwind and to receive guests in style. The architectural configuration is designed to satisfy these dual requisites of calm and conviviality within a single space, just as, in the streets below, the hubbub of galleries and shops rubs shoulders with quiet, residential housing. The building containing the Renaud residence – which occupies the sixth floor, right at the top – was once used for commercial purposes but is now completely residential.

This loft reflects all the diversity and complexity of its environment. The design exploits elements which, although once at the cutting edge of modernity, now seem almost traditional; it uses a variety of materials to create strong contrasts and establish an interplay between forms and planes, between transparency and opacity.

This approach respects the architectural rules prevailing at the time of the building's construction but reinterprets them in the light of modern experience. Movement, space, and volume work together to satisfy functional requirements.

There is, first of all, a basic division between private spaces and public ones. The former are cocooned in cherry wood and topped with a false ceiling dotted with skylights that introduce light into even the most intimate corners of the loft.

The use of movement on the vertical planes, via sliding and pivoted doors, enriches the perception of the overall structure and also emphasises the feeling of light and space.

Architects: Cha & Innerhofer
Location: New York, United States
Photographs: Dao-Lou Zha

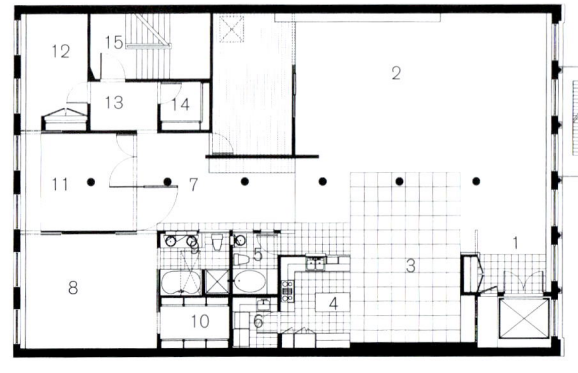

Ground plan
1. Entrance
2. Living room
3. Dining room
4. Kitchen
5. Bathroom
6. Laundry
7. Connecting area
8. Main bedroom
9. Main bathroom
10. Dressing room
11. Family room
12. Bedroom
13. Connecting area
14. Storeroom
15. Service staircase

The relationship between the public and private areas does not rest solely on the geometric interplay of lines and volume; it is also expressed in a sensual interaction of different materials, from cherry wood to limestone, from walnut to frosted glass.

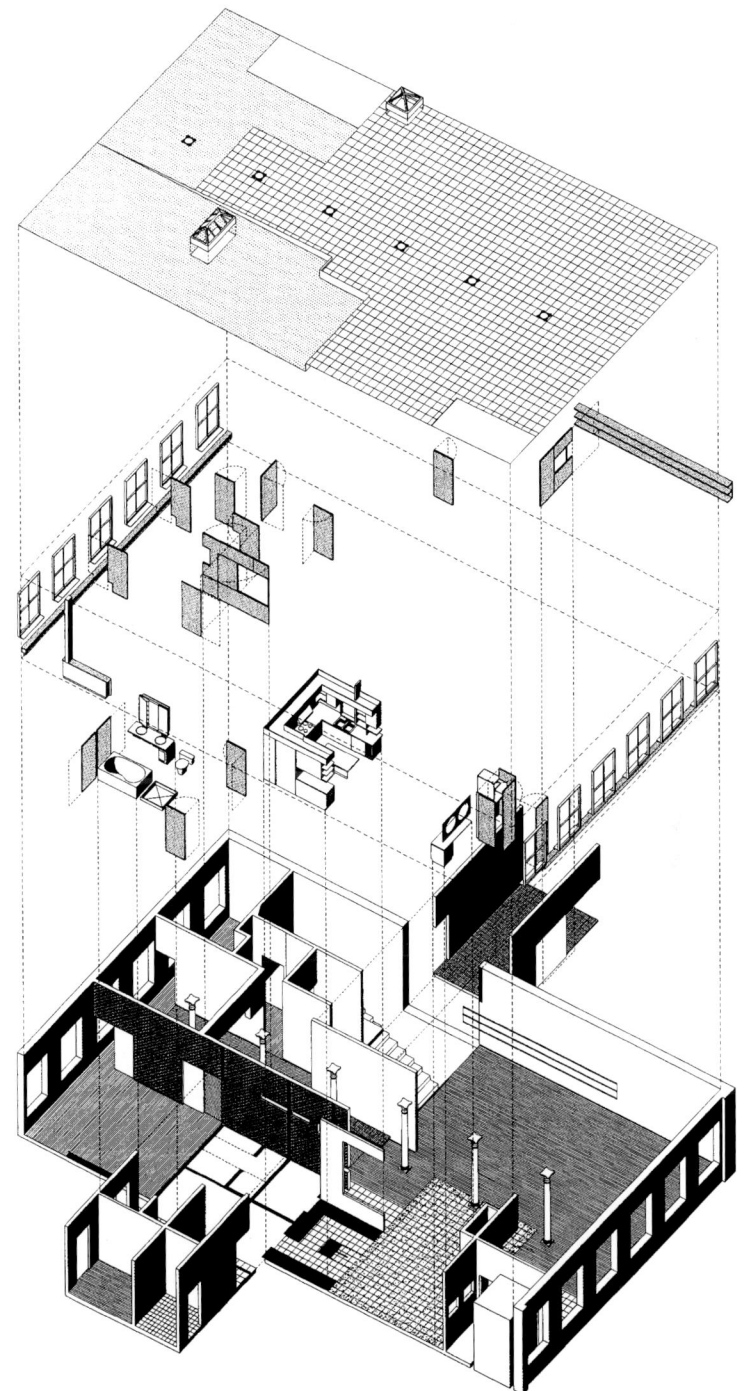

Spatial flexibility

Kar-hwa Ho
Architecture & Design

An old warehouse is the setting for this 2,100-square-foot (195 sq m) loft under the shadow of the Empire State Building, in New York's Flatiron district. One of the briefs for the conversion of these premises was the introduction of as much natural light as possible, without losing the essential characteristics of a loft.

The original distribution of the space was retained and so the renovation focused on supplying comfort and serenity. Generous amounts of storage space are set into the existing walls; the artificial lighting system reinforces the sunlight that enters through the north-facing windows overlooking the street; air conditioning has also been installed, but every effort was made to ensure that it fits in with the overall design of the apartment. Similarly, the new plumbing installation uses very discreet piping which does not clash with the surroundings.

The walls were clad with panels that came complete with baseboards. The color scheme is extremely simple, with the walls and doors all painted in a very luminous, pale cream color. The built-in glass bar provides a striking center of attention and serves as a link between the kitchen and the dining room. The meticulous concern for detail is apparent in the decision to avoid handles on the closet doors so that they blend in more smoothly with the walls.

Architects: Kar-hwa Ho Architecture & Design
Location: New York, United States
Photographs: Björg/Photography

191

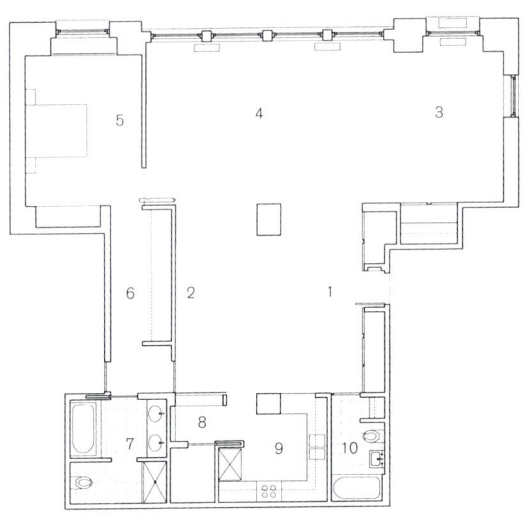

1. Hall
2. Dining room
3. Studio
4. Living room
5. Bedroom
6. Walk-in closet
7. Bathroom
8. Bar
9. Kitchen
10. Bathroom

The hanging light in the dining room – a creamy, hand-blown glass cylinder with stainless-steel support – was designed by the architect Kar-hwa Ho

The lines in the main suite have been stripped down to achieve an elegant refinement.

New trends | Hardy Holzman Pfeiffer Associates

This building at 117 East 24th Street lies in New York's historic center and predates its more famous architectural neighbors: Burnham's Flatiron Building, Le Brun and Corbett's Metropolitan Life Building, and Hardenberg's Western Union Building.

The architects responsible for the renovation of this 13th-floor apartment have not attempted to erase all traces of the past. The elevator shaft has not been disguised and many architectural features were left unaltered, even when they were the worse for wear, as in the case of the girders. The skylight has been re-covered with the Fersnel translucent glass that was used on the original building. The floor, which was extremely worn and cracked, has been repaired, polished, and dyed dark red. Wavy fiberglass panels have been put up, with fluorescent lights inside that gleam and dramatically transform the space. A neon light signals the kitchen space and presides over the collection of plates that has been built up from gifts brought by friends.

Terra cotta has been used to cover the walls and floors in the bathroom, as an alternative to the more customary ceramic tiles in such contexts.

This loft is also home for paintings by prestigious artists like Philip Pearlstein and Jack Beal, which hang in the midst of collections of chairs, tables, and carpets from various eras and places. This exciting, eye-catching space, which was designed and is also inhabited by the architects Landsman and Holzman, opened up new perspectives in interior design, which were later explored in subsequent projects for other homes.

Architects: Hardy Holzman Pfeiffer Associates
Location: New York, United States
Photographs: Hardy Holzman Pfeiffer Associates

The walls are lined with galvanized sheets adorned with a relief resembling brickwork.

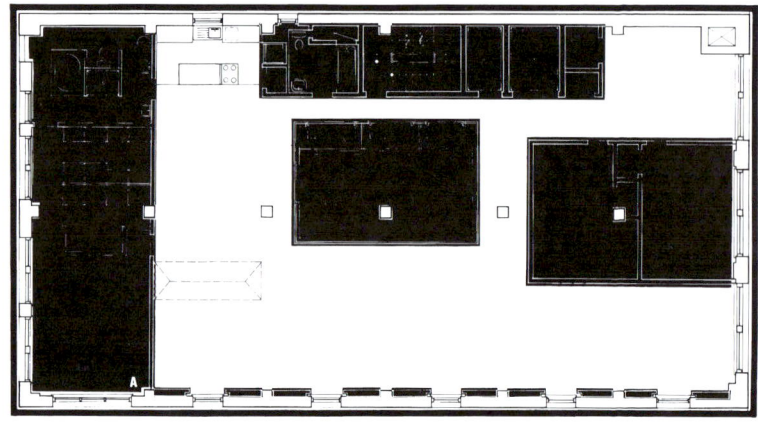

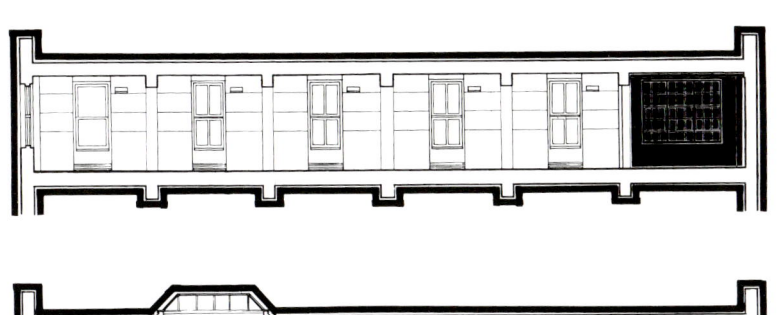
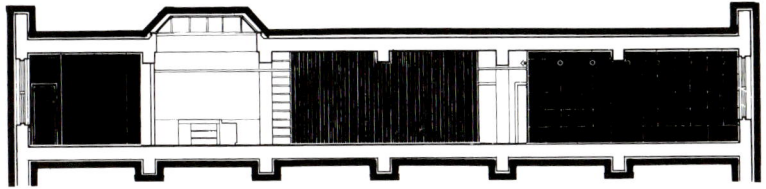

Apartment in Manhattan

Shelton, Mindel & Associates

The approach to the renovation of this 2,150-square-foot (200 sq m) apartment was essentially a practical one, based on the recognition of problems and their subsequent solution. The main priorities were to integrate the project into the city, to exploit the possibilities of the four outer walls and the roof, and to house a collection of 20th-century furniture and decorative art.

The lower level is very clearly divided into a public space and a private one. The area for social gatherings occupies the southern face and is organized around a central element, in this case a water tank. A big sitting room with a fireplace and a dining room are set on either side of the apartment's central feature – a glass box with a double-spiral stainless-steel staircase.

The mobile panels play an important role as the perception of the space changes according to whether they are open or closed. Aluminum, stainless steel, glass, as well as oak and cherry wood (on the floors) are some of the materials used in this apartment. Prouve, Richard Serra, Hoffman, Jacobsen, Aalto, Charles Eames, Caldés, Wagner, and Robert Ryman are some of the artists, sculptors, potters, and architects whose work is on display.

Architects: Shelton, Mindel & Associates
Location: New York, United States
Photographs: Michael Moran

The staircase sweeps up to the roof, providing a conduit for the sunlight that pours into the lower floor, particularly its most public area. Upstairs, another sitting room also serves as an exhibition space.

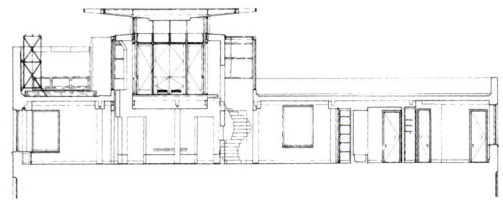

The elevator and storeroom disrupt the regular lines of the western face. An L-shaped area with functional properties marks off this more public space from the private one beyond. The part of the "L" occupying the eastern face connects up with the rest of the building below, via the entrance, and also contains a bathroom and the kitchen, which opens out onto the dining room. The double bedroom and two single bedrooms, sheltered from the public areas by bathrooms and dressing rooms, provide wonderful panoramic views from the northern side.

Residence for artists | Abelow Connors Sherman Architects

The writer Joel Siegel and his wife, the painter Ena Swansea, bought this loft in New York to create a space where they could both live and work. The main aim was, therefore, to integrate these two functions while retaining a degree of flexibility.

The renovation did not do away with the small vaults in the ceilings, the plastered walls, or the industrial details. They were all restored with the same materials originally used to build them, and the electrical wiring and plumbing pipes have been left exposed. All these factors help to evoke the atmosphere that reigned in the building when it was first put up.

The painting studio is set in the northern part of the house, allowing Swansea to enjoy the magnificent views from the huge windows and take advantage of the cold and unremitting northern light. The center of the loft holds the office – a veritable multimedia space equipped with an audiovisual system and computer, as well as facilities to receive clients.

The more private areas – the bedrooms, bathrooms, and dressing room – are on the edges of the loft, separated from the center by screens. The kitchen, dining room, living room, and studio subtly merge into each other, without any sharp differentiation between the spaces.

The old floor has been replaced with a compound of epoxy resin and urethane. The vertical partitions have not been painted, just treated with a product usually used to fill in cracks or holes. The use of such distinctive materials creates a subdued, balanced setting and a perfect backdrop for the colors and forms of the furniture and works of art.

Architects: Abelow Connors Sherman Architects
Location: New York, United States
Photographs: Michael Moran

1. Bedroom
2. Sitting room
3. Dining room
4. Multimedia space
5. Kitchen
6. Painting studio
7. Bathroom
8. Dressing room

The neutral finishes set off the various pieces of furniture and artworks, and the plants and small decorative objects also add splashes of color to the dominant white tone. The rustic details soften the loft's overall industrial look.

Urban interface | Dean/Wolf Architects

The urban interface loft explores the idea of a home that seeks to become an extension of the cityscape around it and to blend in with the new horizons typical of modern living – in this case the skyline formed by the six-floor buildings of Duane Park in New York. The plane of the roof is cut off dramatically and opened up to the sky, revealing urban structures that match the bold thrust of its lines. The views of the buildings outside infuse the interior of the loft and dictate the bold, angular lines within.

The inner spaces seem to be in thrall to the outside world, as glimpsed through a series of skylights. The cuts slashing through the building's outer casing further enhance the complex interplay between the domestic cocoon and the vastness beyond. The copper cladding on the roof belongs to both the private and public domains at the same time, and provides a further link between the two worlds.

This challenging, idealized environment, lurking in the heights of the city, seems like a peculiarly modern version of the haunted house, in which one space imperceptibly merges into another.

Architects: Dean/Wolf Architects
Location: New York, United States
Photographs: Peter Aaron/Esto

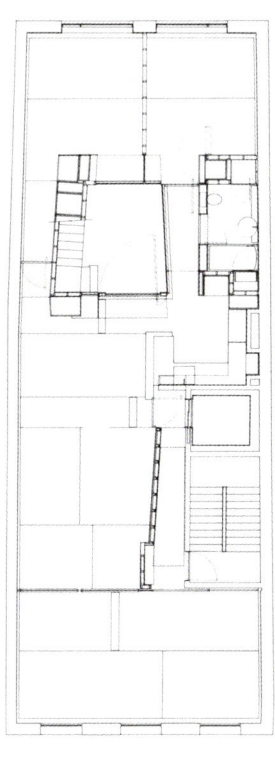

The vacuum in the middle of this loft provides a wide range of views of the sky from the spaces on either side.

The eye is gently led from the interior to the exterior of the building, through yet another hole cut in the roof of the loft.

The vertical panels act as boundaries between the different spaces and provide a degree of privacy.

An industrial touch | Alexander Jiménez

Unlike many of the spectacular projects in this book, this New York loft is not huge nor does it have any luxurious finishing; what makes it stand out is the simplicity and effectiveness of the functional and structural ideas on display. Like most lofts, it takes advantage of former manufacturing premises and so still has an industrial touch, although its installations are adapted to the requirements of a modern lifestyle.

The eating area and lounge are side by side, and are only differentiated by the rugs under the furniture, without any need for partitions. Both areas are flooded with sunlight from the large windows that look out onto the street.

In contrast, the kitchen, bedroom, and bathroom in the back are marked off from the rest by an element that spans the side walls but does not reach the ceiling, leaving plenty of storage space on the top. This part of the loft also houses all the installations for electricity, water, and heating. The partitions only close off the bathroom and the bedroom; the kitchen is left open.

It was possible to restore the redbrick walls and the wooden beams, but the original floor was very deteriorated and beyond repair, so it has been replaced with pale wood.

Architect: Alexander Jiménez
Location: New York, United States
Photographs: Jordi Miralles

Some views of the kitchen.

The bathroom is the only area that is completely enclosed.

A blank canvas | Vicente Wolf

The designer Vicente Wolf's loft in Manhattan is, by his own admission, a blank canvas, "an ever-present setting where I experiment with the things I want to form part of my work." He spends some two months of the year traveling and always comes back loaded with an array of objects that inevitably find a place in his home. This loft, measuring almost 1,600 square feet (148 sq m), has stunning views of the skyscrapers that dominate the south, north, and east of Manhattan.

Wolf has a special talent for finding harmonious combinations of striking but diverse objects that seem to have been left around at random, like the studded 1940s chair picked up in a flea market and the magnificent 18th-century Chippendale armchair, which Wolf has had in his home for over 15 years.

A Louis XVI-style divan is set at an angle opposite an exquisite French armchair from the 1940s. Similarly, a 19th-century wooden table is confronted with a simple stool acquired in a market in Thebes. Wolf's desk, dating from 1950, is complemented by an elegant studded armchair that he managed to pick up at a bargain price.

Although the furniture in this loft is always being rearranged, the designer's collection of 20th-century photographs provides a constant presence, with black-and-white photos by major artists like Man Ray, Robert Mapplethorpe, Alexander Rodchenko, and Diane Arbus. Vicente Wolf's loft is itself a perfect subject for a photographer, and it is Wolf who knows best how to capture its magic on film.

Designer: Vicente Wolf
Location: New York, United States
Photographs: Vicente Wolf

Play of light | Moneo Brock Studio

The building that houses the Davol loft lies in an old industrial area in the south of Manhattan that has been transformed by the conversion of its old manufacturing premises into housing.

The original structure presented all the elements typical of an industrial warehouse: a central row of pillars, huge windows at both ends, and a ceiling over 10 feet (3 m) high. The renovation had to stay within the bounds of a tight budget, leaving open the possibility of adding better-quality finishing at a later stage.

The architects' basic approach was to put the service areas on the windowless north and south sides. In order to avoid the impression that they were totally disconnected from the rest, these areas were treated as forms inserted into a container. Their walls do not reach the ceiling and the materials used are iridescent, creating a wonderful play of light.

Translucent mobile panels were put in, so that the open space can be redistributed at will. The choice of a new material called Panelite was crucial in this respect, as it is not only translucent, but also changes color according to the incidence of the light. Moreover, there is a complex system of overhead rails, allowing the panels to be moved at a different angle or placed one behind the other to obtain a more opaque effect.

The occupants were involved in the project from the start and accepted the challenge presented by this experimentation with new materials. This enthusiasm has endowed them with an opalescent oasis where the sunsets in particular offer an incredible experience.

Architects: Moneo Brock Studio
Location: New York, United States
Photographs: Michael Moran

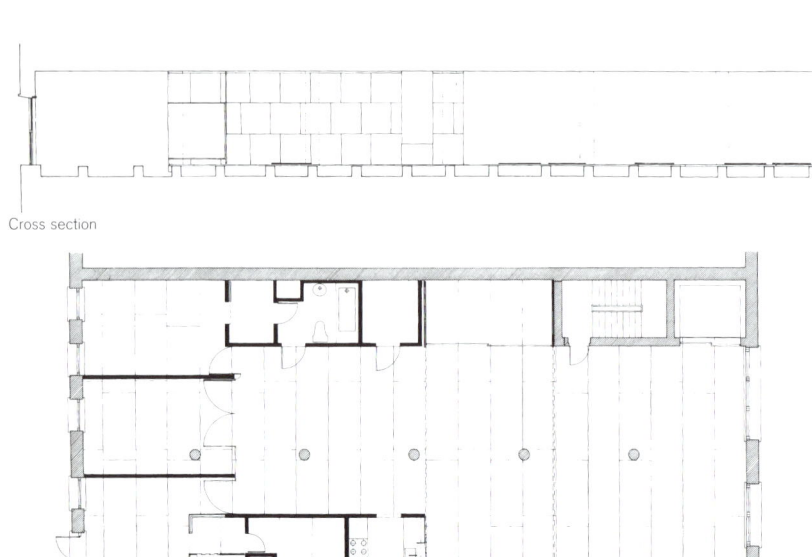

Cross section

Ground plan

The finishings create a play of colors, reflections, and transparencies. This distinctive perception of the spaces is the result of intense experimentation with the materials used.

Some of the vertical partitions are mobile, making it possible to redistribute the space within the loft, so the compartmentalizing is never definitive. The translucence of the panels also means that there is always some contact between the different areas.

Rosenberg residence and studio

Belmont Freeman Architects

Finding a space suitable for both living and working in the lower side of Manhattan can be a challenge. This loft is situated in a former commercial building that was constructed in 1900 and converted into housing in the 1980s.

Two apartments in a single property, both measuring 1,506 square feet (140 sq m), joined vertically and stripped of any unnecessary walls, provide both a studio and a living space for their art-loving occupant. The vertical relationship between the two units is one of the loft's distinguishing traits, as the architects have handled their materials with such skill that the spaces complement each other, while remaining independent.

The upper floor is a home comprising a living room, a kitchen, and two bedrooms. The expanse of the exterior wall is unbroken by any partitions, to take full advantage of the northern light that pours in through the window. The lower story, with part of the original sandblasted concrete floor and walls clad with zinc, is used as an office and studio. Two mobile walls, one of plaster and the other of frosted glass, make it possible to alter the distribution of the loft. A sailors' ladder connects the two levels, while also marking the boundary between the work areas and the private rooms upstairs.

A limited range of materials – concrete, maple wood, stainless steel, and laminated glass – has produced structures that look so natural that they seem to be integral parts of the original building. This architecture, which is stripped of artifice, is ideal for the owner's collection of mid-20th-century furniture.

Architects: Belmont Freeman Architects
Location: New York, United States
Photographs: Christopher Wesnofske

243

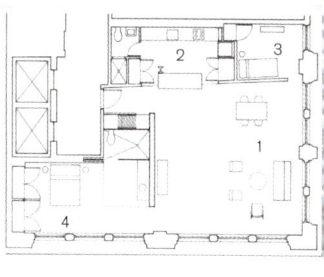

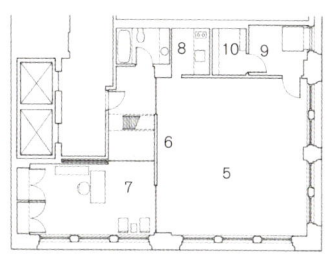

1. Sitting room
2. Kitchen
3. Bedroom
4. Main bedroom
5. Studio
6. Wall on castors
7. Office
8. Larder
9. Strongroom
10. Installations control

Minimalist continuity | Form Werkstatt

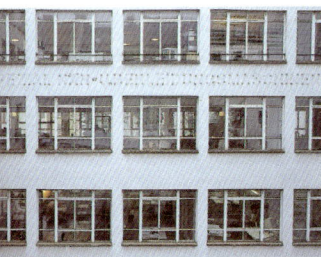

The German architect Siggi Pfundt converted this loft in an old sewing-machine factory in the center of Munich. The renovation of this 750-square-foot (70 sq m) space was completed in 1997, and since then Pfundt has used it as both home and workplace.

The architect recalls that she used "simple materials and construction methods for the renovation of the loft, in order to preserve the original character of the old factory."

The project envisioned a main space given over to the living and work areas, stretching along the entire façade, with the bathroom and bedroom in the back of the apartment. The lighting and privacy of the most intimate rooms can be controlled by arranging five panels of birch plywood, suspended from a steel rail, that mark a boundary along the longitudinal axis. A custom-made stainless-steel sink has been installed to create a kitchen area, while the old bathtub was rescued by the architect from her grandmother's garden.

The original concrete floor has been painted only in the living room, while the bedroom is set apart from the rest by the planked birch floor, giving added comfort and warmth to the sleeping area.

The ingenious and flexible system of panels not only maintains the continuity and coherence of an open space but also solves practical problems at very little expense.

Architects: Form Werkstatt
Location: Munich, Germany
Photographs: Karin Hessmann/Artur

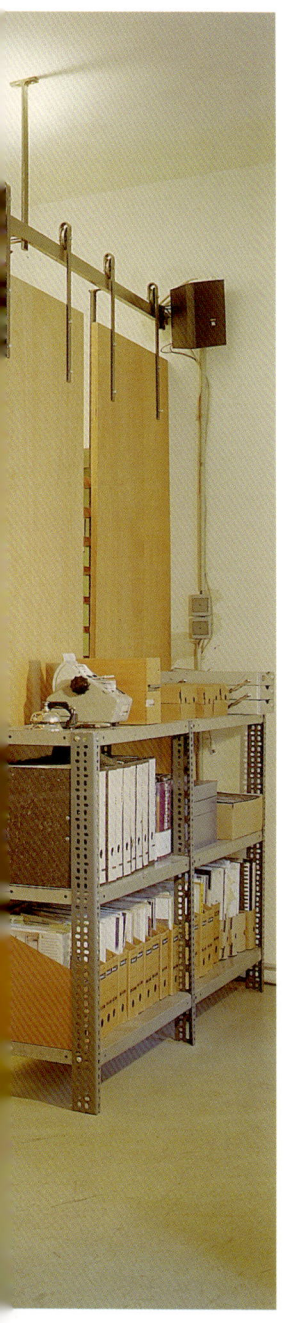

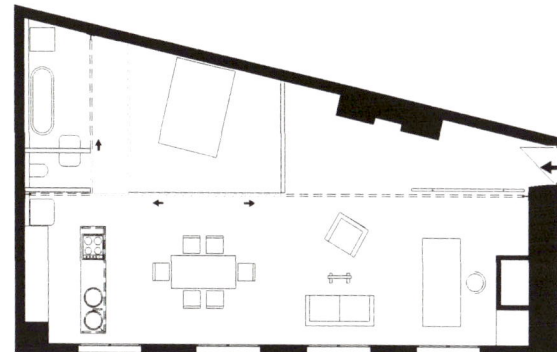

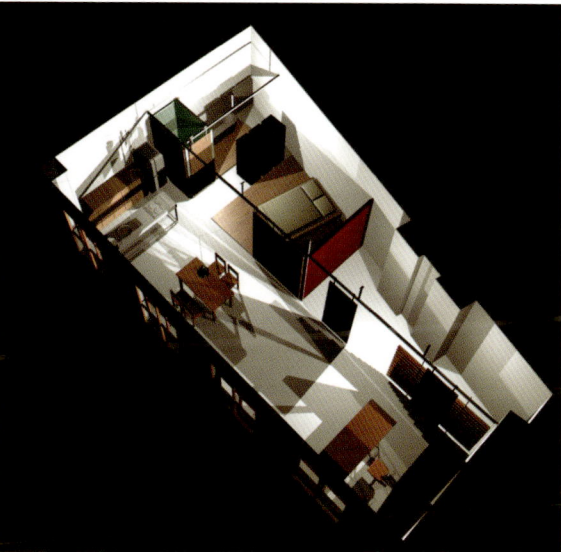

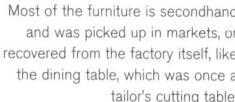

Most of the furniture is secondhand and was picked up in markets, or recovered from the factory itself, like the dining table, which was once a tailor's cutting table.

In the daytime, the mobile birch plywood separations make it possible to control the light and privacy in the more intimate areas.

Versatility | Abelow Connors Sherman Architects

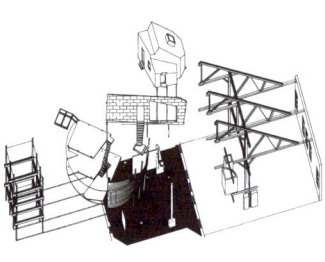

Axonometric perspective

The most immediately striking characteristic of this loft in Jersey City is the industrial scale of the design. The space preserves the basic structure of the original building, which was once a warehouse and stable. The sloping roof, the framework of wooden beams and pillars, and the redbrick walls have all been preserved, virtually untouched since the building's construction in 1880. The architects have sought to preserve the spirit of the building, but the present-day contents have been selected by means of the abstraction of radial diagrams and formalizations based on the musical scale.

The brief provided by the client, a musician and producer, demanded all the usual domestic appliances, an office, and a complete recording studio with all the necessary equipment.

A large versatile area on the first floor, connected to the inner courtyard, serves as a sitting room and recording studio. This space soars unconfined over the height of the other two floors, taking advantage of the acoustic advantages of open spaces. Apart from the studio, the first floor also contains the kitchen, dining room, library, and computer room. The two upper levels contain the bedrooms and other work areas, like the control room and editing suite. Private and public spaces lie side by side on every floor.

The materials used vary. A galvanized metal wall was brought in for one of the inserted pieces, the structural pillars and beams are made out of wood and the curved wall out of flexible wood. This mixture of materials emphasizes the exuberant disparity of the project.

Architects: Abelow Connors Sherman Architects
Location: Jersey City, New Jersey, United States
Photographs: Michael Moran

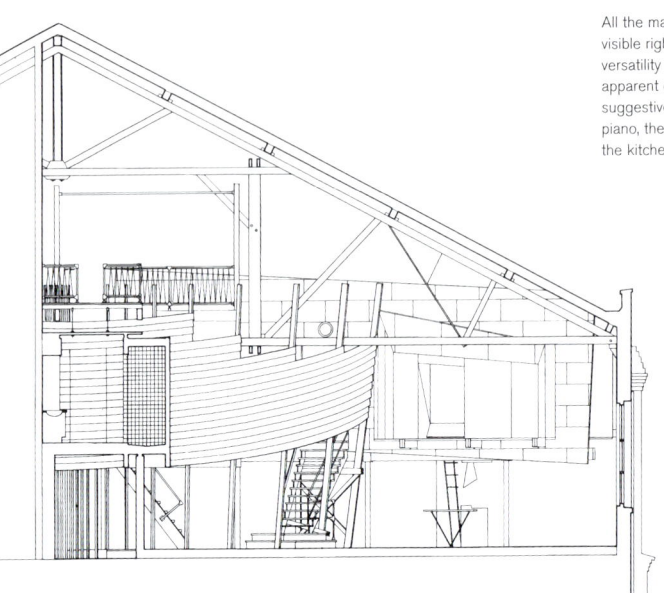

All the main features of this project are visible right from the entrance. The versatility of the spaces is particularly apparent on this floor, with elements suggestive of various activities: the piano, the basketball hoop, the library, the kitchen.

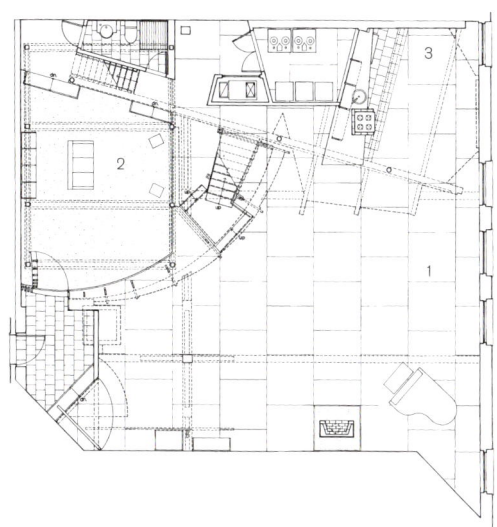

First floor

1. Adaptable space
2. Living room
3. Kitchen

O'Malley residence

Carpenter/ Grodzins Architects

The O'Malley residence is situated in Avoca, a small town on the outskirts of Scranton, Pennsylvania. The building was originally a warehouse and, although its outer walls were demolished, the interior pillars, beams, and walls have been retained, providing a space filled with light.

The loft, measuring around 1,500 square feet (140 sq m), was designed for a single occupant, whose main requirement was as much open space as possible and the incorporation of large storage areas. So, a series of closets was installed along the north wall and the kitchen and bathroom were put together on the south side. As the apartment has only one occupant it was possible to use transparent or translucent partitions for most of the space dividers, allowing the sunlight that floods in on three of the loft's four sides to penetrate into the interior.

To take further advantage of the light entering from the south, both the bathroom and the kitchen were conceived as intermediary spaces that allow the light to pass through them, in the former by means of translucent glass panels and in the latter via a big horizontal opening that also serves as a counter for eating.

The floor is covered with oak boards and also incorporates strips of marble that accentuate the lines of the circular pillars like shadows. The continuity of space and light is apparent from every vantage point in the O'Malley loft.

Architects: Carpenter/Grodzins Architects
Location: Avoca, Pensylvania. United States
Photographs: Chun y Lai/Photography

Two closets made of ash and glass flank the entrance, evoking the idea of an industrial locker room.

The pattern marked out by the marble strips on the floor helps distinguish the different areas used for eating, relaxing, and sleeping.

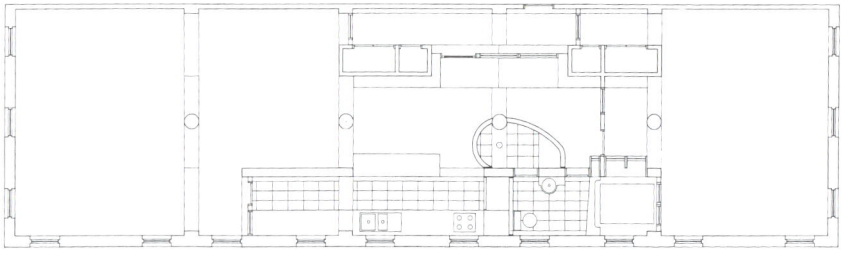

Ground plan

Accessibility
Paul Guzzardo, Ray Simon

The objective was to convert the second floor of an old industrial building – originally a four-story shoe factory – on Washington Avenue, Saint Louis, into a loft.

The second floor, some 4,520 square feet (420 sq m) in size, is a long, narrow space bounded by brick walls and divided by five thick cement pillars along its central axis. The architects resolved to maintain the width of the space by minimizing the partitions and avoiding the visual obstructions created by the pillars.

Isolation and accessibility were the key problems to resolve, as the brief required the separation of the first and second floors and, therefore, direct access from the street via the building's back staircase. An outside staircase led straight from the first to the second floor, but there was no direct communication with the street, as a chimney blocked the way in from the exterior. So, a curved wall was built to link the second floor with the nightclub on the first floor, and the chimney was sealed with a skylight.

Additional comfort was brought to the home by two wooden elements, made from planks recycled from old crates, which contain, on one side, kitchen equipment and, on the other, the bathroom, laundry, and air conditioning. The pine wood of these planks was treated with several coats of a colored sealant.

The apartment takes advantage of many of the leftover factory furnishings, such as the benches used for the assemblage, now improvising as wooden tables, and the metal staircase. Even the window shutters and fire doors are part of the original building.

Architects: Paul Guzzardo, Ray Simon
Location: Saint Louis, Missouri, United States
Photographs: Jeffery Johnston/Photography

Ground plan
1. Hall, lounge, and music area
2. Unit divided into bathroom and laundry
3. Bathroom and shower section
4. Closets with kitchen equipment
5. Kitchen counter
6. Building's interior staircase
7. Drainage pipe
8. Metal shutters
9. Elevator
10. Sleeping area
11. Curved screen
12. Cabool buffet
13. Staircase to Cabool Club

The ceilings and circular pillars are made of concrete. The floor has been covered with maple wood treated with oil and a special urethane preparation.

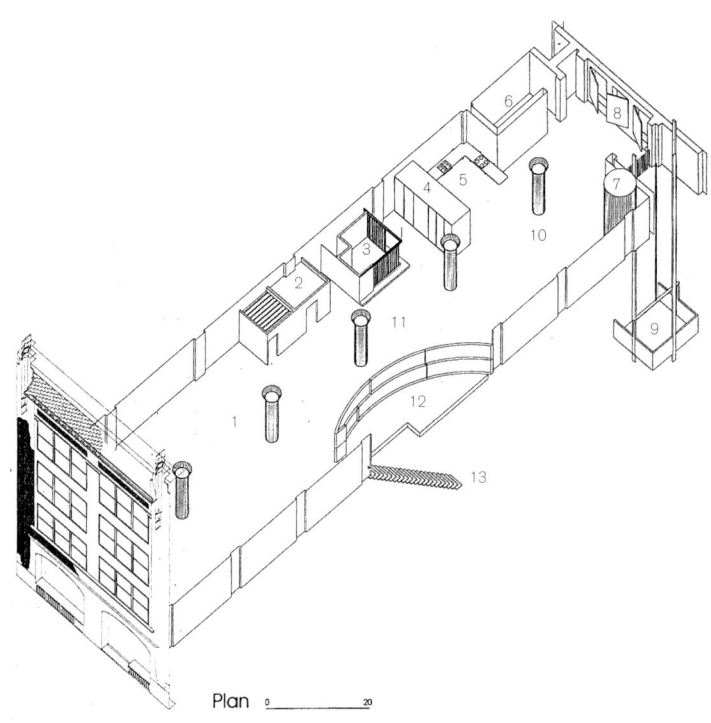

Plan 0 ___ 20

Number 1709 Studio | Paul Guzzardo, David Davis

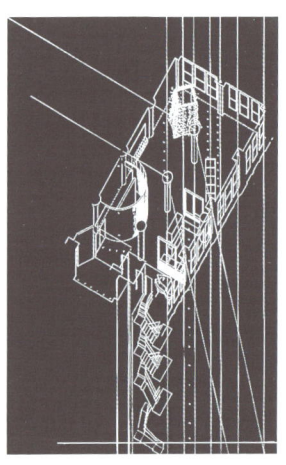

This building at 1709 Washington Street in Saint Louis was put up in 1903 and was originally used by a company dealing in animal skins.

This rectangular loft, measuring 26 x 39 feet (8 x 12 m), occupies the fifth floor. It has a line of large windows on the two sides that meet at the street corner; it is a continuous space, interrupted only by the bulky cement pillars that help to mark off the different spaces.

The dazzling gleam of the floor was obtained by thoroughly sanding and polishing the maple-wood floorboards that cover the entire space.

The main concerns of the client's brief were the provision of comfort and convenience without overly reducing the extension of the open space or detracting from the views of the city and the industrial legacy of the building. A corrugated-iron semi-circle shields the bathroom and dressing room, while the Plexiglas panels along one side allow the sunlight from outside to seep in.

The kitchen area is bounded by two transparent glass walls with metal bases placed at a right angle to the exterior wall. The sleeping area features a novel device designed to afford greater privacy; it consists of counterpanes hanging from tubes, like giant handkerchiefs, and when the mechanism is opened out these surround the bed like curtains. This all-embracing invention is not only visually attractive – it also cuts out a great deal of the noise entering from outside. Other atmospheric touches are provided by the steel counters, the hotchpotch of kitchen equipment, and the storage area.

Architects: Paul Guzzardo, David Davis
Location: Saint Louis, Missouri, United States
Photographs: Joel Marion

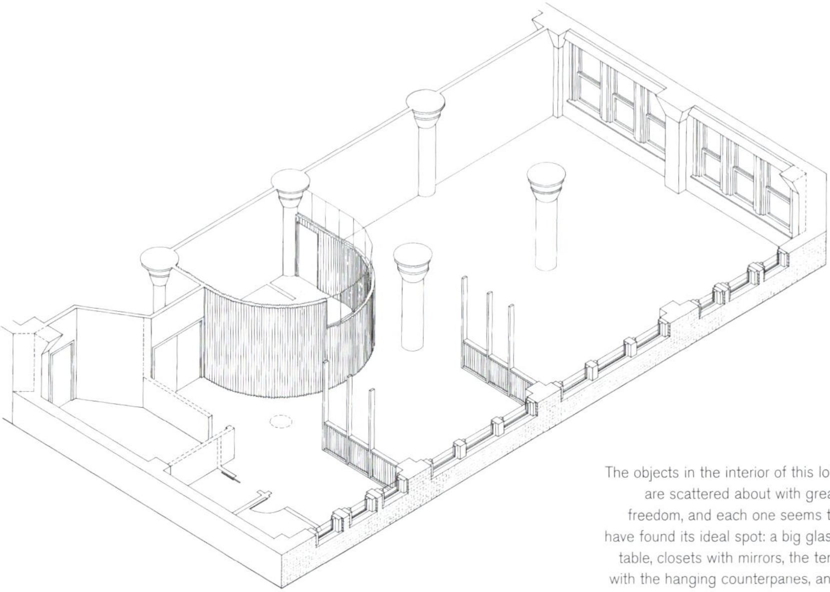

The objects in the interior of this loft are scattered about with great freedom, and each one seems to have found its ideal spot: a big glass table, closets with mirrors, the tent with the hanging counterpanes, and a 1924 white Cable Nelson piano

Sophisticated innovation | Cecconi Simone, Inc.

The multidisciplinary team formed by Elaine Cecconi and Anna Simone advocates new forms of design. "Life is experience. Transmitting experience to other people, something to talk about, something that makes them feel alive – that's what it's all about. When people can move around in an environment and feel it, touch it, breathe it, then we've achieved our aim, whether they like the result or not. Our design doesn't just consist of solving problems, it also provides a new feeling, as if our presence always lingers on in everything we do."

In this apartment, which has been the model for the conversions in the Sears warehouse in downtown Toronto, the aim was to preserve the intrinsic expansiveness of the spaces while accommodating them to the needs of a modern home by applying modern technology to provide workspaces that offer flexibility and versatility.

An axis running from the entrance and dividing the apartment symmetrically isolates those areas that need to be separated, like the laundry, tucked away by the entrance so as not to rob space from the main suite. The high ceilings, cement floors, pilaster columns, and industrial lighting all reflect the building's former life as a warehouse. A restful bathroom and a modern kitchen add a feeling of comfort to the space. The juxtaposition of different materials and finishes, along with the combination of cool and warm environments, puts this sophisticated and innovative loft at the forefront of Toronto's modern urban residences.

All the main areas look out on the exterior, and they can also be closed off by mobile panels that serve as sliding doors.

Architects: Cecconi Simone, Inc.
Location: Toronto, Canada
Photographs: Joy von Tiedemann

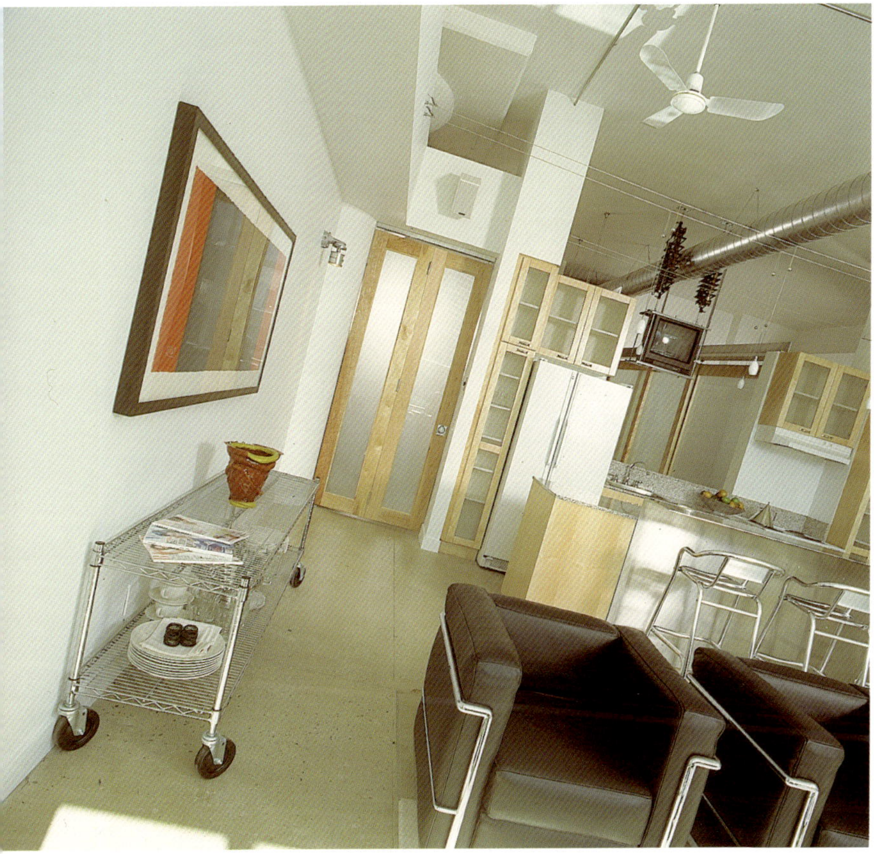

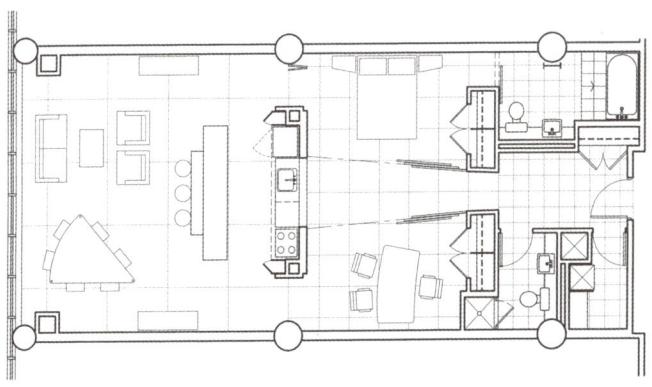

Color is supplied by the materials used – natural birch, granite, aluminum, and concrete – rather than by any new finishes applied to their surfaces.

Private residence | Cecconi Simone, Inc.

This private residence is situated in an up-and-coming area in Toronto's East End, an industrial neighborhood that has recently witnessed an influx of artists and photographers taking over the disused old warehouses. The project involved the recovery and re-creation of an environment in which the old and the new live side by side.

This loft was originally two separate spaces, which have been connected to form a single whole. The project has preserved the building's structural features and both the floor and the pillars have been treated to restore their original appearance and texture, thus imbuing the entire space with a special sensuality.

Although many of the elements in the kitchen were recycled from an old cafeteria, the counter was custom-made by Cecconi Simone, Inc. The architects were also personally responsible for the canopy over the bed and the desk in the office area.

The windows were left unaltered, and their huge expanse allows air to penetrate the large area inside, as well as offering exceptional views of the Toronto skyline outside.

The space was designed to be absolutely flexible. Drapes hang throughout the loft from bars fixed to the ceiling, and they can be drawn in any number of ways to unify or divide the space at will. This concept extends to the bed, where an adjustable canopy can be set according to the privacy required, or opened out to reveal the view of the city. Using this approach, Cecconi Simone, Inc. have created a home in which the occupants are free to follow their own lifestyle and exercise control over the use of the space.

Architects: Cecconi Simone, Inc.
Location: Toronto, Canada
Photographs: Joy von Tiedemann

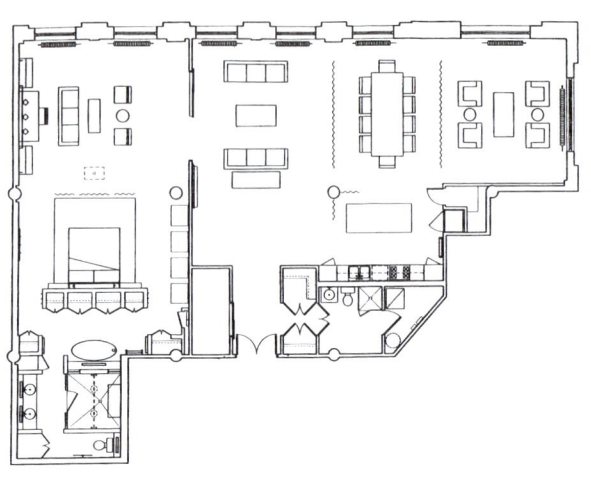

A palette of neutral colors is enriched by the various wood tones in this huge space bathed in sunlight.

Restored food lockers and elements recycled from an old cafeteria add a nostalgic but functional touch to the kitchen.

The drapes allow the occupants to put their personal imprint on each area and divide the space according to their needs.

The planning of a completely flexible space does not allow for individually designed rooms. The headrest of the bed was specially designed by Cecconi Simone, Inc., with a mobile canopy that can be maneuvered according to the degree of privacy desired.

House and studio | Fernando Campana

This building, put up in 1940 in a residential zone in the Brazilian city of São Paulo, was originally a warehouse. The architect responsible for its loft conversion, Fernando Campana, remarks: "We have some beautiful industrial spaces here in São Paulo. Many of them are lying empty and deteriorating; they are buildings that were constructed by Italian immigrants in the early part of the 20th century. Sometimes these areas look just like a suburb of Milan or Turin."

The original structure consisted of two cement boxes, one in the back and one in the front, with an intermediary bathroom section connecting the two. The loft project got rid of these bathrooms to leave an open courtyard measuring 345 square feet (32 sq m). The first floor of the finished building contains a studio in the back section, along with the kitchen and a living area and large an gallery in the front. The basement contains the bathroom and bedroom. In all, the loft occupies a total floor space of 2,475 square feet (230 sq m).

Campana first started designing a studio for his own work, but he ended up living on the premises as well. He stresses the adaptability that this decision has given him "The only thing that is firmly in place is the ivy in the courtyard. This means that I have the flexibility to transform the space every day from a home into a workplace, or vice versa."

Architect: Fernando Campana
Location: São Paulo, Brazil
Photographs: Andrés Ortero

The studio and the kitchen are on the other side of the patio. The cement floor has been burnt, polished, and waxed and the walls have been covered with thick plaster to emphasize the roughness of the original construction.

The furniture has been designed by Fernando Campana and his brother Humberto; who have an international reputation and whose work is produced by various companies around the world.

Round armchair by Ricardo Fasanello (1972) and black armchair on castors by Pedro Schimitd (1954); the rest of the furniture is designed by the Campanas.

Formal unity | Knott Architects

The wooden wall that turns into glass when it reaches the ceiling; it is this element that gives the project formal unity.

The empty shell of a loft can instill panic in many clients. Potential buyers often underestimate the amount of space available or are deterred by the lack of functional demarcation. These worries can induce a desire to divide the space along the lines of traditional rooms, despite the fact that this squanders all the advantages of a loft.

Knott Architects tackled this dilemma not only when they were required to install two bedrooms and two bathrooms, but also a kitchen, and living room in a 1,290-square-foot (120 sq m) loft in a refurbished building in London's Soho district. Their inspired solution has not insensitively chopped up the space; it is instead based on a rigorous design conception that makes a clear distinction between the inserted elements and the surrounding space.

Turning this large area into a domestic environment required decisions about the materials and finishings that would define each space. Once the materials had been established, the choice of a single visual language applicable to the entire conversion was the crucial factor in endowing it with formal unity.

Architects: Knott Architects
Location: London, United Kingdom
Photographs: Jefferson Smith, Laurent Kalfala, Knott Architects

All the added elements are made out of wood, steel, and glass, in order to make the new additions stand out from the original walls – which have been plastered and painted white. The wooden floorboards similarly help to define the partitioned areas.

The rooms are treated as pieces of furniture that do not touch the ceiling or party walls, except in the case of the glass tops on the partitions.

Translucent floors | Fraser Brown McKenna Architects

In the opinion of the architects, the simplicity of the new elements, like the screen and the copper box, does not merely determine the quality of the space, but also suggests a new, unencumbered way to occupy that space.

This project involved refurbishing the top two floors of an industrial building in Bethnal Green, east London. Although the arch that covers part of the old terrace had been built before the renovation carried out by Fraser Brown McKenna Architects, most of the spaces were small, dark, and excessively compartmentalized.

The architects installed a translucent floor in the kitchen and dining room under the arched roof, creating the effect of a theater stage when seen from the adjacent sitting room. The first floor was completely stripped of partitions and reconceived as a single space for working and sleeping, although it is still partially divided by a 32-foot (10 m) translucent screen that marks off the bedroom and bathrooms, as well as the small storage area clad with copper sheets. The screen is cut off at one end, providing a great deal more space for the bedroom.

This conversion revels in the extraordinary quality of its materials, such as the wood on the floor and the beautifully finished complementary metalwork.

The sunlight that pours through the arched roof, the translucent floors, and the screen all bear witness to the primordial role played by light in this project.

Architects: Fraser Brown McKenna Architects
Location: London, United Kingdom
Photographs: Nick Hufton/View

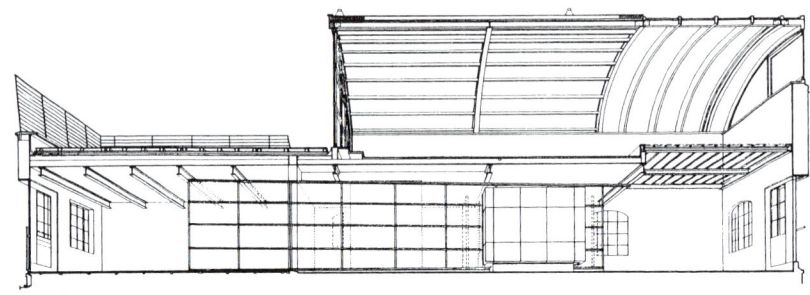

Longitudinal section

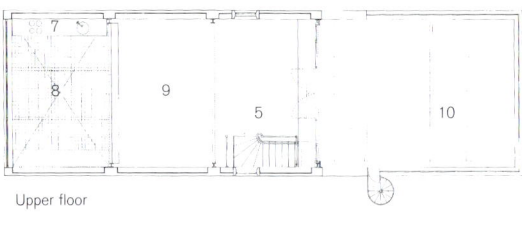

Upper floor

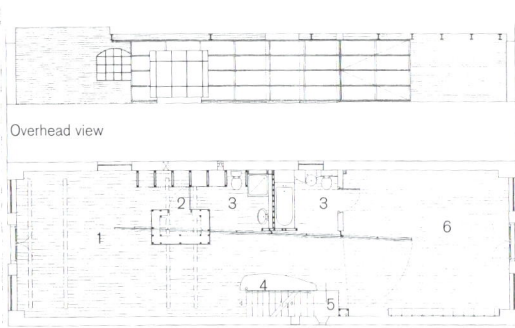

Overhead view

Lower floor

1. Studio
2. Store
3. Bathroom
4. Balustrade
5. Staircase
6. Bedroom
7. Kitchen
8. Dining room
9. Bedroom
10. Terrace

The translucent screen is formed by a series of aluminum T-shape supports screwed together.

White and empty | Hugh Broughton Architects

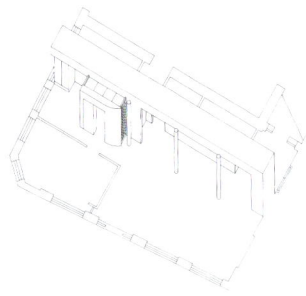

This loft was part of a program to convert four industrial buildings in London into housing.

Hugh Broughton's architectural studio converted an old industrial space into an apartment for a married couple. The team came up with a project for the 1,600 square feet (150 sq m) of floor space that guaranteed both communication between the different spaces and privacy where it was required (bedrooms and bathrooms). Two differentiated spaces were created, one for the day and one for the night, each defined by its particular functions and architectural ideas: on one hand, the kitchen, living room, and dining room, situated near the entrance; and, on the other, the private space, comprising the bedrooms and one of the two bathrooms.

The daytime area is where the building's former industrial use is most apparent, mainly on account of the large light-filled expanse of floor, the exposed brickwork on the walls, and the wrought-iron pillars. No doors were considered necessary here; the kitchen and dining room run into each other, although the living room is separated from the kitchen by a wall that contains the door leading onto the hall.

A structural axis formed by a line of wrought-iron pillars divides the whole apartment lengthwise. In the more private area, this disappears as it is absorbed into a wall with a fitted closet.

Finally, the curved wall that marks off the bathroom breaks with the linearity established by the pillars and provides a sculptural effect that sets off this bright space.

Architects: Hugh Broughton Architects
Location: London, United Kingdom
Photographs: Carlos Domínguez

The white finish of the walls and ceilings contrasts with the exposed brick walls, the acid-treated glass insets, and the African wood of the floorboards. The illumination combines the sunlight streaming through the windows with a series of built-in ceiling lights and atmospheric light sources, as well as the light passing through the translucent wall pieces.

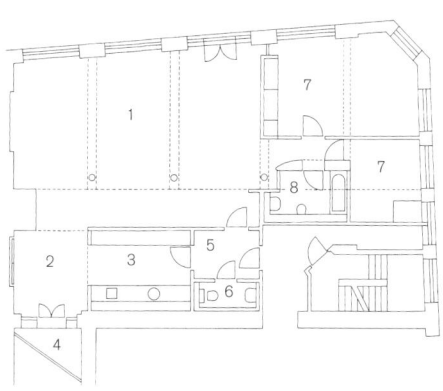

Ground plan

1. Living room
2. Dining room
3. Kitchen
4. Balcony
5. Hall
6. Bathroom
7. Bedroom
8. Bathroom

New Concordia Wharf | Mark Guard Architects

The client bought 2,000 square feet (185 sq m) on the sixth floor of a warehouse overlooking the river Thames – an irregular shape dominated by beams and round pillars, an array of windows, and dark brick walls.

The architects came up with a 75-foot (23 m) wall to separate the guest room, kitchen, service room, and bathrooms from the main space. This wall contains all the apartment's service installations, and it is cut off to allow the light entering from the east into the entrance area. The squared pattern created by the slabs on the floor emphasizes the role of the wall as the dominant geometrical element and the pivot around which the space is organized. This wall creates a false perspective when the apartment is seen from the entrance, leading the eye to the view of the river. The unit with the clothes closet distorts this false perspective, turning the attention back to the living room area.

The end of this wall forms part of the main bedroom, which can be closed off or opened out onto the large living space at will by means of a sliding 13-foot (4 m) wall. The glass screen separating the stone bathtub from the bedroom is electrically activated by a Priva-Lite system; this alters the opacity to make it more transparent.

The whole space is cocooned in white; this chromatic uniformity serves to hide the heating system and other installations carefully and appropriately incorporated within the architectural setting.

Architects: Mark Guard Architects
Location: London, United Kingdom
Photographs: Allan Mower, John Bennett

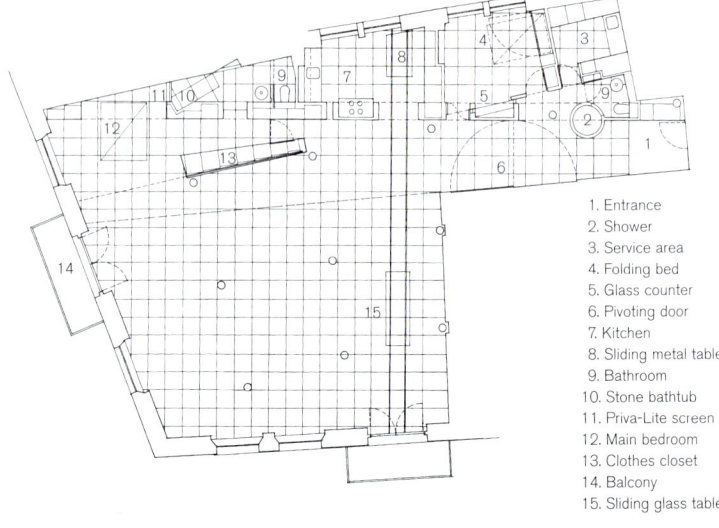

1. Entrance
2. Shower
3. Service area
4. Folding bed
5. Glass counter
6. Pivoting door
7. Kitchen
8. Sliding metal table
9. Bathroom
10. Stone bathtub
11. Priva-Lite screen
12. Main bedroom
13. Clothes closet
14. Balcony
15. Sliding glass table

Stainless-steel rails set into the stone floor can be used to slide the tables into different positions, increasing their versatility.

Oliver's Wharf | McDowell + Benedetti Architects

Oliver's Wharf, a tea warehouse built in 1870, was one of the first of London's old dock premises to be converted for residential use, back in the early 1970s. The attic on the top two floors, with stunning views of the city, was originally occupied by the architect responsible for the conversion. After the present owner bought it, it was left unused for several years.

It is a two-story 2,700-square-foot (250 sq m) space with cast-iron pillars supporting enormous oak beams and an elaborate roof. The conversion by McDowell & Benedetti Architects restored many elements of the existing structure but it also involved the total transformation of the space through the installation of intermediate levels and the addition of two terraces on the roof.

The layout of the loft on the main level revolves around the kitchen, which gives onto a series of different spaces: hall, staircase, gallery, fireplace, and a living room with panoramic views. Next to the entrance there is a small guest room with a folding bed and its own toilet.

The main divider of the space is an 8-inch (20 cm.) thick limestone wall, right in the center of the floor space, which stretches up to the top of the building. This wall is fitted with a number of closets and shelves, which provide storage space both for the kitchen and for the main bedroom.

Architects: McDowell + Benedetti Architects
Location: London, United Kingdom
Photographs: Tim Soar

The new elements serve to articulate the space; they are made of natural materials that contrast with the roughness of the original construction.

Two attics have been built on the top level: one for the main bedroom and bathroom; the other for a small studio with a big pivoting window that overlooks the Thames.

The enlargement of the roof ha[s] provided an enclosed room with larg[e] glass windows and a terrace wi[th] panoramic views of London. The walls [of] the terrace, fitted with glass benches [on] steel supports, have been left low [to] allow sunlight to penetrate the interio[r]

London post office | Orefelt Associates

A new approach to domestic living allows buildings to change their function if a little imagination is used.

This project involved converting an old post office into a studio and home for a painter. One of the challenges was to avoid the conventional layout of a single-family residence, even if the building seemed best suited to this arrangement.

One of the outstanding features of this loft is the feeling of spaciousness inside, both vertically and horizontally. The constantly changing perspectives afforded by the distribution of the space are evidence of the mastery of this conversion. The brief required a sitting room, kitchen, painting studio, two bedrooms, two bathrooms, and a terrace on the roof. The most obvious approach would have been to put the sitting room on the bottom and the bedrooms, kitchen, and the bathrooms on top. However, Gunnar Orefelt has quite literally turned this concept upside down. The first floor is given over to the bedrooms and bathrooms on one side and an extensive reception area – complete with a pool table – on the other; at the back a double-height space is used as a studio. An open area on the top floor contains the living rooms, kitchen, and dining room; it is lit by large skylights and offers views of the studio.

Right: The house is designed with large parties in mind, hence the visual connection between all the floors – via the split levels and the skylight in the roof – and the 16 loudspeakers dispersed around the various rooms.

Architects: Orefelt Associates
Location: London, United Kingdom
Photographs: Alberto Ferrero

The owner's eye-catching collection includes a leopard-skin couch, a dog sculpture by Jeff Koons, a selection of toy figures given away by McDonald's lined up on the bathroom shelf, an assortment of miniature Eiffel towers, and a rug depicting Snow White and the Seven Dwarfs.

Home for a painter | Simon Conder Associates

The furniture was also designed by Simon Conder Associates. All the pieces were conceived as mobile units and contain fitted artificial lighting.

The need for a free space, with no compartmentalization of any kind, was the determining factor for this conversion of an old factory. The client, a painter living in Kent, wanted an apartment in London as an operational base for getting into the city's art world.

The aim was to fully exploit the entire 1,250 square feet (116 sq m) available by enhancing the feeling of spaciousness and luminosity intrinsic to the original building. These criteria overrode any division of the space but did not prevent an efficient functional distribution of the space.

Furthermore, the floor area available was relatively limited, which was another reason for maintaining a single space – although this is broken up by the staircase that boldly separates the living area from the bedroom. Three vertical elements define the style of the loft: the stainless-steel kitchen unit and the two cylinders containing the shower and toilet. The party walls serve various functions: they house closets, electrical installations, and even a folding bed for guests.

This concentration of storage space frees up the rest of the loft for a variety of functions and does not interrupt its flow.

The lighting is reinforced by the different materials covering the surfaces: the white paint on the walls and ceilings reflect light, and the metal sheets also gleam and intensify the effect of the artificial lighting.

Architects: Simon Conder Associates
Location: London, United Kingdom
Photographs: Simon Archer

The central part of the home opens up vertically to provide access to the terrace on the upper floor. The studio looks out on both the West End of London and the southern part of the city.

The materials used in the project give the setting a certain minimalist touch. The kitchen, the structure of the staircase, and the fittings in the glass gallery are all made of stainless steel. The floorboards, which are of white oak, hide the underfloor heating system.

FOA London | FOA. Foreign Office Architects

This loft in London's Pimlico neighborhood is L-shaped; it is 16 feet (5 m) high and it has been divided into two levels, one of which leads directly onto the street. The main space, containing the living area and the dining room, has large windows looking out onto the street, as well as access to the inner courtyard.

The high wall on one side of the living area also serves as a huge screen on which all kinds of images are projected, brightening up the area and creating an other-worldly atmosphere. The 645-square-foot (60 sq m) mezzanine overlooking this space contains a bedroom – which can be divided by a system of sliding panels – a bathroom, and a library that is visible from below. Only a few materials are used, but these are used repeatedly throughout the loft to highlight the qualities of the original building. All the walls and ceilings have been painted white, except for the wall at the end of the kitchen, which is clad in slate.

The floors are covered with wide oak boards. The furniture, characterized by its complex, curving forms, is the work of famous designers like Paulin, Jacobsen, and Eames. The indirect lighting of incandescent tubes and halogen lamps complements the light reflected by the walls. The lighting can be programmed by a computerized control system.

Architects: FOA. Foreign Office Architects
Location: London, United Kingdom
Photographs: Valerie Bennett

All the steel has been painted dark gray; the hinged doors are coated with unpolished black lacquer, the sliding ones with the same matt paint as the walls.

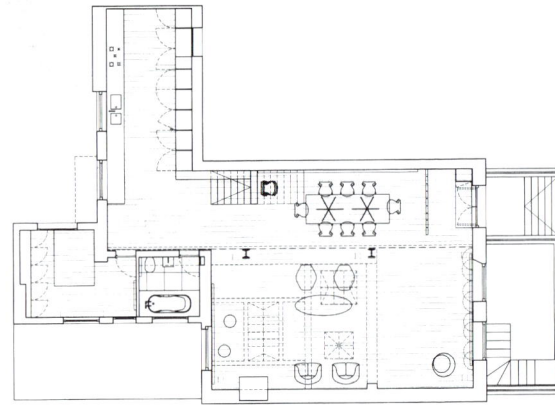

First floor

A centralized control system makes it possible to program the lighting in different sequences.

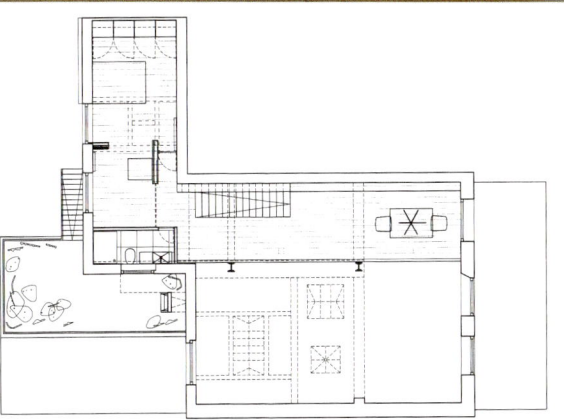

Mezzanine

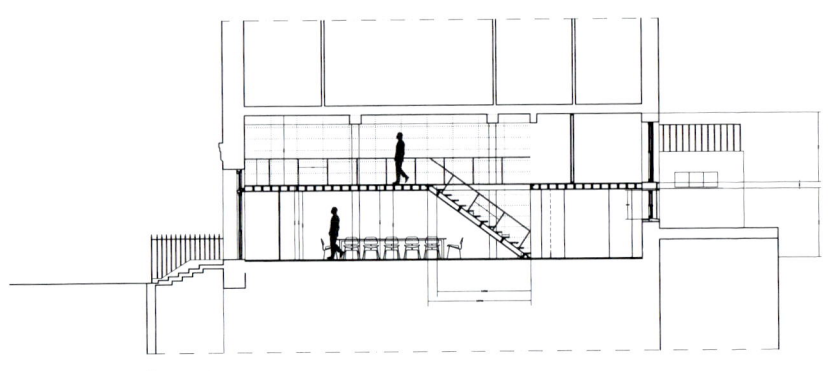

Cross-section

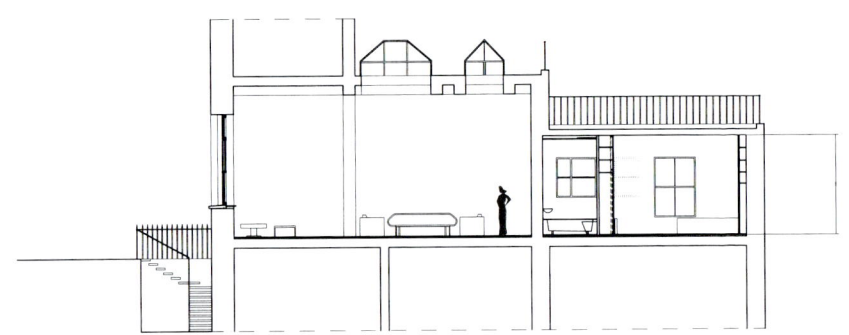

Cross-section

The wall at the end of the kitchen is clad with slate.

Because the closets are fitted into the walls, they do not disrupt the flow of the space.

Conversion of a warehouse

Adam Caruso, Peter St. John

This project involved several vows of chastity: minimal division of the space, minimal relationship with the street, minimal furniture, and minimal finishing of the wall.

The idea was to convert an old two-story warehouse in Islington, north London, into a home and studio. It was originally built with brick walls and wooden beams. Both the rectangular floors were completely unobstructed, without any partitions or pillars; they measured 15 feet (4.7 m) along the front by 32 feet (9.8 m) in depth, resulting in a useable space of 480 square feet (46 sq m) on each floor.

Caruso and St. John decided to replace the old façade with a glass wall. This screen, made with Climalit double glazing (8+24+6), helps to insulate and soundproof the space. The panes are translucent and provide the same effect as a Chinese silk or paper screen. During the day the façade is inscrutable, as if it were covered by a layer of metal; by night it is like a lantern glowing on the street outside.

Not all the divisions are fixed, as some – such as the main entrance door and one of the first-floor windows, which are covered with an opaque Eternit Eflex panel and can be opened.

Architects: Adam Caruso, Peter St. John
Location: London, United Kingdom
Photographs: Hélène Binet

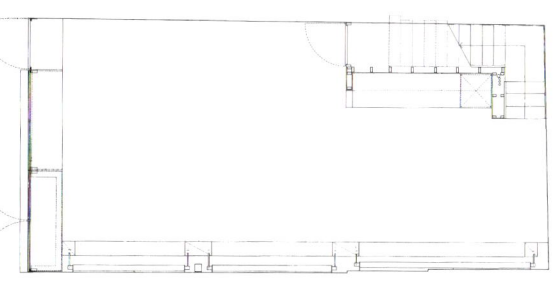

All the wrought-iron fittings were removed from the back area and an opening was made in the roof to provide a source of light. The stairwell was put in this area, along with the toilet, bathroom, and kitchen.

Upper floor

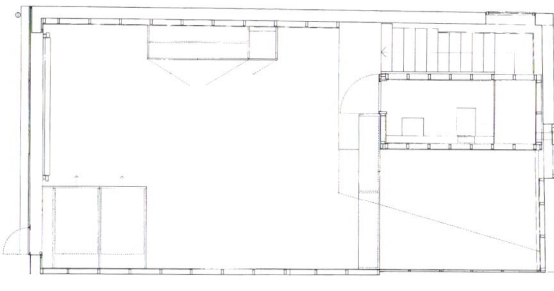

The rough finish of the old warehouse dictated the type of materials used for the new elements. The end result is an austere, unpretentious, and totally introverted space.

First floor

Wall Street lofts

Chroma AD. Alexis Briski + Raquel Sendra

The Chroma AD team formed by Alexis Briski and Raquel Sendra drew up a project for 13 lofts at number 15, Dutch Street, in the heart of New York's financial district. As they explain, "Wall Street is a business neighborhood in lower Manhattan full of high buildings and narrow streets. Often the only sunlight that reaches the façade of a building is reflected from another building across the way. The dramatic shadows and penetrating rays of sunlight typical of Wall Street provided the inspiration for this project. By creating luminous white boxes and breaking them down with elements of black, we tried to reflect the neighborhood itself."

The seven-floor building, put up in 1957, houses 13 lofts, ranging in size from 1,400 to 1,600 square feet (130–150 sq m). The Mayor's 1995 Revitalization Plan provided a legal framework for the conversion to residential use of commercial buildings such as this one – which had been lying empty since 1961.

Two types of loft were created, one with an "L" shape and the other rectangular with a central line of pillars marking off the kitchen area. The dressing rooms, equipped with industrial fittings, provide both privacy and ample storage space. Monumental bathrooms with imported tiles, specially designed lighting, and granite counters 6 feet (1.80 m) long all add to the grandeur of the setting. All the installations for state-of-the-art communication technology are at the disposal of the lofts' cosmopolitan owners, from the US Canada and Europe.

Architects: Chroma AD. Alexis Briski + Raquel Sendra
Location: Manhattan, New York, United States
Photographs: David M. Joseph, Bart Michaels

Windows stretching from wall to wall, 11-foot (3.3 m) high ceilings, and the reflection of the epoxy resin on the floor flood the interior of each loft with natural light. Monolithic black kitchens and other granite elements in the same tone bring this ethereal space down to earth.

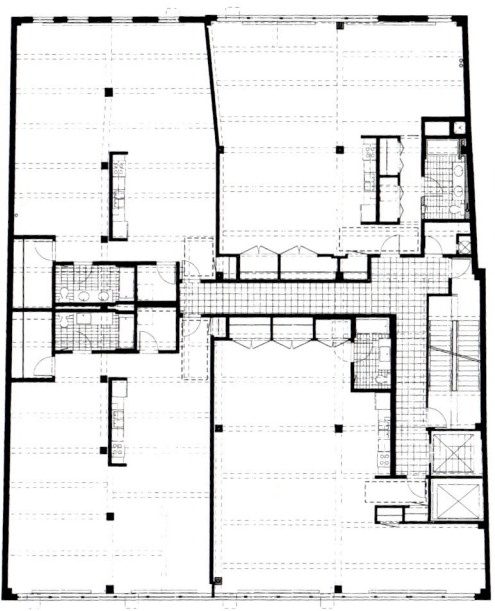

Attics on Wardour Street | CZWG Architects

The addition of two attics to an industrial building in London's Soho was intended as a continuation of the floors immediately below, in both visual and practical terms, thereby avoiding the marked division between the old and new so beloved of many architects working on pre-existing buildings of this type.

The transformation of this industrial building by putting new elements on top is indicative of a new way of thinking that promotes superimposition and mixture over the demolition and substitution that were so popular until recently.

The concrete structure on the roof was fitted out with a series of steel doors. This use of steel was extended to the frames of the large windows, so that metal is the element that dominates the exterior. The linearity is softened by a softly curving layer of zinc on the roof

The terraces offer superb views of the rooftops of London's Soho. The architects stressed that their aim was not only to take advantage of these stunning panoramas, but also to make the building an integral part of them and contribute to the neighborhood'. urban landscape. This explains the arched roofs topped with zinc

Architects: CZWG Architects
Location: London, United Kingdom
Photographs: Chris Gascoigne

The interior of the top floor is visually dominated by the arched roof. The architects have aimed for a warm, homely interior, with reddish colors on the walls and parquet floor.

One of the features that CZWG Architects treated with particular attention was the connection between the lofts and the exterior; the façades were provided with huge windows stretching from the floor to the ceiling, while each apartment was allocated a spacious terrace.

Lee House | Derek Wylie

A century ago Clerkenwell was a craftsmen's neighborhood. It went down rapidly in the 1950s and is now experiencing a revival as a fashionable alternative to the center.

Lee House is situated in Clerkenwell, to the west of London's financial center. It was the architect Derek Wylie himself who found this abandoned apartment building in St. John Street, with a two-floor industrial building in the back that had once been a silversmith's workshop. Although the total floor space of the workshop amounted to 4,845 square feet (450 sq m), the premises were very long and thin and completely surrounded by other buildings that shut out the sunlight.

So Wylie and his client, a local builder, were taking on a considerable challenge when they set about restoring the building. To complicate matters even further, the brief demanded a home for a couple with two children, a small office with an entrance on the street, and another apartment to sell (to finance some of the building work), also with direct access onto the street.

A small courtyard separates the building giving onto the street (containing the office and second apartment) from the old workshop, which contains the main home, measuring 2,700 square feet (250 sq m). The light enters through the courtyard and several galleries covered with translucent glass. The new architectural elements – staircases, walkways, flooring, partitions, and doors – and the furniture all define the space but do not radically alter its appearance. One of the priorities of both the architect and the client was to preserve the original character of the silversmith's workshop.

Architect: Derek Wylie
Location: London, United Kingdom
Photographs: Nick Kane, except kitchen (Mainstream) and the courtyard balcony (Derek Wylie)

The aim of the project was to highlight the building's original structure and create a home with flowing spaces that would take the maximum possible advantage of the natural light.

Long conversations about lifestyles made it apparent that the client was insistent on a democratic distribution of the space, with equal parts for children and adults.

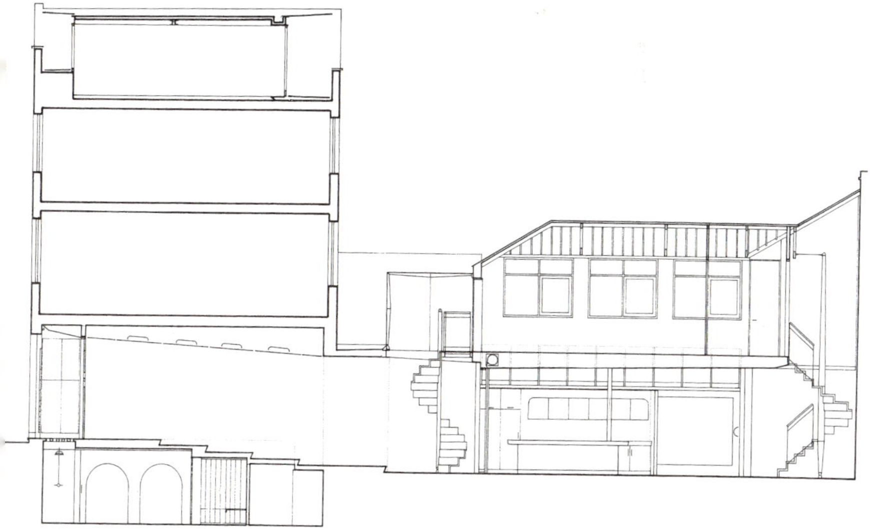

The main structures of the new elements are deliberately robust, to withstand the wear and tear of domestic life; the details and finishing, however, are delicate and polished, to contrast with the rough surfaces of the original building. The oak parquet on the lower floor extends from the entrance to the living room, while the kitchen, dining room, and courtyard are paved with limestone slabs.

The staircase is strategically situated to separate the various parts of the living area without interrupting the continuity of the space.

Loft in Clerkenwell | Circus Architects

The skeletal structure of the steel staircase is inspired by the Rem Koolhaas Dance Theater in The Hague.

This loft is the result of the conversion of two apartments in Clerkenwell, a London neighborhood with a large number of old industrial buildings of this type. This example, a former printing shop which was built in the 1930s, was refurbished by the Manhattan Loft Corporation (MLC) to give it a residential use. At the suggestion of MLC, the clients, a family of four, engaged Circus as the architects for the project.

The basic structure, with large concrete beams and enormous metal windows, bears witness to the building's industrial past. The main innovation of Circus Architects was the addition of an attic and a series of rounded metal sheets that mark off the bathrooms and serve as a visual separation between the different parts of the loft.

The children's bedrooms are on the first floor, right by the main entrance, while that of the parents is in the attic.

Circus Architects decided not to alter any of the building's original structure in the attic; similarly, part of the front wall has been left untouched.

Architects: Circus Architects
Location: London, United Kingdom
Photographs: Martin Levint (collage), Richard Glover

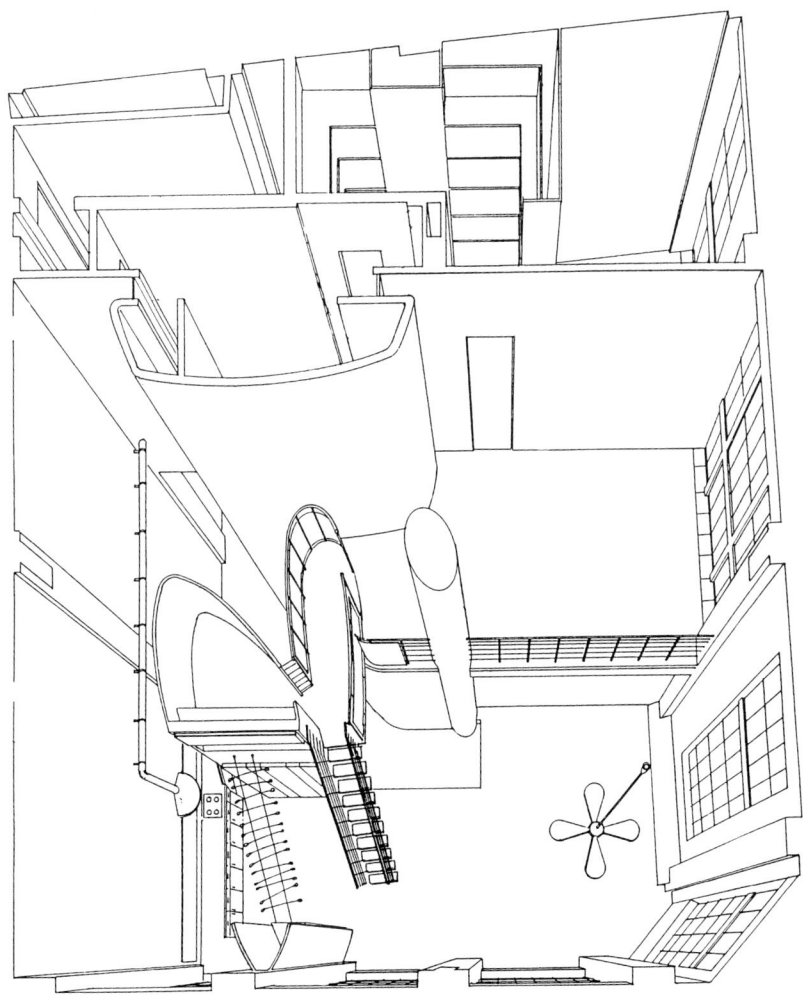

The balcony overlooking the main space not only offers great views, it also provides a more intimate space, set back from the large windows of the façade.

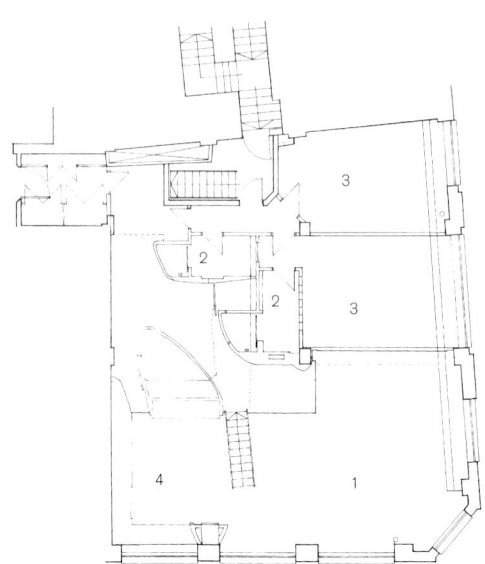

Top floor

1. Living room
2. Bathroom
3. Bedroom
4. Kitchen

Bottom floor

1. Hall
2. Study
3. Emergency exit
4. Bathroom
5. Bedroom

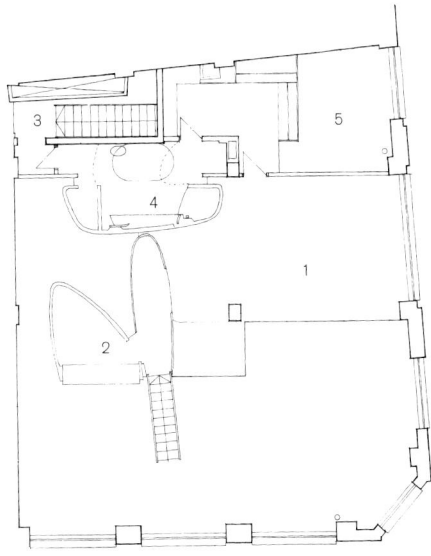

The kitchen takes up one corner of the lower floor. The closet doors were recovered from a 1950s kitchen.

An elliptical metal tower houses the washing machine and pantry.

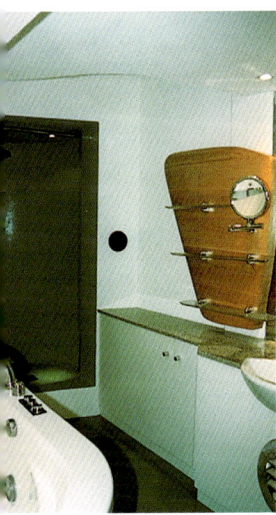

The bathrooms, like the other service areas, are conceived as hermetic forms.

Unit 203 | Buschow Henley & Partners

This 1,940-square-foot (180 sq m) apartment in Clerkenwell was designed to be occupied by a single person. The conversion tried to avoid diminishing the powerful impact of the original building. The client himself suggested that concrete should remain the predominant element in the design.

The loft is divided from east to west by four large pillars which create five different areas. These columns are built with a mixture of brick and concrete, with some tiled areas, reflecting the mixture of materials on the walls: the concrete of the original structure and the blocks making up the new partitions between the areas.

The main aim of the project was to delineate each space in a different way by putting in new walls, linked to the outer walls by a concrete floor. These new walls also serve to hide service areas, like the shower and pantry, as well as creating different spaces for relaxing, eating, and sleeping.

The new walls are made up of concrete blocks 5 feet (1.5 m) long, with a cross-section of 4 x 6 inches (10 x 15 cm), which set up a visual interplay with the 2½-inch (6.5 cm) bricks on the perimeter walls. Special pieces measuring 2½ feet (0.75 m) are added to the ends of each wall to create a striking indented pattern.

The bare mass of the floor gives the space unity, even when its form is irregular. The harsh lighting from the hidden tungsten and fluorescent bulbs reveals the convergence of the different planes and corners of the loft.

Architects: Buschow Henley & Partners
Location: London, United Kingdom
Photographs: Nick Kane/Arcaid

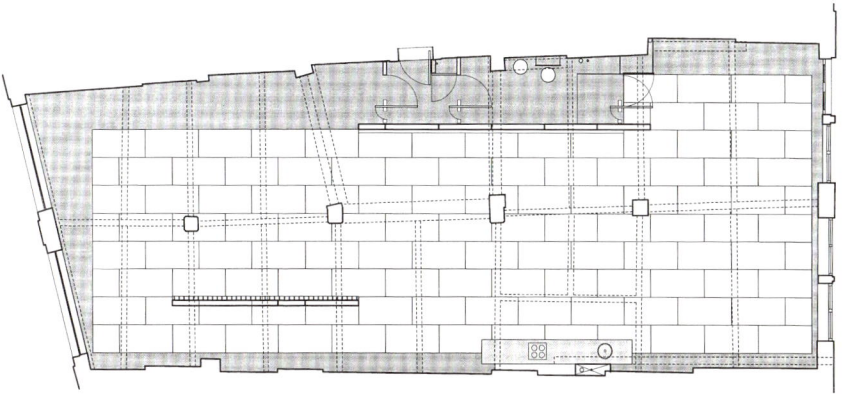

Chromatic treatment | AEM

Glyn Emrys and Pascal Madoc Jones, the two directors of AEM, instinctively understood that the conversion of a loft into a home demands not only aesthetic decisions but also entails a particular lifestyle on the part of the client that must be taken into account by the architect. One of the factors in this complicity is the love of spaces that are empty and stripped bare, almost without furniture. Eliminating all that is unnecessary means reinventing the very art of furnishing, and therefore redefining the boundaries of a space.

This process implies a commitment from both architect and client. The former must avoid partitions and camouflage any storage areas, while the latter has to learn how to combine various activities in a single space. This loft in Clerkenwell comes up with perfect solutions to these problems, as the chromatic treatment of the few pieces of furniture and the modulation of the light with filters not only respect the commitment to leave the existing structure barely untouched. It also brings out the underlying lyricism of such buildings.

The kitchen counter is mobile and can be placed where desired. The splash of color is guaranteed to set off any part of the space.

Architects: AEM
Location: London, United Kingdom
Photographs: Alan Williams

The architects appreciated that the existing metal structure serves as a sculptural element that enriches the spaces.

Apart from the most intimate activities (isolated in the bathroom and bedroom), everything takes place in a single big space. The magic of this room lies in its very emptiness. For this reason, the furniture is reduced to the bare minimum.

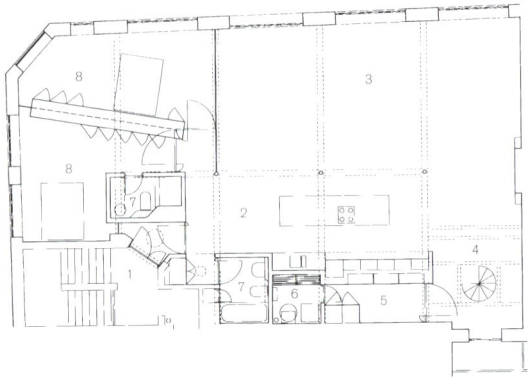

Ground plan

1. Entrance
2. Kitchen
3. Living room
4. Staircase to the terrace
5. Storage space
6. Sauna
7. Bathroom
8. Bedroom

The glass treated with acid is not merely an architectural resource, it also has a poetic quality. Figures behind the glass lose their form and become fragile and spiritual, like the woman levitating in the painting, or the reader beyond, sitting on a transparent inflatable armchair, seemingly floating on air.

Interior landscape | Florian Beigel Architects

This apartment is long and thin (26 x 69 feet/8 x 21 m) and covers a single story of an old shoe factory in Clerkenwell, with a reinforced concrete structure, that was built in the 1930s.

The loft conversion was conceived as an inner landscape. The new free-standing elements, dotted about like boats anchored in a bay, include very confined but striking spaces for the bathroom and bedroom. The shower, for example, boasts a blue floor and walls and a transparent polycarbonate ceiling that reveals the building's concrete beams and fluorescent lighting. Also tucked away are a small enclosed room, the size of a double bed, used to put up guests, and a 20-foot (6 m) long counter made of stainless steel and laminated wood that marks off the kitchen. The privacy of these areas contrasts with the unexpectedly large open spaces in the rest of the apartment.

The original ceiling, supports, beams, and walls were all painted in the same yellowish-white color. The undulating irregular forms of the walls and the strong presence of the concrete supports and beams are a reminder of the building's former use. The floor is made of hardened mortar with a grayish-green matt epoxy resin finish; it has been raised to put in the kind of underfloor heating more usually found in large industrial workplaces or hospitals and other public buildings.

Architects: Florian Beigel Architects
Location: London, United Kingdom
Photographs: Hélène Binet

High-frequency fluorescent tubes are set at strategic points a little below the ceiling.

The doors of the bedroom and bathroom have been clad with sheets of plywood finished with a coat of transparent matt polyurethane.

Ground plan

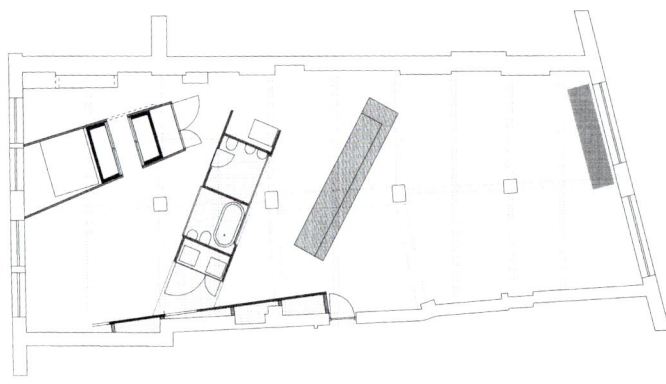

The big polycarbonate panels are linked together using a system that allows the material to expand or contract according to the temperature.

The blue tone on the walls and floor of the shower, after Yves Klein.

Neutral space | Felicity Bell

This loft is situated in a 1930s building in Clerkenwell; it was originally intended for light industry but, in the opinion of the Australian architect Felicity Bell, its real attraction did not lie in its industrial past. Bell, who shares this home-studio with the interior designer Christian Papa, did not consider this circumstance very relevant as many of the original features had been changed over the years and the end results were neither interesting nor beautiful.

The main idea for the 820-square-foot (76 sq m) apartment was to create a totally neutral space that could be used for either work or play as required. The owners of this loft like to cook for their guests and do not consider their work as being divorced from their daily life, so the two functions could not be kept apart rigorously. "Work is such an important part of my life that I would be squandering space if I reserved a whole room for it," admits Bell.

The layout of the space is divided by a central axis marked by a long wall with fitted kitchen equipment and hidden garbage cans. The counter is made of *jarrah* wood, from a tree native to Australia, which radiates an intense color that contrasts with the subdued tones of the rest of the furniture. The floor is covered with shiny gray rubber and disguises an underfloor heating system that eliminates any need for obtrusive radiators in the small apartment. The overall effect is finished off by designer furniture, such as the dining room table and chairs by Charles and Ray Eames, which champion the ideals of the modern movement in a domestic environment. This loft is a excellent illustration of flexibility and multiple uses in a single space.

Architects: Felicity Bell
Location: London, United Kingdom
Photographs: Chris Tubbs

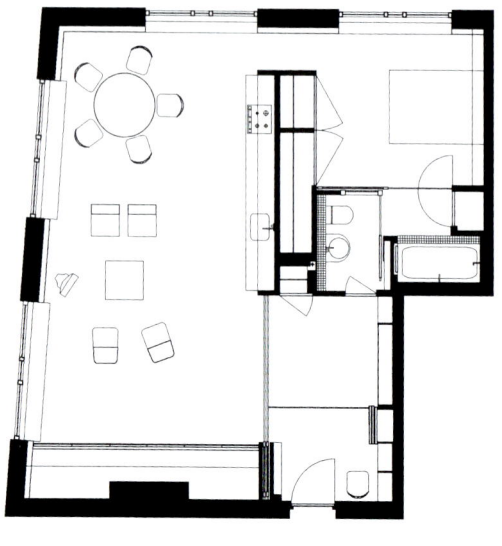

Layout option for an exclusively domestic use.

Layout showing all the work areas open, with the table for meetings with clients in the entrance area.

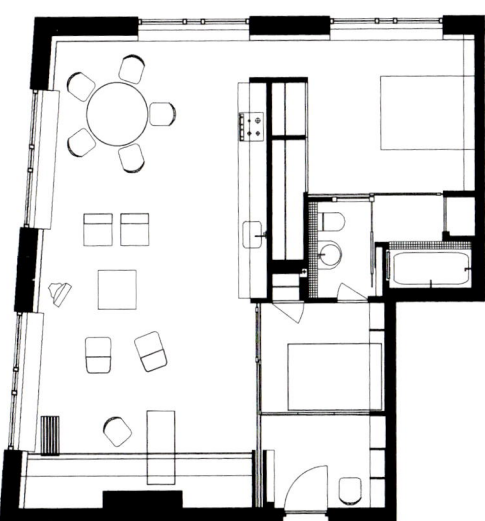

Layout with the table in the main space and the entrance area converted into a bedroom for guests.

No restrictions

Blockarchitecture:
Graeme Williamson + Zoe Smith

All the projects undertaken by Blockarchitecture (formerly known as 24/seven) are governed by a series of parameters or variables that govern the solutions to any problem that may arise in the design process. Their approach to a project is direct and free of any restrictions, and sufficiently flexible to be able to react to any unforeseen requirements.

The design of this loft in London bears witness to their courage in experimenting with space and materials in a constant reconfiguration of our modern cultural context, based on the principle of "cut and paste." The aim was to keep the concrete structure that defines and contains the space as open and uninterrupted as possible. The apartment's shape and length are boldly emphasized by the wooden floorboards aligned toward the balconies on the building's eastern façade. A long 30-foot (9 m) wall, made of recycled steel panels, dominates the space and determines how it is organized. Behind it lie the hall, a small storage space, the toilet, and the dark room; when all the doors on this wall are closed, the apartment seems to be cut off, with no way in or out. The lights pointing toward the ceiling emphasize the octagonal structure of the beams crossing the space. The bathroom elements are set on a free-standing concrete platform and stand exposed, just like any other pieces of furniture.

"We're involved in architecture and design because we're interested in taking a stand on certain social issues and reacting against the standardization of lifestyles and the homogeneity of design."

Architects: Blockarchitecture: Graeme Williamson + Zoe Smith
Location: London, United Kingdom
Photographs: Chris Tubbs

The architects' social concerns have led them to experiment with new configurations capable of matching the changes in modern lifestyles.

Both the kitchen counter and the platform for the bathroom are made of concrete.

Kopf Loft | Buschow Henley

The Kopf loft forms part of a renovation of a Victorian building in Shepherdess Walk, east London, originally a warehouse, with a total floor space of 110,000 square feet (10,200 sq m). The entire project was realized by the Buschow Henley team of architects. The rhomboid building has seven floors on the west side and six on the east, with a central courtyard following a longitudinal axis running from north to south.

The project's aims did not include the creation of commercial spaces; the whole building was given over to residential units, each one with its own parking space. Given the size of the building, this meant that the total number of units, as well as the impact on the neighborhood, was limited.

Curiously enough, the demarcation of the separate units coincided with the original dividing walls. On the eastern and western sides of the courtyard the stories are divided into two to four apartments, while the other sides are divided into three or four.

The architectural team who were responsible for the project came to the following conclusion: "The building has already demonstrated its durability. Our work has given it a new meaning and no doubt it will be able to support subsequent reconfigurations."

In an era when most new building work serves the purposes of speculation, Buschow Henley's project is both conventional, because it does create homes ripe for speculation, and unusual, in that it unequivocally mediates between the use of the original building and the budget for the project.

Architects: Buschow Henley
Location: London, United Kingdom
Photographs: Nick Kane/Arcaid

The work acts as an intermediary between the homogeneities and heterogeneities of the composition and the construction, between the ideal and real.

"With only limited means, the transformation sought to be quite honest." (Buschow Henley)

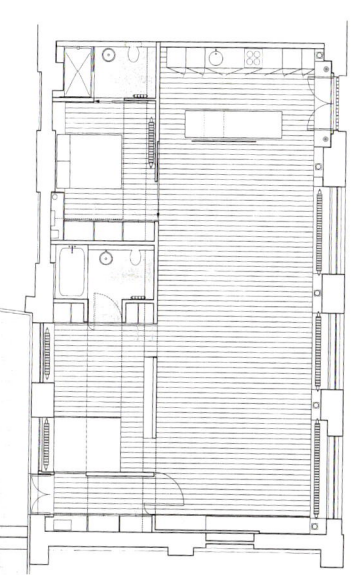

Light from all sides | Buschow Henley

This loft forms part of another building in Shepherdess Walk, Hackney, that was also restored by the architectural team of Buschow Henley.

The builder wanted to create a mixed-use building that combines homes with commercial premises. The preliminary studies showed that the conversion could accommodate some 50 apartments on the upper floors, with commercial units on the first floor and a parking lot in the basement.

The plan for this loft in particular involved the creation of an apartment with two bedrooms for a couple who had tired of living in the typical loft with exposed brick walls and a concrete floor. The design of the new 2,200-square-foot (205 sq m) apartment, which was sold unfurnished as an empty box, sought to take the maximum advantage of the bright, high space next to the mezzanine.

The light enters the apartment from all sides, from the array of windows and the skylights over the bathroom, the attic, the lower toilet, and the open space on the lower floor.

In the words of Buschow Henley, "Our adaptation of this building corresponds to a vision from a new perspective that gives vital new impulses, so that when our work is over we leave behind wide, empty spaces waiting to be filled."

Architects: Buschow Henley
Location: London, United Kingdom
Photographs: Nick Kane

The lower level contains the bedrooms, dining room, and living room areas, arranged in two blocks on either side of the inner space.

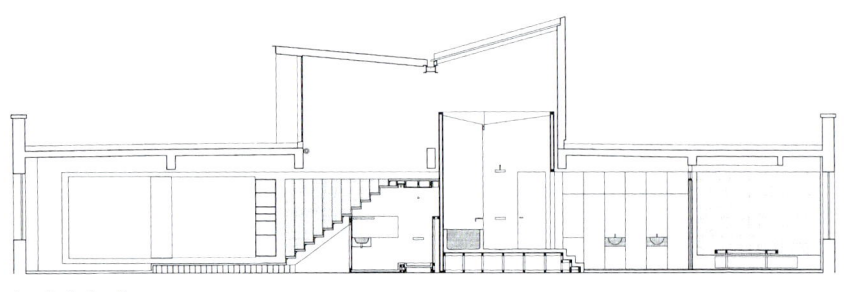

Longitudinal section

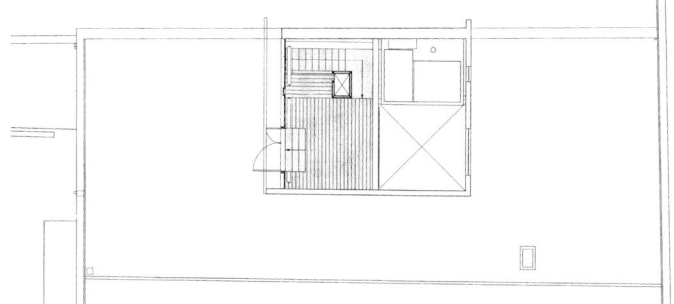

Top floor

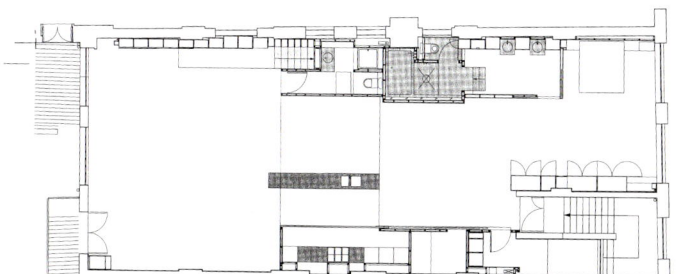

Lower floor

The mezzanine defines the lower space and allows light to penetrate into the interior, as well as establishing visual contact with the area below.

Piper Building

Wells Mackereth Architects

The Piper Building is a concrete office block originally built at the end of the 1950s. It owes its name to the painter John Piper, whose murals decorate the building. In the year 1997 the Lifschutz Davidson studio rehabilitated the building, and subsequently several loft apartments were created by architects such as Ron Arad, John Pawson, and, in this particular case, James Wells and Sally Mackereth. The apartment, which was completed in 1998, was designed for a young businessman; it is distinguished by its wide open spaces, flooded with light, and a flexible and highly intelligent layout.

This young but very experienced team maintains that an architect's principal challenge is the creation and organization of space. A static, rigid architecture does not express anything, whereas a living organism — which any building is capable of becoming — immediately gives rise to flowing spaces that can be changed according to the requirements of its occupant.

The entire floor was covered with large birch plywood boards, as Mackereth considered this material to be ideal for the proportions of the loft. Some high pivoting doors made of reinforced glass — set in dividing walls that do not reach the ceiling — make it possible to alter the space at will.

This team finds its inspiration in a wide range of sources, from its experience with its own studio in Soho to movies, music, or the beauty of the natural world.

Architects: Wells Mackereth Architects
Location: London, United Kingdom
Photographs: Chris Gascoine/View, Dominic Blackmoren/Mitchell Beazley Picture Library

1. Living room, dining room, and kitchen
2. Furniture unit behind sliding panel
3. Pivoting glass panel
4. Bedrooms
5. Sliding blinds
6. Dressing room
7. Bathroom
8. Bathtub on slate support
9. Sliding doors made of engraved glass
10. Storage area

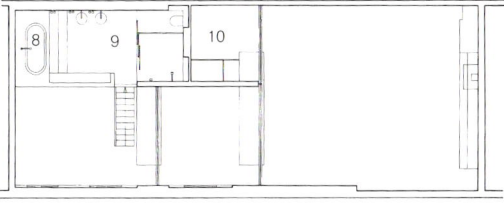

Attic

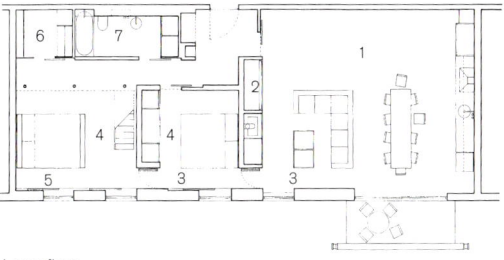

Lower floor

The television and sound system are incorporated into the closets. The couch was designed by Terence Woodgate.

The bathroom, in the attic off the bedroom, seems like another living area.

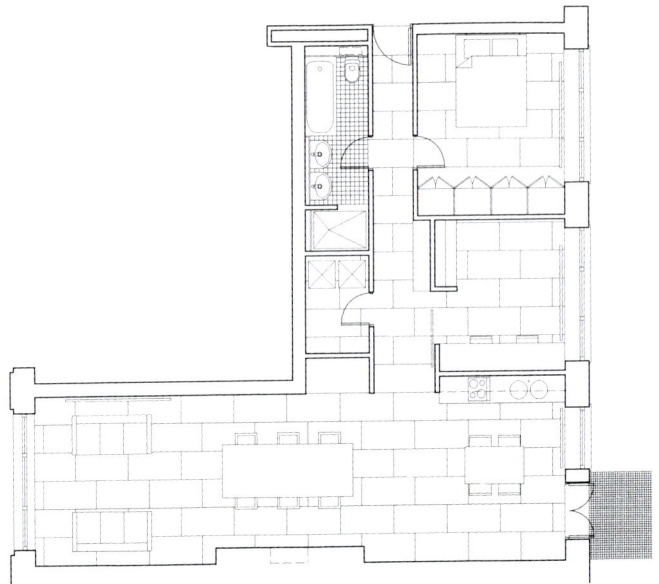

Number 8C, French Place

Project Orange: Christopher Ash, James Soane

Project Orange was formed in 1997 by the architects Christopher Ash and James Soane, who are committed to following the architectural process through from the birth of an idea to the last details of the design. "Our work does not seek to establish a set of aesthetic rules or practices, it explores the process. It's a way of understanding design and buildings from a hybrid approach to their architecture."

Number 8C, French Place lies on the third floor of a late-19th-century building in Shoreditch originally used for the clothing industry. The rental contract specified that, in the three years during which it was applicable, the loft could be used as both a workplace and a home, and the interior could be modified provided the building's basic structure was unaffected. The building was in a parlous state, with no heating and a primitive plumbing and sanitation system. As the people living in the apartment did not own it they decided to invest the basic minimum in its renovation.

With these criteria in mind heating was put in and the place was generally smartened up. The main architectural contribution was a large terracotta wall at the northern end of the space, which made it possible to create two private bedrooms and a new bathroom. The latter is situated behind the corner created for the kitchen, which takes advantage of a stainless-steel counter left on the premises.

The tenants, who are architects, did most of the conversion work themselves, and were, therefore, directly involved in every phase of the design and construction process.

Architects: Project Orange: Christopher Ash, James Soane
Location: London, United Kingdom
Photographs: Alicia Pivaro

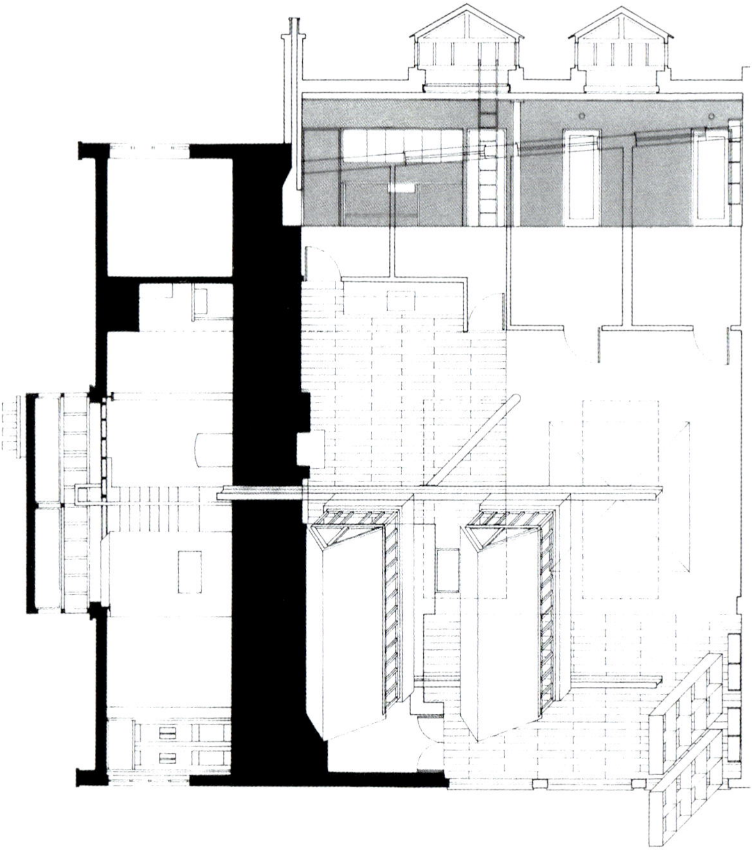

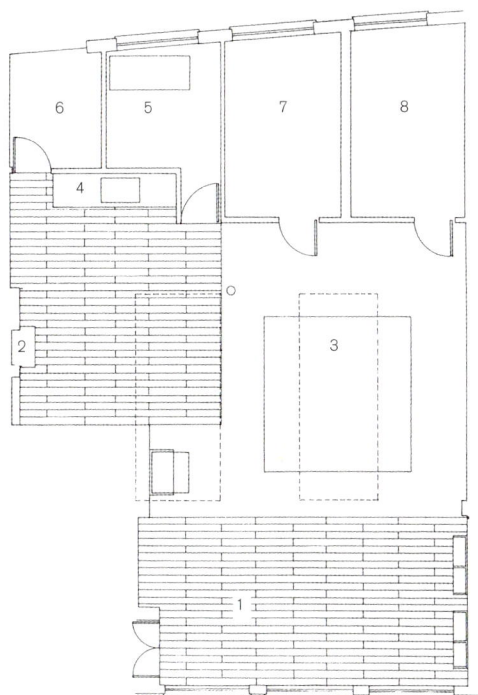

1. Work area
2. Living room/fireplace
3. Dining room
4. Kitchen
5. Bathroom
6. Pantry
7. Bedroom
8. Bedroom

The main space has three areas: the living room, centered around the fireplace; the dining room, under the skylight; and the work area, next to the windows on the front of the building.

Spatial contrast
María Rodríguez-Carreño Villangómez

This 2,480-square-foot (230 sq m) studio-home is on the third floor of a building that was once a gym. The first stage of the refurbishing was the installation of a waterproof surface on the terrace above the loft, as the roof had been damaged by the infiltration of water. Then the entire ceiling was painted white. The building's structure seems to be based on the number 12: 12 windows, 12 large beams crossed by 12 smaller ones. The conversion sought to emphasize the original structure and avoid any compartmentalizing that would diminish the dynamism of the space. All the furniture introduced was free-standing and always set some distance from a wall.

The new architectural elements also stood out strongly from the old building, which is solid and heavy with thick walls, buttresses, and robust beams measuring 10 x 16 inches (30 x 50 cm) with a span of 20 feet (6 m). The new additions, in contrast, are made of metal, wood, exposed concrete, and glass – lighter and more sophisticated materials that are easier to transport and install.

Striking spatial contrasts have been achieved with respect to the original structure by raising the ceiling to 8 feet (2.3 m) in the entrance, and by adding a graffiti painting to one of the end walls to create a visual reference point that dominates the whole space.

Architects: María Rodríguez-Carreño Villangómez
Location: Barcelona, Spain
Photographs: Joan Mundó

The staircase leading to the upper level is made of steel steps set into the wall. These have a T-shaped cross-section and inlaid aluminum strips painted with gray oxiron. The sleeping area is on a smaller scale than the rest, to provide greater intimacy.

A wall made of *iroko* wood hides the kitchen closets and bathroom near the entrance area. The kitchen unit is also made of *iroko*, topped with a fitted 1-inch (3 cm) thick slab of Greek marble.

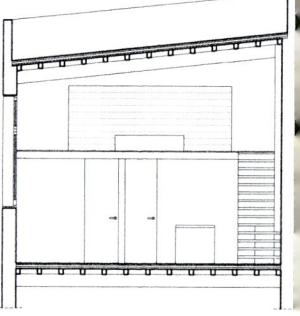

Lower level
1. Entrance
2. Kitchen
3. Dining room
4. Living room
5. Studio
6. Bathroom

Cross-section

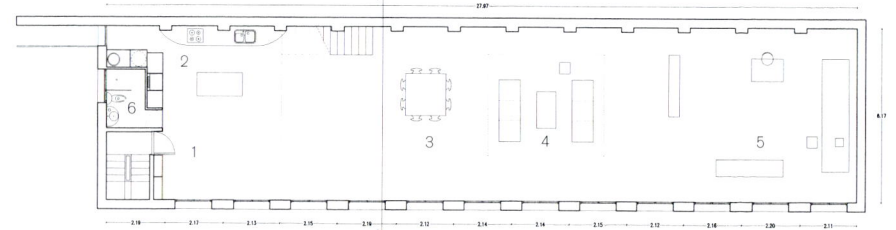

The studio is dominated by a photo by Julio Rodríguez-Carreño of graffiti on the island of Ibiza.

The varnished *iroko* closet at the head of the bed with metal edges is fitted with inbuilt lighting.

The bathroom is clad with stone slabs measuring 10 x 20 inches (30 x 60 cm), for protection.

Leisure and business | Ramón Úbeda / Pepa Reverter

Barcelona's Poble Nou neighborhood, once the city's industrial center, is now popular with artists and other creative professionals looking for a space in which they can both work and live. The area still abounds in beautiful buildings that were once warehouses or factories for light industry. The recovery of these buildings has confirmed the relevance and creative dynamism of the loft lifestyle.

The home-studio of Ramón Úbeda and Pepa Reverter, on the second of the four floors in one of these old buildings, is a good illustration of this phenomenon. According to them, "It was the easiest design job in the world. The main aim of the conversion of old industrial premises is always to have large spaces and take full advantage of the sunlight. These things are so basic yet they can be so difficult to achieve, but in this case they were already there. The strong, solid structure of this old factory provided over 3,000 square feet (280 sq m) of floor space, and then there are two impressive windows that flood the place with light. So much space is a luxury that can't be found in conventional homes."

The decorative work had to strike a balance between the conflicting tastes of its occupants: Úbeda tends towards minimalism, while his partner likes exuberant colors and forms. The resulting compromise is an austerity tempered with a few lively but sophisticated touches in the accessories and furniture.

Interior designers: Ramón Úbeda/Pepa Reverter
Location: Barcelona, Spain
Photographs: Pere Planells

"Writing an article, designing a book, illustrating a poem, painting a canvas, or carving a sculpture can all be just as enjoyable as making a paella or having a siesta in the loft." (Úbeda/Reverter)

Space and total freedom in a setting that caters for both leisure and work. The open rectangular space houses a living area, an office, and a studio, all clearly delineated and separate from each other.

The generous height of the ceiling made it possible to insert a mezzanine that visually enriches the space, as well as accommodating the two most intimate spaces: the main bedroom and the drawing studio.

La Nau | Carol Iborra, Mila Aberasturi

Over 60 years have passed since this distinctive building, once a spinning mill, took its place among the impressive buttresses and domes of Barcelona's Poble Nou neighborhood. La Nau is the loft on the third floor; its name "La nau" — which means "ship" in Catalan — pays tribute to its past industrial history. Once Mila Aberasturi and Carol Iborra (Forma 7) had found this architectural treasure, with its massive walls and typical Catalan arches, they set about turning it into a home for the Pou-Iborra family.

La Nau is surrounded by a maze of streets and small buildings of varying heights that seems to be continued inside. The result is a panorama of shapes and white walls that draws on the wisdom of the popular vernacular architecture of the *kasbah*. The bold perspectives of the series of receding walls and sharp corners hide intimate spaces tucked away for the bathrooms and toilets, the kitchen, and the storage area.

The materials chosen for the renovation were unpretentious but effective: pine floorboards; thin, untreated plaster partitions; concrete on the walls and floors of the bathrooms; and simple metal structures.

Although the Pou-Iborra house is a space without doors where conviviality rules, the great distances between each area ensure domestic and personal privacy. Living in La Nau is an adventure that offers its inhabitants the luxury of living immersed in a huge space.

Architects: Carol Iborra, Mila Aberasturi (interior designer)
Location: Barcelona, Spain
Photographs: Xabier Mendiola

An inner enclosure made of fiber-glass panels creates a mother-of-pearl effect when light pours in through the large windows.

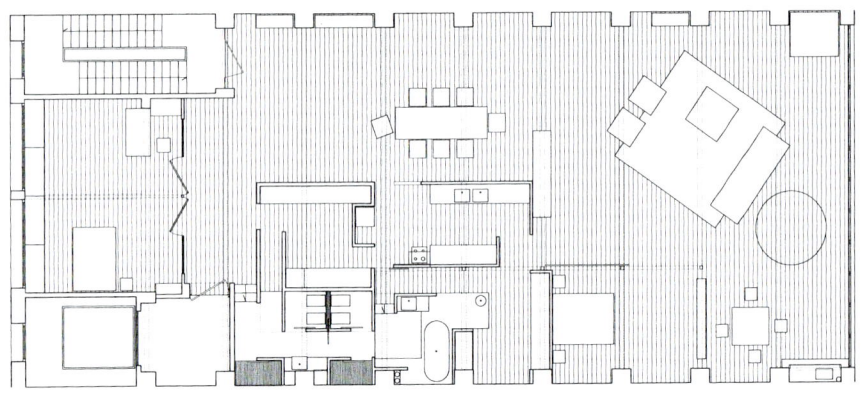

The conversion has retained the metal frames of the large windows that look out onto the rear courtyard.

An abstract geometry of white forms delineates the different settings in the house.

There is a plan, as yet unrealized, to put an attic space above the bathroom area.

Urban panorama | Antoni Arola

The top loft in this old spinning mill in Poble Nou, Barcelona, is situated on the fourth floor, tucked under the roof. A web of metal girders looms over the studio and even invades part of the domestic space. Because the loft's designer (and owner), Antoni Arola, wanted to set up his home and workplace in the same space, the two settings are both in a continuous state of flux, creating a vibrant laboratory of ideas.

In the privacy of his home, Arola is surrounded by sources of inspiration: lights, reflections, and other elements that constantly play off the outside world to stir his imagination and offer hidden beauty or emotion

In the studio, the designer has all the tools required to produce his attractive, ingenious, but functional designs. Although Arola is responsible for the interior decoration of countless buildings, most of his projects are intended for production on an industrial scale: lamps, chairs, couches, display cabinets, and even packaging materials.

The studio retains the original frames of the enormous window that looks out on the unequivocally urban panorama at the back of the building. A small partition, treated with paint specially made for blackboards, also serves as a bookcase. The floor is made of sand-polished concrete.

The new layout created by the loft's owner makes it a changing, dynamic space, imagined with total freedom, that reaches out to the exterior but retains an intimate atmosphere

Interior designer: Antoni Arola
Location: Barcelona, Spain
Photographs: Pere Planells

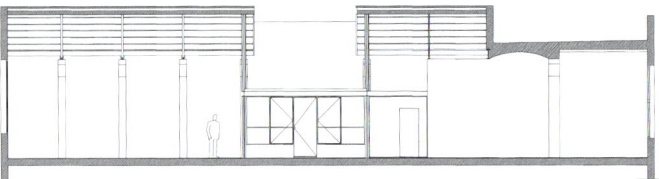
Longitudinal section

Cross-section

Ground plan

The bathroom and toilet are integrated into the bedroom and play an important visual role in the most intimate area of the home.

Vapor Llull

Cirici & Bassó, Inés Rodríguez, Alfonso de Luna, Norman Cinamond, Carla Cirici

Cristian Cirici and Carles Bassó converted an old four-story chemicals factory into a residential building. The external references to its industrial past are plain to see: a tall brick chimney that practically scrapes the building, materials until recently used exclusively for industrial purposes. These aspects probably influenced the decision to respect the original features of the factory. The architects kept the outer brick walls, the wooden rafters, and the wrought-iron work on the small ceiling vaults, but they did add three glass-fronted vertical communication blocks, each with a staircase and an elevator shaft, in order to provide all the 18 homes with independent access. The sophistication of the new elements contrasts with the structures that have been preserved and with the orange and blue tones of the façade. Although aesthetic considerations did not govern the construction of the original building, the conversion has created some attractive living spaces with modern touches. The exposed metal structure, the big windows letting in sunlight, and the configuration of the open spaces all help to make the old factory a homely and welcoming place to live.

Cirici and Bassó left the interiors of the apartments unfinished, so that various interior designers could complete the process and leave a personal imprint on each home. We have chosen the very different solutions of four of these designers: namely Inés Rodríguez, Norman Cinamond, Alfonso de Luna, and Carla Cirici.

Architects: Cirici & Bassó, Inés Rodríguez, Alfonso de Luna, Norman Cinamond, Carla Cirici
Location: Barcelona, Spain
Photographs: Rafael Vargas

Inés Rodríguez has designed an austere attic where the wooden beams create a powerful presence.

The floor is made of polished concrete and the walls have been plastered and painted white. There is barely any furniture and the paintings stand against the walls.

Norman Cinamond put in a counter to separate the kitchen from the sitting room and serve as an informal eating area. The Jamaica stools were designed by Pepe Cortés.

The extensive use of wood, the ceramic tiles, and the primitive sculptures give the apartment designed by Alfonso de Luna a decadent, tropical atmosphere.

Carla Cirici's version is the one that makes the least modifications to the original space.

Apartment for an actress | Franc Fernández

In this building, originally an old industrial warehouse, the high ceilings (15 feet/4.5 m) were left intact to retain the industrial feel of the space and give a distinctive personality to the new homes that were created after the conversion.

Each floor was divided into four 1,600-square-foot (150 sq m) lofts, although the apartment shown here, measuring 1,200 square feet (110 sq m), was the result of a further subdivision of one of these areas. It has the advantage of occupying one of the corners of the building, which guarantees a supply of natural light from two directions. The owner's work as an actress determined the type of space she was looking for; the loft sometimes needs to be used for rehearsals and even performances, so the main criteria for the conversion were open spaces, plenty of light, and versatility.

The original structure was maintained, from the metal pillars and summers to the wavelike ceramic arches on the ceiling and the large windows. The floor space was divided into two areas: on one side, the kitchen, dining room, and living room, with no divisions between them; on the other, the bedroom, bathroom, toilet, and study. The first, more public area has kept the high ceilings and receives generous amounts of sunlight, while the vertical space in the second area is divided in two by a platform ceiling to provide greater intimacy. The upper section, an open space 5 feet (1.5 m) high, houses the library, which can be reached by a wooden staircase.

Architect: Franc Fernández
Location: Barcelona, Spain
Photographs: Joan Mundó

The walls and the ceilings were all painted white to emphasize the building's original structure.

The floor of the apartment is entirely covered with boards of *ipe* wood. This adds warmth, to contrast with a decoration that stresses the original building's industrial features.

The rooms are connected to each other by sliding doors, in some cases translucent, which ensure that no space is wasted.

Franc Fernández has created an apartment that boasts a high degree of tension in each space and a great richness of form, despite the austerity of the materials used.

Verticality | Pere Cortacans

The Barcelona neighborhood of El Born – a maze of narrow, winding streets – is the setting for this conversion of an early 20th-century L-shaped block that once loomed over a workshop specializing in street signs.

The Pere Cortacans' project involved not only a total overhaul of the building, but also the demolition of the old workshop to make way for a central garden. Cortacans also made sure he reserved one of the homes on the top floor for his own use.

His apartment has three levels: the original floor, an upper story resulting from the dismantling of a ventilated air chamber – a primitive form of air conditioning – and, finally, a glass-lined studio on the roof that leads onto the terrace. It is therefore a home that functions on a vertical plane, in contrast to the horizontal planes generally associated with lofts. Each level corresponds to a set of activities with varying degrees of privacy and intensity. The three-tiered layout is not merely a byproduct of the high ceilings typical of old industrial buildings, it also reflects the architect's use of the roof as an extension of the domestic setting.

The garden in the central patio, on the site of the old workshop, provides access to the building. This layout is reminiscent of the Spanish colonial *corrals* in Latin America, where the patio not only led on to the homes but also housed their communal services, such as toilets, laundries, and bathhouses.

Architect: Pere Cortacans
Location: Barcelona, Spain
Photographs: David Cardelús

A bookcase-bench specially designed to fit along the banister marks the separation between the bedroom and the living room area.

The studio offers some wonderful views of the city's rooftops. Even though the apartment is in a neighborhood full of dark, narrow streets, it enjoys the benefits of Mediterranean sunshine.

Austerity or design | Joan Bach

Even though these two apartments are in the same building and have both been converted by the same architect, they represent two different approaches to a loft space. The selection of materials, finishings, and furniture gives each loft a very different personality: one is austere, while the other is almost palatial.

In the first, most of the structural elements have been left unaltered (the little vaults in the ceiling, the front wall, and the latticed girders) and a mass-produced material – polished concrete – has been put on the floor. Its appearance is deliberately industrial, even harsh. The apartment is divided into two areas, one with the bedrooms and bathrooms, the other a large square sitting room, with one corner cut off to house the kitchen/dining room.

In the second loft the walls have been painted yellow. Parquet has been installed on the floor, the artificial lighting has been designed to give a warm light, and the furniture is new and functional. This loft has a big living room that includes an open kitchen, as well as a side area divided vertically into three levels. The lower level is taken up by the dining room, the staircase, and a toilet; the second by the main bedroom with an adjoining bathroom and dressing room; the third by an independent area designed for children, with two bedrooms, a bathroom, and a room used as a playroom and study.

Architect: Joan Bach
Location: Barcelona, Spain
Photographs: Jordi Miralles

Most of the furniture has been recycled from a variety of sources, adding variety to the space.

The partitions do not reach the ceiling and so do not give the impression of interrupting the space. The pillar with exposed brickwork does not support any weight – the building's basic structure is metal – but it does serve to hide the plumbing.

Even though the bedroom and living room are on different levels, there is still a visual communication between them. The main bedroom is reached through the bathroom.

The architect has established an interplay between the large surfaces painted in yellow and isolated touches of pale brown on the beams, pillars, staircase, air ducts, in the kitchen, on picture frames, and so on.

Working from home | Helena Mateu Pomar

This building in Barcelona's Gràcia district was once a factory that produced electrical goods. The loft shown here occupies the top floor, and it has the special advantage of having direct and exclusive access to the terrace situated on the roof.

The client wanted to refurbish the space and convert it into a home and office, but he insisted that the bright open space, which had immediately captivated him, should not lose its essential qualities. It was also important that the most private rooms and the service areas could be closed off independently of each other, but without any interruption in the continuity of the space. Some freestanding units were designed for the service areas, which in turn served to mark off the sitting room, the office, and the bedrooms. This allows the sunlight to pour into the main spaces in the home and penetrate into its deepest recesses.

The new units are equipped with sliding doors to allow the client privacy as required, but they also give a sense of uninterrupted flow to the floor space. Large oil paintings by the artists Imma Alonso and Miquel Planas add a highly personal touch to each space. Given the generous spaciousness of this loft, the paintings can be fully appreciated from a distance.

A metal staircase leads to the upper level, which contains a small room that serves as an office, with access to the garden on the terrace.

Architects: Helena Mateu Pomar
Location: Barcelona, Spain
Photographs: Jordi Miralles

The dimensions of all the furniture and partitions match the scale of the building.

The metal girders and the strong lines of the small vaults on the roof, typical of Catalonia, contrast with the continuous polished surface of the wooden floor.

The most private rooms are incorporated into the rest of the space, with controlled elements like sliding doors.

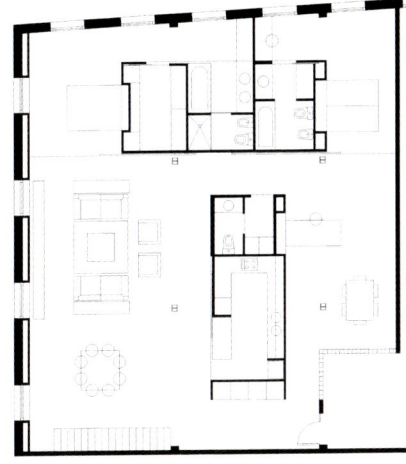

Each bedroom has its own bathroom, to ensure greater privacy.

Efficient distribution of space

Joan Bach

This loft occupies the bottom part of a building in Barcelona's colorful Gràcia neighborhood. The whole building was refurbished by the architect Joan Bach, who took advantage of the lower floors to set up his home and office.

The loft has four distinct levels that mark off the different functional areas without any need for extra walls. The entrance from the street gives onto a small office and reception area and a toilet. A mechanical platform links this level to the upper bedroom and bathroom, while three steps lead down to the high-ceilinged living room and the courtyard – which is small but, thanks to its low walls, lets abundant sunshine into the house. The double height of the living room affords sufficient space for a small mezzanine that serves as an office, complete with a view of the exterior.

The logic that has led to such an efficient distribution of space has also determined the criteria for the decorative elements: the choice of furniture (some designed especially, and some mass-produced), the Zen-style outer garden, and the lighting.

The building work was planned with care to provide impeccable finishing and comfort. A good example of this intelligent approach is the skylights, which are equipped with an electrical mechanism that adjusts their opening and closing in accordance with the amount of ventilation required.

Architect: Joan Bach
Location: Barcelona, Spain
Photographs: Jordi Miralles

Both the floor and the finishing on the pillar are made of synthetic resin, a material more commonly associated with industrial buildings.

The entrance provides a view of the elevator that goes up to the bedroom.

All the spaces, with the exception of the bathrooms, have views of the rest of the house, emphasizing the relationship between them.

Camden Lofts | Cecconi Simone Inc.

Camden Lofts is a new loft-style residential building in the center of Toronto. It was formerly a conventional apartment building; it now contains 55 housing units, ranging in size from 600 to 1,200 square feet (55-110 sq m), and an underground parking lot.

From the architectural point of view, the layout of the building was considered propitious for the creation of lofts right from the start. The interior decoration brought out the qualities of the original building, showing that creativity and imagination open up limitless possibilities with respect to the organization of living space.

Cecconi Simone, Inc. have designed not only the individual lofts, but also the building's communal areas, passageways, and entrance hall. The project reveled in the classical features of the loft lifestyle: the wide, open spaces for the dining area and living room, the high ceilings, and the huge windows looking out on the city. First, however, a model for potential buyers was set up in another building directly opposite the block. This made it possible to promote and sell the lofts before the construction work even began. One of the features common to all the lofts was the exposed reinforced concrete walls, which serve as a reference and invite the strong contrasts needed to create an individual and homey atmosphere for the space.

Architects: Cecconi Simone Inc.
Location: Toronto, Canada
Photographs: Joy von Tiedemann

The coldness of the concrete is counteracted by the use of warm materials like wood, soft fabrics, and candles, to reflect the strong contrasts and exuberance of the neighborhood.

The open kitchen's industrial-style lighting and counter, particularly designed for having breakfast, are the main defining features of this space.

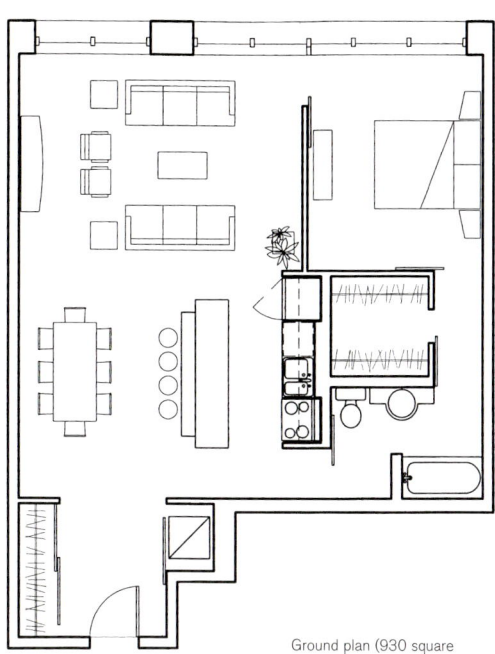

Ground plan (930 square feet/87 sq m).

The bathroom is finished with stainless-steel washbasins and faucets mounted directly onto the wall. The furniture in the bedroom has been specially designed by Cecconi Simone, Inc.

House in Igualada | Pep Zazurca i Codolà

The main façade — made of wood, galvanized metal sheets, and glass — is completely independent of the rest of the building.

Pep Zazurca experiments with structures, materials, and finishings more commonly associated with industrial architecture than domestic settings. He built this house as a large, open rectangular space, with metal pillars and an arched roof made of galvanized steel supported by curved latticed girders spanning some 33 feet (10 m). The whole steel structure was prepared in a workshop and then transported to be installed *in situ*. This method allowed the building's curved "ribs" to be put up in just a few days. In contrast, the house's end walls were built by laying bricks by hand; these have been left exposed inside and clad with steel on the outside.

A big space backing onto the main façade houses all the areas used for day-to-day activity: the living room, dining room, kitchen, and library. A corridor running along the longitudinal axis leads to the bedrooms in the back.

The girders supporting the roof add an extra dimension to this innovative and highly distinctive domestic environment.

Architect: Pep Zazurca i Codolà
Location: Igualada. Spain
Photographs: Eugeni Pons

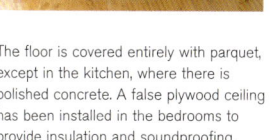

The floor is covered entirely with parquet, except in the kitchen, where there is polished concrete. A false plywood ceiling has been installed in the bedrooms to provide insulation and soundproofing.

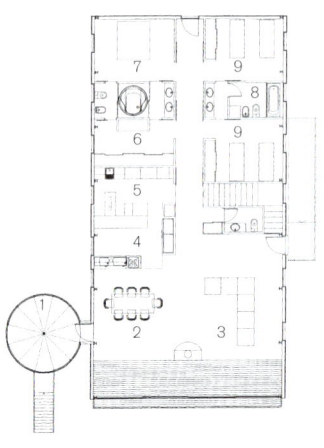

Ground plan

1. Library
2. Dining room
3. Living room
4. Kitchen
5. Pantry
6. Dressing room
7. Main bedroom
8. Bathroom
9. Bedroom

The divisions between the rooms are made of DM panels.

All the wiring has been left exposed.

Fitting out an attic

A-cero estudio de arquitectura y urbanismo SL

This irregularly shaped attic, measuring approximately 860 square feet (80 sq m), induced a craving for light. It originally presented a narrow entrance giving onto a space that was excessively divided and lacking in light. The demolition of all the existing partitions and the insertion of new windows made it brighter and gave it some views of the outside world. Some walls were opened up to allow more light in, the whole place was painted white, and partitions were reduced to a minimum to allow the light to penetrate more thoroughly.

The mezzanine was originally supported by a pillar, but it is now sustained by a cable fixed to the roof, seemingly in defiance of the law of gravity. The conversion reduced the number of enclosed spaces, and the area containing the kitchen, dining room, living room, and bedroom was unified. Only one problem remained: the untidiness which, as he willingly admits, is part of the owner's nature, along with his love of playing host to all his friends. Therefore closets were dotted all over the space, fitted into the walls, so that his personal effects can remain largely out of sight: there are closets in the entrance, in the pantry, near the sink; there is another just for suitcases, not forgetting the larger one designed for the washing machine, dryer, and cleaning equipment.

All the furniture and fittings were specially designed for this loft, from the armchairs right down to the picture frames.

Architects: A-cero estudio de arquitectura y urbanismo SL
Location: La Coruña, Spain
Photographs: Juan Rodríguez

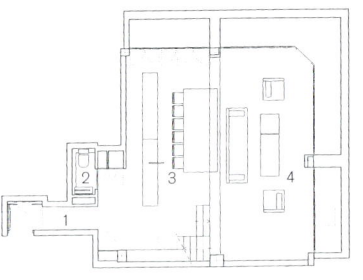
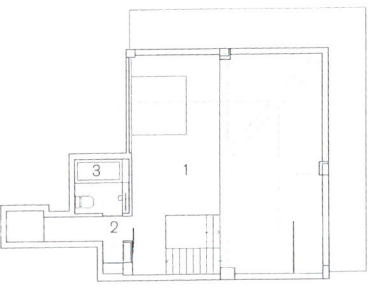

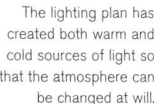

Lower floor
1. Hall
2. Bathroom
3. Kitchen-dining room
4. Living room

Upper floor
1. Bedroom
2. Dressing room
3. Bathroom

The lighting plan has created both warm and cold sources of light so that the atmosphere can be changed at will.

The white paint on the walls, floors, and ceilings is matched by the austerity of the finishing. This is not the case in the bathroom where glass panels have been installed to provide impermeability without losing the continuity of the space

Interior garden |

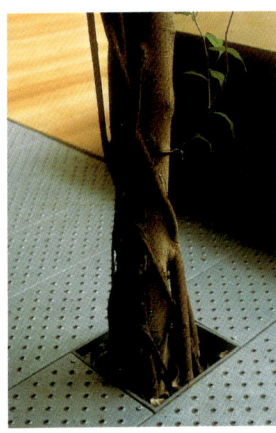

This 3,230-square-foot (300 sq m) loft is situated in a private alleyway near Stalingrad Square in north-east Paris, in the middle of a typical 19th-century industrial complex. The architect decided to create an interior landscape that provided a refuge from its ugly surroundings.

The original structure of this old electric motor factory comprised two stories, along with a shed on the roof and a garage. A spiral staircase was put in at the back, thereby creating a light source to brighten up the gallery leading to the dining room. A series of new rooms on the first floor – on the site of the old garage – accommodate the library, the guest bedroom, and sauna-bathroom. On the same level, the kitchen acts as a link between the entrance, on one side, and the dining room, living room, and gallery, on the other.

The bedrooms are on the upper floor, which is reached via a gangway made of perforated metal sheets. In the main bedroom, thin, angled metal pillars support the portico, increasing the amount of space available.

A stroll through all three floors, starting from the entrance to the terrace, offers a wonderful sequence of interior views. The design intelligently incorporates double- and triple-height spaces giving rise to sculptural forms and poetic perspectives, artfully bathed in sunlight.

Architect: Alain Salomon
Location: Paris, France
Photographs: Chris Tubbs, Gilles Trillard, Alain Salomon

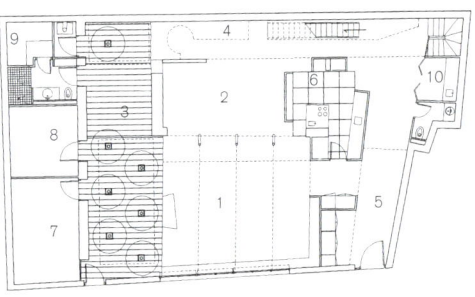
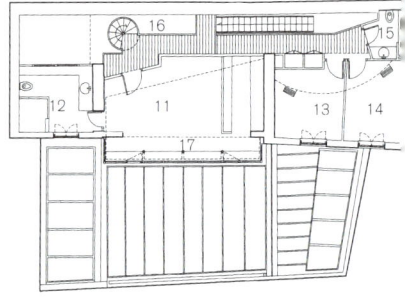

First floor

1. Living room
2. Dining room
3. Interior garden
4. Gallery
5. Entrance
6. Kitchen
7. Library
8. Guest bedroom
9. Bathroom and sauna
10. Office

Second floor

11. Main bedroom and dressing room
12. Bathroom
13. Child's bedroom
14. Child's bedroom
15. Children's bathroom
16. Staircase to the terrace
17. Gallery

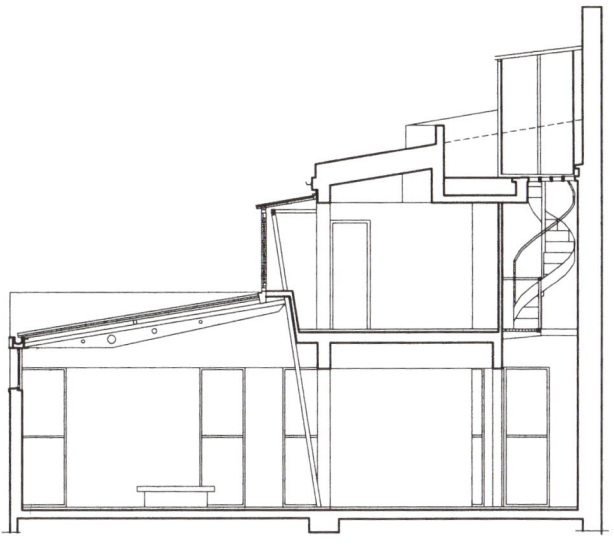

Cross-section

The trees, which hide an automatic sprinkling system activated in the case of a fire, are planted between latticed metal paving – a reminder of this garden's urban setting.

The inner garden contains rows of trees, arranged symmetrically in typical French style.

A metal spiral staircase connects the house with the terrace on the roof. The gallery offers views of the interior garden.

A trapezoidal concrete bench separates the garden from the living room.

The main bedroom receives light from the glass roof of the portico on top of the leaning pillars. This system means that windows can be opened both on top and in the front.

Visual connections | Christophe Pillet

The occupant of this loft is a design connoisseur who works freelance and who decided to set up his operational base in the same space as his home.

The two-floor layout has allowed him to divide the loft into two functional areas: downstairs, the daytime area, with the kitchen, dining room, toilet, studio, and sitting room; upstairs, the bedroom, with its own bathroom. The two are linked by a metal spiral staircase with steps in the form of petals soldered to the balustrade.

All the spaces are visually connected, giving an impression of spaciousness to a house that is in fact quite small. This effect is further enhanced by the circular windows set into the partitions closing off the kitchen and bathroom. Similarly, part of the floor on the upper level is transparent, creating a further visual link between the two levels.

As Christophe Pillet's client has a special predilection for works of art and furniture by top designers, he created a neutral space against which both the strictly functional and the more purely decorative elements can stand out prominently. Simple, natural finishes were chosen: stone on the floor, plaster and pale blue, gray, and white paint on the walls, to match the tones of the other materials used.

The finishings may be subdued, but the bright colors of the furniture and other decorative objects add warmth and create a space that is dynamic and rich in contrasts.

Interior designer: Christophe Pillet
Location: Paris, France
Photographs: Jean François Jaussaud

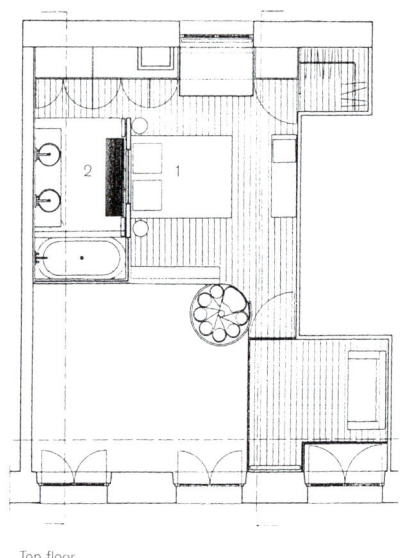

Top floor

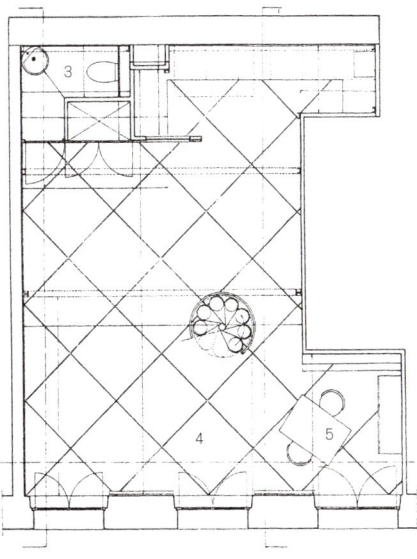

Only one of the loft's walls has windows, so it was essential to find ways for light to penetrate into the interior.

1. Bedroom
2. Bathroom
3. Bathroom
4. Sitting room
5. Studio

Lower floor

The loft is functional but imaginatively laid out to combine its occupants' professional and domestic activities.

Home and studio | Christophe Pillet

The French interior designer Christophe Pillet works for prestigious international companies on projects for stores, hotels, and homes. His own home in Paris is a 1,350-square-foot (125 sq m) apartment next to the historic Père Lachaise cemetery; which also contains his studio.

Pillet himself took charge of the conversion. The main interventions were the removal of as many partitions as possible to gain space in the sitting room, the restoration of the structural elements, and a coat of white paint throughout the whole house. The result is a stark setting that highlights empty space and the light that floods into the house through several windows and two big skylights above the central area.

The apartment is divided into two main spaces: the studio, spread over two separate rooms, and a living area containing the sitting room and dining room, with its original wooden beams exposed to view.

The design studio emanates the same simplicity. The apartment has retained all the original wooden window frames (again painted white), a series of radiators with all the pipes visible, and wooden floorboards.

Pillet has managed to create a versatile environment that serves as a stage for a continuous stream of prototypes of his own furniture designs, as well as examples of the work of other famous designers, sent by various companies so that their resistance and comfort can be assessed.

Interior designer: Christophe Pillet
Location: Paris, France
Photographs: Agence Omnia

Prototypes of Pillet's designs rub shoulders with RAR chairs from Charles and Ray Eames, a table from Jacobsen, and a lamp from Sotsass.

When these photos were taken, the apartment included furniture from xO, Domeau & Péres, Ceccoto, Cappellini, and Toutlemonde Bouchard.

Cluster of lofts | Alain Salomon

This 1,600-square-foot (150 sq m) house near the Porte de Pantin in Paris belongs to a film actor and his wife. It forms part of a group of 30 lofts created for a community of artists in a 19th-century warehouse. In this case, the loft is spread over three levels: one giving onto the street (complete with garage), the entrance area, and a mezzanine.

The owner's office has direct access to the street, but the loft's private entrance can only be reached through the building's courtyard. An interior staircase connects the office and the garage with the home on the upper floor.

This domestic area contains the high-ceilinged sitting room and dining room, an open kitchen, a bathroom, and a guest room, normally used for taking breakfast, which has sliding glass doors that open onto the corridor to allow air to circulate in summer.

The curved mezzanine imitates the shape of a grand piano. The loft's owner uses it as a rehearsal space, but it also houses the main bedroom and bathroom. The concrete floor has been given a coat of gray industrial paint. The staircases and the counter in the kitchen are made of laminated oak. The furniture is an eclectic mix, with a table by Le Corbusier and lamps by Ingo Maurer. The walls are decorated with paintings by Polish artists who are friends of the loft's owners.

Architect: Alain Salomon
Location: Paris, France
Photographs: Chris Tubbs, Alain Salomon

1. Garage
2. Office
3. Entrance
4. Guest room
5. Kitchen
6. Dining room/sitting room
7. Bedroom
8. Main bathroom
9. Mezzanine

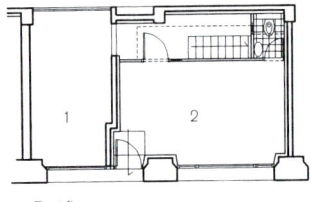

First floor

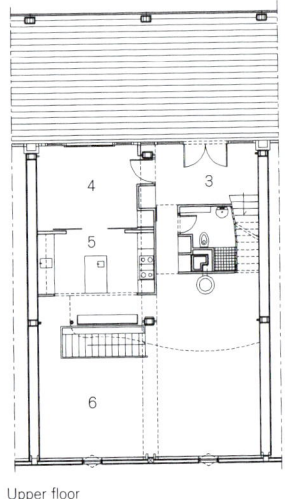

Upper floor

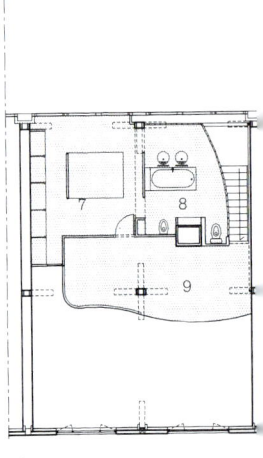

Mezzanine

The guests' bathroom receives light through the translucent concrete wall; which also reveals the form of the staircase leading to the mezzanine.

The concrete bathtub in the main bathroom contrasts with the black unit separating it from the stainless-steel washbasin.

Spaciousness | Patrizia Sbalchiero

This loft, measuring almost 2,150 square feet (200 sq m), is situated in the old Naviglia neighborhood in Milan. It was once a cabinetmaker's workshop comprising two buildings, one with a wooden roof, the other covered with fretted sheets.

The first stage of the conversion, which was carried out by the BAUQ studio, comprised the restoration of the entire roof, conserving the old rafters and putting a big skylight over the central area. The building was then divided into three separate units, each of which was refurbished by different architects, as chosen by the respective owners of the lofts.

The main challenge in this studio-home was to provide a sufficient amount of light in the studio area, which is fitted out with desks and computers and functions independently of the rest of the house, even though it is an integral part of it.

The focal point of the building is the roof, and the conversion sought to highlight this feature to emphasize the spaciousness. The use of high doors reaching almost to the roof enhances this effect.

The staircase going up to the studio dominates the center of the house. It is built of metal girders and Canadian wood, and its two large landings are broken by a chimney with a metal fireplace that warms the kitchen and living room.

The floor is made of wide planks of Canadian pine, dotted with mats and frosted glass panels to mark out specific areas: the entrance, the chimney, the kitchen, and the bathroom. The orange tone of the partitions creates a warm and inviting atmosphere.

Architect: Patrizia Sbalchiero
Location: Milan, Italy
Photographs: Andrea Martiradonna

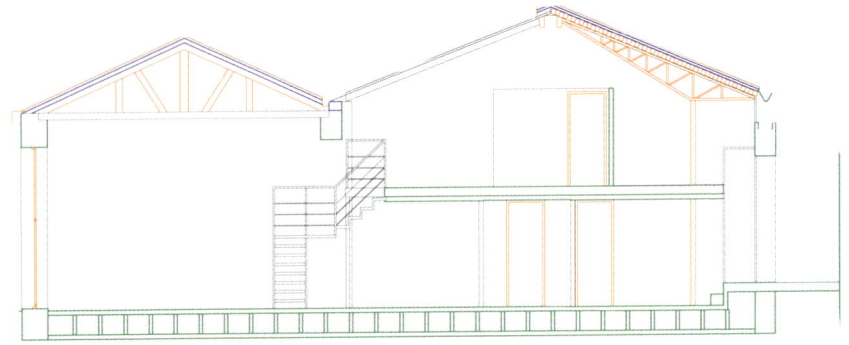

Longitudinal section

Two tall orange closets which contain the music equipment separate the kitchen from the living room.

The studio combines privacy with a view of the entire house.

An old typographer's cabinet, with drawers for keeping type, presides over the studio, which is lit by two old-fashioned industrial lamps hanging from the ceiling.

The little girl's room is decorated with small lights inserted in the roof and a big, atmospheric mural designed by her mother.

Second floor

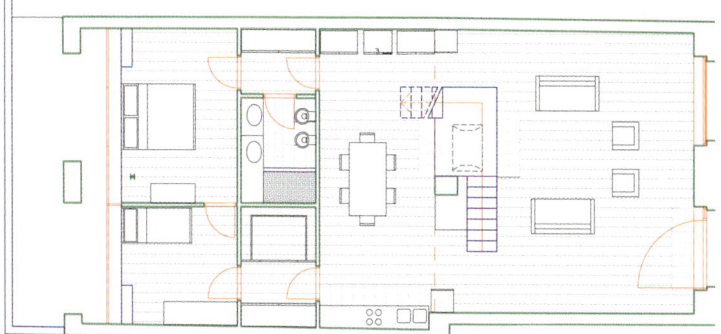
First floor

House for a painter | Antonio Zanuso

The artist Anna Muzi Falcone lives on the fourth floor of an early-20th-century industrial building in one of Milan's most colorful neighborhoods. The conversion was entrusted to the architect Antonio Zanuso, who came up with a space free of physical or visual barriers. The cordial relationship between the young painter and the architect allowed them to create a style to the liking of both.

The loft has a surface area of 2,600 square feet (250 sq m), divided into two blocks that form an "L" shape. One area looks out onto an inner courtyard, while the other offers views of the city. The sunlight pouring through the large windows – retained from the original building – illuminates the entire space. The considerable height of the ceiling – 16 feet (5 m) – made it possible to add a mezzanine for the most private areas: the main bedroom, with its bathroom and dressing room.

This layout, suggested by the architect, perfectly satisfies the client's practical requirements. The entrance opens out onto an enormous industrial-style kitchen, then a long corridor leads to the living room and the two studio areas. Two bedrooms and a bathroom are situated on the opposite side. The work spaces have no doors and join onto each other. To emphasize the interconnection between them, they both share the same gray resin floor.

This apartment was conceived as a big space in which to live, work, and hold social gatherings, a neutral background to set off the client's paintings dotted over the walls.

Architect: Antonio Zanuso
Location: Milan, Italy
Photographs: Henry Bourne/Speranza

The decoration, dreamed up by the owner, mixes pieces by top designers with others rescued from flea markets and antique shops.

The mezzanine can be reached by two staircases, one in the studio and the other in the corridor.

The main bedroom, on the mezzanine, has windows that overlook the living room. It also has its own dressing room and private bathroom.

House in San Giorgio | Studio Archea

The conversion or restoration of a building for a new use means that its architectural characteristics can be seen in a new light.

Any modification of a period building is always a complicated affair. If the quality of the workmanship is in doubt, it is best to start from zero. The restoration need not involve a great financial investment if time and effort are put into making a series of technical decisions beforehand. A study must be made of both the premises and the period in which they were built; this research will make it easier to decide which elements are to be refurbished and which are beyond repair. The recovery of these old buildings involves, above all, a specific construction method, which must be tailor-made to the requirements of the particular space.

Italian architects have long been experts in this field, as their rich architectural heritage has provided them with many great opportunities to research unceasingly and act on the results. A good example of this trend is the apartment near the Ponte Vecchio, in the heart of Florence, designed by the Studio Archea firm.

The original building, dating back to the Renaissance, was dominated by big wooden beams that loomed imposingly over the interior. The problem was to create a residential setting that both took advantage of the exceptional qualities of the Quattrocento and functioned as a practical modern home.

The project gave the architects the freedom to design every element in detail, avoiding mass-produced products and creating one-off objects of an almost sculptural intensity.

Architects: Studio Archea
Location: Florence, Italy
Photographs: Alessandro Ciampi

The space is distributed around a curved stone wall that determines the various functions of the home, as well as supporting the beams that hold up the sleeping area in the mezzanine. A gangway connects this platform with a small swimming pool.

The staircase leading to the mezzanine was designed by Studio Archea and was built by Módulo Laser, who were also responsible for the kitchen, the stone wall, and the wooden floor.

Transparencies | Rüdiger Lainer

The architect Rüdiger Lainer has created a two-story space to replace the area once occupied by the attic of one of Vienna's oldest reinforced-concrete buildings. It is a transparent box, a house designed to sit on another, pre-existing house.

The brief required five units, usable as either living quarters or offices, or a combination of the two. The central space uses laminated glass on the roof to break up the horizontal plane and mark out two different, but related, spaces. The veneered, molded ceilings supported by a steel structure create an open, flexible space that can be adapted to various layouts.

The building's façade, built in 1911, is typical of its period, despite the fact that it was made of reinforced concrete. Similarly, Lainer uses the language of his own era for the element he has added to the top of the building.

Architect: Rüdiger Lainer
Location: Vienna, Austria
Photographs: Margherita Spiluttini

The interior extends horizontally toward the city, and vertically toward the sky.

The interior finishings (a combination of plywood and treated glass panels) let in plenty of light allowing privacy.

The building is two minutes away from Vienna's historic center and offers a fine view of Saint Stephen's cathedral. One surprising aspect of this project is the fact that it obtained a building permit, in view of the strict regulations governing any reform to this part of the city.

The service areas (bathrooms, kitchens, storage, etc.) are conceived as independent units that can be adapted to any reconfiguration of the main spaces.

Ecological apartment | Lichtblau & Wagner

The term "loft" can also refer to an attic space under the roof — a setting that has always fascinated the popular imagination. The conversion of this attic in Vienna revels in the architecture typical of these spaces, where the walls and the roof are one and the same.

This project also applies various energy-saving techniques that are usually more common in architecture for public buildings. The main criteria for the scheme drawn up by the team of Lichtblau & Wagner were flexibility, versatility, and cost-effectiveness in terms of energy consumption in the attic.

It is divided into two apartments, each again divided into two basic 540-square-foot (50 sq m) areas. These both share a central space; to compensate for the restricted dimensions of the homes, the architects decided to create an area common to all of them, with a storage space, a laundry, and a multipurpose room suitable for parties, meetings, and other social activities.

The conversion encourages a flexible use of space, as there are no conventional dividing elements. Every space can be exploited according to a whim of the moment, or the passing of the seasons. The space under the windows, for example, can serve as a terrace or a glasshouse, according to the time of year.

Architects: Lichtblau & Wagner
Location: Vienna, Austria
Photographs: Andreas Wagner, Margherita Spiluttini

Energy-saving devices like the solar panels that provide hot water for all the eight apartments in the building represent a saving on living space; the same is true of the centralized heating system.

Some installations have been integrated into the floor to avoid any need for pipes on the wall. The kitchen and bathroom modules can be dismounted and moved elsewhere; no extra connections are needed, as they can be directly connected to the plumbing system via holes in the floor.

Partitions have been reduced to the bare essentials; even the bathrooms can be directly connected with the living spaces. The rooms are not conceived as enclosed spaces but intended to take advantage of the light and the views of the rest of the apartment. The absence of internal walls also helps bring down the building costs.

Loft in Bruges | Non Kitch Group

The old factory chimney can be seen through the parallel skylights on the roof.

The most decisive operation in the conversion of this old canning factory in Bruges was undoubtedly the refurbishing of the roof. This was formerly a conventional, tiled affair, supported by the latticed girders. William Sweetlove and Linda Arschoot, the designers in the Non Kitch Group, decided to replace the upper part of all the parallel rows of tiles with glass. The result not only provides an extraordinary increase in the amount of sunlight that enters into the loft but also, as a result of the considerable height of the space (19 feet/6 m) turns the interior into virtually an outside city square. On the first floor, the sitting room opens out onto a small garden with a covered swimming pool on one side, so every part of the home affords views onto the exterior.

The loft is divided into three levels. The center is dominated by a big sitting room, open right up to the roof; this is flanked by a mezzanine comprising the kitchen, dining room, bar, and television room. Under this platform, and three steps below the sitting room, there is a pool room, bedroom, dressing room, gym, and bathroom, which is directly connected with the covered pool.

Architects: Non Kitch Group
Location: Bruges, Belgium
Photographs: Jan Verlinde

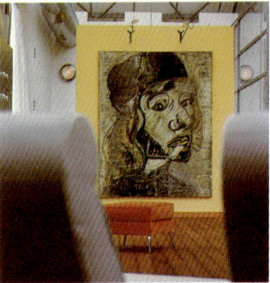

Many of the accessories and decorative elements emphasize the building's industrial legacy: the galvanized steel staircase, the heating pipes, the lamps, and the free-standing kitchen unit.

Non Kitch Group reject the asceticism of minimalist materials and consider themselves heirs to the humor and colorfulness of the Memphis Group.

Old spinning mill
Ernst & Niklaus Architekten ETH/SIA

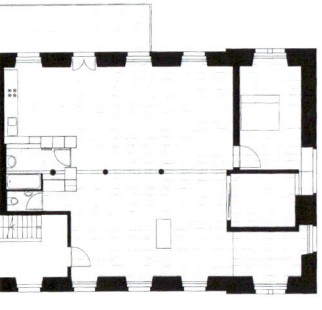

Third-floor loft

The architects Bertram Ernst and Erich Niklaus have converted an old spinning mill in Suhr, northern Switzerland, and designed lofts for Peter, a graphic designer, Nicole, a journalist, and Konrad, a manager of cultural organizations.

When the architects were approached to refurbish the building, the owners had already divided it into eight parts. The conversion sought to minimize alteration to the original structure, in order to enhance its defining characteristics.

The layout of the third-floor apartment takes the form of a "Z," following the line of a new staircase and the space created by the original elevator shaft. The entire loft is spanned by varnished oak floorboards.

Blue is the dominant color, as it is used for the single unit that opens up to reveal a kitchen, bathroom, toilet, and closet. The unit is easy to assemble, and its modern finishing contrasts with the original wrought-iron girders.

The apartments on the fifth and sixth floors take advantage of the roof structure, which has had skylights put in to increase the illumination.

The central axis of pillars creates an imaginary wall that connects the areas devoted to relaxation, working, cooking and sleeping. The L-shape unit that defines the kitchen, made up of wooden components, is set against the back wall and leads onto a clothes closet.

All the materials – compressed birch, oak, and fir, aluminum, stainless steel, plaster and glass – have been left in their original colors, or just given a very pale coat of varnish.

Architects: Ernst & Niklaus Architekten ETH/SIA
Location: Suhr, Switzerland
Photographs: Hannes Henz

Cross-section

Longitudinal section. Fifth- and sixth-floor loft.

A central landing with metal banisters runs along the top of the whole building.

Sopanen/Sarlin Loft | Marja Sopanen + Olli Sarlin

The center of Helsinki contains many old buildings that were originally built for offices or light industry but have been converted for other purposes in the last few years.

The two young architects Marja Sopanen and Olli Sarlin designed a loft apartment on the first floor of an old redbrick textile factory built in 1928; whose upper floors had already been converted into housing.

The Sopanen/Sarlin loft covers an "L" shape measuring 915 square feet (85 sq m). The architects decided to completely recover the original structure of the interior, which had been hidden by all the additional construction that had taken place during the 70 years of the factory's life. This meant removing the array of false ceilings and dividing walls that had been installed to make offices.

While clearing away all these encumbrances, the architects discovered a network of concrete beams; these were cleaned and then sealed with a mixture of beer and wallpaper. (Beer mixed with pigment is a traditional method of coloring wooden walls.) The redbrick walls, on the contrary, were left exposed, without any treatment.

The bleached and oiled pinewood floor was laid on top of lengths of timber that were originally secondary beams in the ceiling. The new floor stops just short of the walls, to make way for the heating pipes.

A piece of furniture recycled from an old hospital serves as a partition between the bedroom and the sitting room.

Architects: Marja Sopanen + Olli Sarlin
Location: Helsinki, Finland
Photographs: Marja Sopanen, Olli Sarlin

The use of recycled materials, even in essential installations – as in the case of the pipes for the heating system – lends the project an air of authenticity.

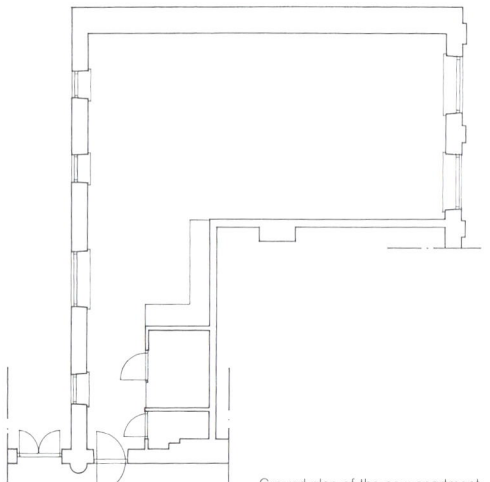 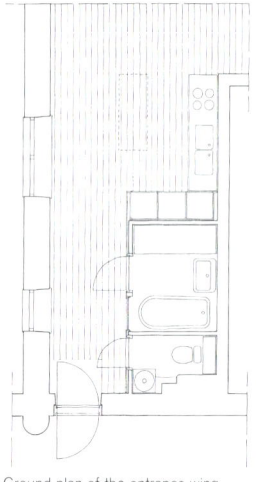

Ground plan of the new apartment.

Ground plan of the entrance wing.

The L-shape layout makes it possible to isolate the toilet, bathroom, and kitchen in the wing containing the entrance to the apartment.

The bathroom and kitchen are defined by a new glossy compressed-wood unit that does not reach the ceiling and that contains not only the bathroom and toilet but also the oven and kitchen closets.

"A loft is ideal for any kind of work that requires space. The initial expense of setting up a business is huge. A loft provides the space to begin"

James Soane and Christopher Ash, Project Orange

working
in a loft

@radical.media | Rockwell Group

The main entrance has a sign on the door reading "@radical.media" and, in smaller print, "never established," printed on a board that looks like a relic from an old 19th-century warehouse. This slogan was coined only partly in jest, because it does in fact sum up the spirit and image that this multimedia company seeks to project.

The same philosophy led its president, John Kamen, to install his new offices in an old industrial building on the edge of Manhattan. The architect David Rockwell was given the brief to convert it into a loft that was as open and spacious as possible, to encourage communication between all the members of a dynamic, flexible and egalitarian team.

The Rockwell Group decided to preserve the character of the building's industrial past by introducing a layout and finishing materials similar to those of an old warehouse. The flow and spaciousness of the building were ensured by the creation of open rooms surrounded by wide, open spaces. The various working areas were marked off by waist-high plywood panels fixed to the building's outer walls.

The pillars and the beams on the high ceilings are criss-crossed by the electrical wiring, air-conditioning ducts, and piping. Down below, the expanse of concrete on the floor gives unity to the disparate spaces.

Architects: Rockwell Group
Location: New York, United States
Photographs: Paul Warchol

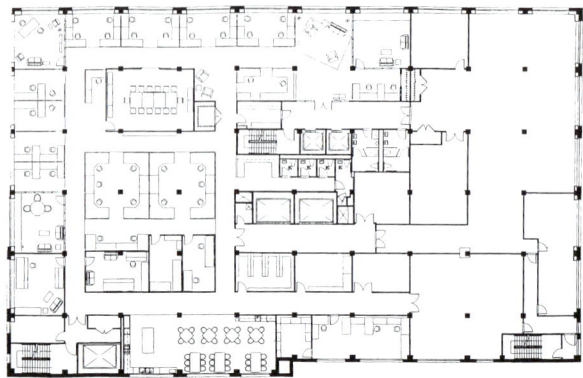

The shelves are recycled pieces of scaffolding, and even the table used for company meetings has been improvised with boards and trolleys, symbolizing the flexibility of these offices.

Only a few partitions have been installed; they are fitted with sliding doors and echo both the exterior windows and the metal interior ones which, like most of the furnishings, date back to the 1950s.

Connors Communications

Lee H. Skolnick Architecture + Design

The conversion of this New York loft into offices for a prestigious public relations company raises thought-provoking questions about the type of spaces needed to foster dialogue, versatility, and teamwork.

Lee H. Skolnick and Paul Alter have come up with spaces that combine private, independent offices with communal working areas, and traditional conference rooms with informal meeting areas.

The architects aimed to create a distinctive, visually attractive space that not only heralds the company's creativity but also its innovative spirit, as well as encouraging a more direct and dynamic relationship with clients. The original structure was simply an empty space with six wrought-iron pillars in the center. The outer walls were left white, except in some areas that serve a specific function, where they have been highlighted with bright colors. The additional partitions, such as those marking off the toilets and the production suite, or the curved wall of the kitchen, were built with lacquered plywood panels, in contrast with the warmth of the furnishings.

Individual work spaces, with eye-catching shoulder-height partitions, were set up in the central area of the loft. The perimeter walls were allotted the more private spaces, which are bounded by partitions made of glass or wood, or translucent fiber-glass panels reminiscent of the *shoji* of Japanese houses.

Architects: Lee H. Skolnick Architecture + Design (Lee H. Skolnick, Paul Alter)
Location: New York, United States
Photographs: Andrew Garn

The dominant material in these offices is wood; it is used on the floor, and for the vertical partitions and furniture. It provides a sense of continuity and a great feeling of warmth. The shelves are made of ash.

Although the kitchen has no door, it is set apart by a green plywood panel.

The conference room on the right is integrated into the rest of the space by means of adjustable, mobile panels.

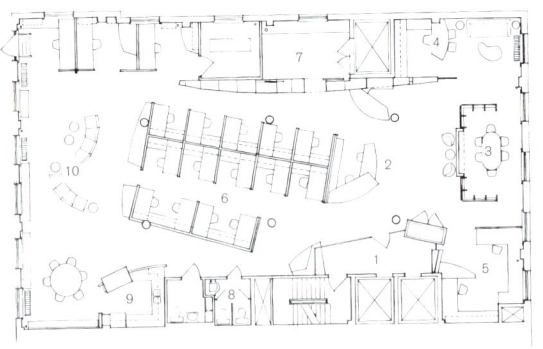

1. Entrance
2. Reception and waiting area
3. Conference room
4. President's office
5. Operations office
6. Open office area
7. Production suite
8. Bathroom
9. Kitchen
10. Relaxation and meeting area

Design studio in Tribeca

Parsons + Fernández-Casteleiro

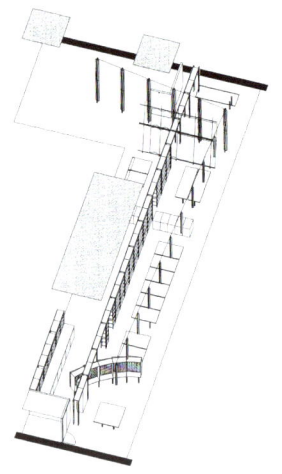

New York's Tribeca neighborhood is famous for buildings that contain some of the best lofts in the whole city. Parsons + Fernández-Casteleiro designed these offices for their own use in one of the five floors of a building that had been completely refurbished.

The L-shaped space is divided along its longitudinal axis by a metal bookcase that forms the backbone of the project. All the electrical wiring and other installations are hidden behind this bookcase, which is interrupted at both ends to make room for two private offices.

It is lit with fluorescent lamps, some hanging from the ceilings, others fitted into metal structures running from the floor to the ceiling. This system not only throws light on both the work tables and the plans and models hanging on the walls, it also provides the office with a distinctive visual rhythm.

Parsons + Fernández-Casteleiro work in an industrial idiom with inexpensive materials: the floor is made of polished concrete, the walls are painted white, and the metal shelves and fittings have been assembled like pieces of Meccano.

Architects: Parsons + Fernández-Casteleiro
Location: New York, United States
Photographs: Paul Warchol

Ground plan

1. Reception
2. Design room
3. Office
4. Conference room

The use of the fluorescent lamps transcends their strictly functional purpose and they become distinctive visual features in their own right, reminiscent of the installations of James Turrell.

Two translucent plastic screens finished with a wavy meshed material cut across both ends of the design room to separate it from the conference room, on one hand, and the reception area, on the other.

Sunshine Interactive Network

Gates Merkulova Architects

Sunshine Interactive Network (SIN) is a communications company that was formed only recently but has evolved and expanded rapidly. It is divided into five departments, each with a distinct field of responsibility: cinema and video, records, multimedia, distribution, and administration. The company follows proposals for projects right up to their production and distribution, so the separate departments are not entirely independent of each other as their work inevitably overlaps.

The new headquarters of SIN are situated in a Manhattan loft building measuring some 10,750 square feet (1,000 sq m) which was formerly lying empty. The architects sought to introduce elements into the space that would serve all their client's diverse needs. The center is dominated by three striking units that contain installations shared by all the company's departments: a cone for audiovisual presentations and small meetings; a long, oval space for conferences and movie and video screenings; and a small blue room for slide shows. These elements also serve as boundaries to the adjacent areas. One corner of the loft completely isolated from the rest, contains a recording studio and video-editing suite. The rest of the office is open, with work tables set along the outer walls only separated from the main space by glass-fiber panels.

Architects: Gates Merkulova Architects
Location: New York, United States
Photographs: J.B. Grant Photographs

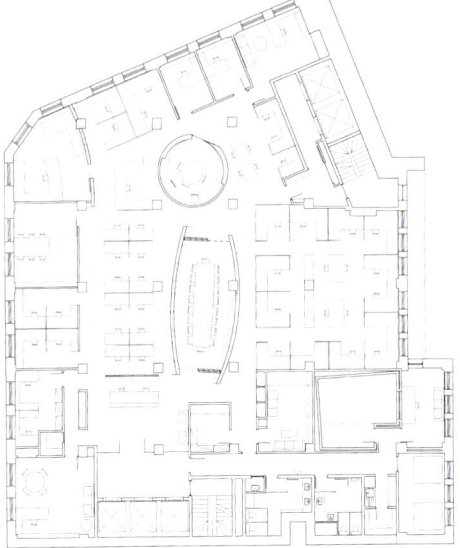

The type of commissions received by the company requires a constant turnover of personnel. Its offices have to be able to accommodate both permanent staff members, with their own personal desks, and temporary collaborators with their particular needs. The space has to be simultaneously communal and private, and sufficiently flexible to adapt to the company's changing requirements.

Ground plan

One of the key ideas of the design was the encouragement of creative synergy by overlapping the boundaries of the company's different activities.

Miller-Jones studio | LOT/EK

The Miller-Jones studio in the heart of Manhattan is both the workplace and home of a couple comprising a fashion photographer and a designer. It is spread over 2,000 square feet (185 sq m) on the 15th floor of a skyscraper.

The loft has some excellent views and, as it faces south, it receives a great deal of sunshine. The scheme devised by the two architects from the LOT/EK team consisted of a single metal wall, made of broken-down aluminum panels, that dominates the interior of the apartment. This huge barrier emphasizes the loft's original industrial function – also evident in the high ceilings, exposed piping, concrete floor, and white walls – and divides the space into two areas, one for work, the other a private living space. The metallic surface also reflects the sunlight, and is almost blinding in hot weather! Most of the domestic installations – the bathroom, kitchen, and closets – are set into the wall, and the others are set next to it. Revolving panels provide access to the space on the other side.

The wall is used in every possible way. The kitchen, seemingly suspended in the air, can be pulled out by means of a system similar to that of the trunk of an automobile. The bedroom behind the wall is reached via three pivoting doors.

Architects: LOT/EK
Location: New York, United States
Photographs: Paul Warchol

Four fridges lying on the floor in the center of the studio serve both as work tables and additional storage space. The computer is set into one of the fridges, while the scanner and printer are in the freezer.

Two sheets of wood have been attached to the top of the fridges, complete with a traction system to adjust them as required.

Stingel studio | Cha & Innerhofer

This 3,980-square-foot (370 sq m) loft is situated on the top floor of the Starrett-Lehigh Building, far from the bustle and noise of the streets of New York's Chelsea district below. As one of the first examples of the American International Style, the building has become an architectural landmark and was featured in the 1932 show of the Museum of Modern Art's *Modern Architecture: International Exhibition*. The windows on two sides of the studio provide a perfect viewpoint for the stunning spectacle of Manhattan's skyline, from the Chrysler Building to the Empire State.

The studio caters for both the private and the public aspects of artistic creation. The private space serves for experimentation, production, and storage of work, while the public area is devoted to exhibitions.

The rhythm of the building follows a circular motion, and the large amount of open space round the perimeter of the loft, free of any obstruction, emphasizes this feature.

As in the Chinese board game *Go*, the first move constitutes the strategy; an enclosed space – the spray room – in the southeast corner of the loft automatically divides the space into four sections: the gallery, the reception area, the work area, and the store. Furthermore, one of the walls of this enclosure has been extended to form a partition that defines the exhibition area, while also masking the areas on the other side that require more privacy. This minimalist intervention creates a neutral setting that does not interfere with the prime function of the studio: artistic creation.

Architects: Cha & Innerhofer
Location: New York, United States
Photographs: Dao-Lou Zha

1. Entrance hall
2. Exhibition gallery
3. Reception
4. Bar
5. Spray room
6. Work area
7. Bathroom
8. Warehouse

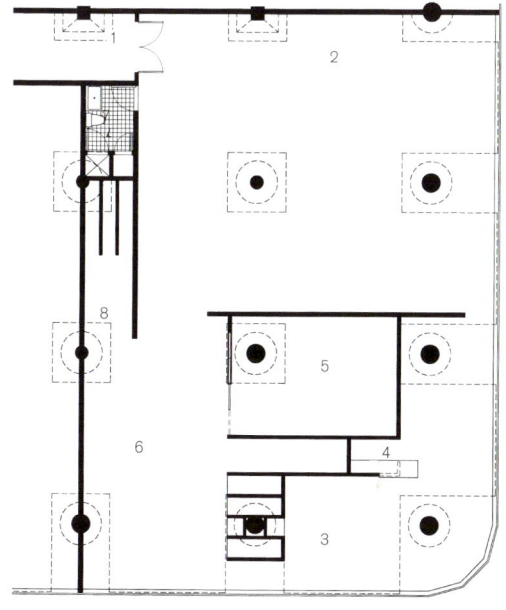

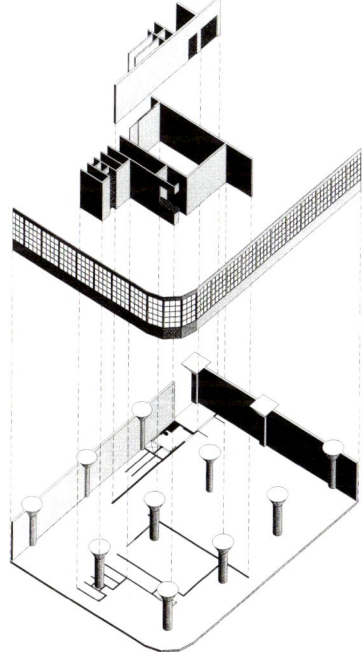

Three spaces in one | Tow Studios Architecture

This 3,000-square-foot (280 sq m) loft in Chelsea boasts a row of north-facing windows with views of the Empire State Building. The conversion aimed to install an office and studio for both a graphic designer and a textile designer, while maintaining the feeling of open space intrinsic to a loft.

The layout established three sharply differentiated spaces. The creative area comprises the design studios, set along the north side. The intermediate area contains the entrance, to the east, and the administrative offices in the central and western parts. The third and final area contains the pantry, the small kitchen, and the meeting room, which is separated from the rest of the offices by the translucent wall that is in the form of an arch.

In order to take advantage of the flow of light through the building's northern windows, the partitions in all three areas are made of sliding translucent panels. The play of light and shade is heightened by the fact that all the opaque walls are on the north and south sides of the premises, and all the translucent ones on the east and west sides. As the conversion had only a limited budget, it used cheap, industrial-quality materials, such as plastic panels screwed onto wooden frames. Finally, the color white is used to unify the different elements and forms in the loft, and the result is a fresh and airy space that exudes a touch of Zen.

Architects: Tow Studios Architecture
Location: New York, United States
Photographs: Björg/Photography

Ground plan

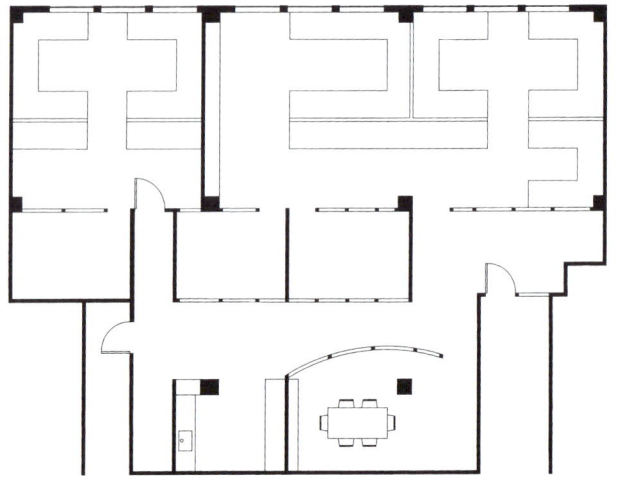

WMA Engineers

Valerio Dewalt Train Architects

The new offices of WMA Engineers, long-time consultants of Valerio Dewalt Train Architects, were designed on the basis of units, each containing an individual work space. Each of these modules is equipped with all the necessary working tools (computer, drawing table, catalogs, handbooks, and so on), and they all join up to form an octagonal pattern. The client's idea was to fit as many work areas as possible into the space available and take advantage of every inch of space. The layout does not envisage enclosed offices; the various modules are separated from their neighbors by low bookcases, and so the employees can consult each other without any inconvenience.

This maze of desks and bookcases covers the large central area; on either side there is a series of enclosed towers containing various back-up services – a store, archives, a kitchen, printers, and photocopiers – as well as offices and conference rooms.

Architects: Valerio Dewalt Train Architects
Location: Chicago, Illinois, United States
Photographs: Karant + Associates/Barbara Karant; Neil Sheehan (exterior photo)

Further imaginative details lie beyond the zigzags formed by the lights, beams, and pillars; other sources of indirect light are set between the windows on the high perimeter walls.

The regularity of the horizontal layout contrasts with the complexity and exuberance of the vertical plane, with its towers, pillars, and lights.

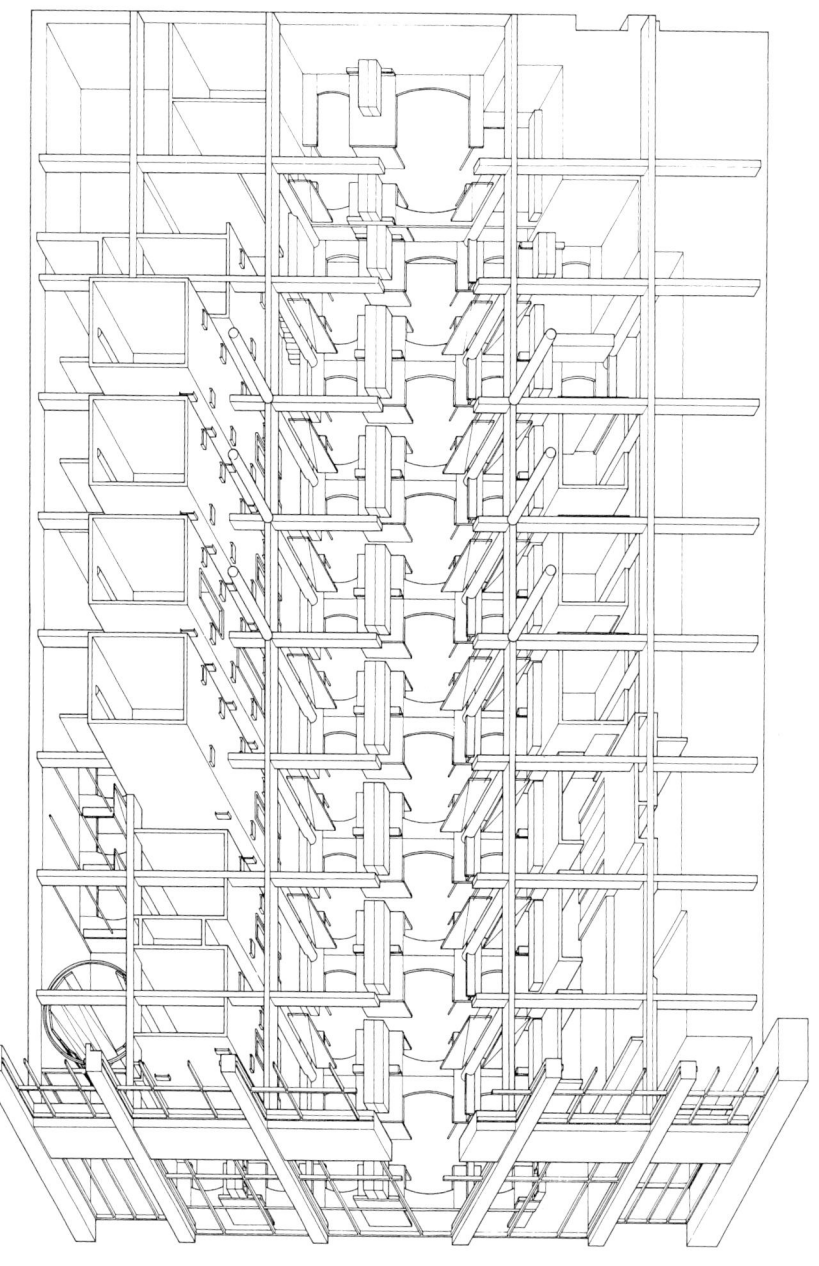

BBDO West | Beckson Design Associates

This architectural project went hand in hand with the restructuring of the company; the old hierarchical structure, based on enclosed offices and independent departments, was replaced by open spaces and flexible teams of employees, each catering for particular clients. The old offices were completely demolished; their original three stories were turned into two, in an attempt to create a more condensed and dynamic working environment.

In this new setup, even the president's work area was the same size as those of the staff. He himself admits that in the old offices people wasted too much time in meetings. "They talked a lot about what they were going to do, but they didn't do much work. I asked Michael Beckson if there was some way of getting the people together as if they were always in a meeting, so that communication could occur by osmosis, by the very fact that employees could see and hear everybody else's work."

The architects set about creating an image that suggested not an office but a factory of ideas, complete with an industrial look: no false ceilings, instead there are exposed structure and installations that achieve the physical impact of a collage.

Over 200 employees use these offices; the sheer size of the workforce meant that the creation of meeting areas was of prime importance. The entrance hall, for example, is designed as a multipurpose space, where it is even possible to play ping-pong.

The countless prizes that have been won by the company are displayed at strategic points around the building.

Architects: Beckson Design Associates
Location: Los Angeles, California, United States
Photographs: Tom Bonner

The most striking feature is the series of modules, with desks and partitions that are easy to assemble and dismount. Various cheap and simple materials are screwed to a galvanized steel, Meccano-style structure.

Rhino Entertainment | Beckson Design Associates

As Michael Beckson himself says, "We created a slightly unconventional environment in a conventional office building for a company that is definitely not conventional at all."

Rhino Entertainment has grown from a record shop in the 1970s to become a fast-expanding corporation specializing in music from the 1950s to the 1970s.

Its new headquarters on Santa Monica Boulevard are spread over 36,000 square feet (3,400 sq m) in a modern office block organized around three atriums. Despite the fact that the time available for the building work (60 days), the budget (around 360 Euros per sq m), and the building itself (with a speculative organization of the space) all cried out for a typical layout based on partitions, straight corridors, and square offices; Michael Beckson, Ed Gabor, and Steven Heisler decided to reflect the youthful, upbeat spirit of the company.

The lack of a false ceiling, coupled with the seemingly random use of bright colors, on both the walls and floor, evoke the aesthetic of Pop Art. The connecting corridors are replete with corners, curves, and amusing details. The sloping planes, curved shapes, and sharp edges of the walls are echoed in the drawings on the floor; each plane is allocated a different color to create a chromatic composition reminiscent of the later works of Sol LeWitt.

Details such as the counters made out of recycled cassette boxes, the 1960s furniture by Eames and Noguchi, and the odd palm tree here and there, all contribute to this loft's laid-back humor.

Architects: Beckson Design Associates
Location: Los Angeles, California, United States
Photographs: Tom Bonner

There is no continuous false ceiling in these offices. However, eye-catching soundproofing has been installed on some ceilings, which helps to define the space.

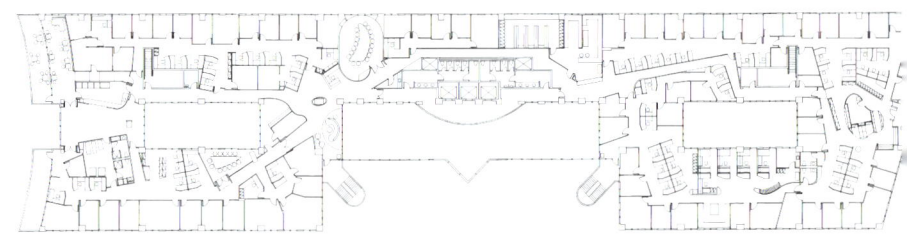

MTV Networks | Felderman + Keatinge Associates

The team commissioned to design this major TV channel's new HQ on the US west coast, Felderman + Keatinge Associates, is headed by the architect Stanley Felderman. His trademarks are a quirky sense of humor and an innovative spirit. These qualities are now impregnated in all of the five floors (totaling 110,000 square feet /10,200 sq m) of what used to be a commonplace office building.

The aim was to reflect the city outside – Santa Monica and the Pacific Ocean that laps its shores – through dreamlike jetties, beach huts, bohemian loft neighborhoods, art galleries, and avant-garde architecture.

An enormous bright red steel boat anchored in the entrance gives an idea of what is to come. A triangular wooden envelope defines the reception area. An oval-shaped hall with a polished aluminum 1957 Airstream trailer serves as a waiting room. Two high (13 feet/4 m) steel structures represent "talking heads" with eyes and mouths made of TV monitors. The corridors depict scenes which illustrate aspects of Santa Monica's urban culture. The floors are decorated with brightly colored carpets, while the white walls provide some respite from the visual assault. Each story has two large rooms – one for conferences and one for waiting – dotted with articles of domestic furniture, such as armchairs, stools, and low tables.

Architects: Felderman + Keatinge Associates
Location: Santa Monica, California, United States
Photographs: Toshi Yoshimi

Praxair Distribution Inc. | Herbert Lewis Kruse Blunck Architecture

Herbert Lewis Kruse Blunck Architecture received the commission to transform a 58,000-square-foot (5,400 sq m) warehouse situated on an industrial estate into a center for processing and distributing soldered items. One third of the space was converted into offices, while the rest became a workshop and store.

All the elements of the project – the layout of the offices, the furnishing, lighting, and installations – were boldly linear and were designed to allow for any future expansion. The meeting and training areas were placed near the entrance, next to the few windows that the building has.

The interdependency of the offices and the workshop is emphasized by the use of the same building materials and visual style in both areas. The shelving system in the workshop, for example, serves as the structure that defines the upper level in the offices.

One of the main problems that the architect had to tackle was the lighting requirements of the offices, which were very different from those of the store and workshop. As it was impossible to put any more windows into the building's prefabricated side-panels, it was decided to put skylights into the roof, with continuous sheets of corrugated fiber-glass underneath to filter the light evenly throughout the office area. This solution also had a great visual impact and has become one of the building's most distinctive character traits.

Architects: Herbert Lewis Kruse Blunck Architecture
Location: Ankeny, Iowa, United States
Photographs: Farshid Assassi

The architects left the basic structure visible throughout, with no cladding on the perimeter walls, in order to emphasize the building's industrial function.

The corrugated fiber-glass wall separates the meeting and training areas from the rest of the offices.

The air-conditioning ducts are the dominant features on both the horizontal and the vertical planes.

Meyocks & Priebe Advertising Inc.

Herbert Lewis Kruse Blunck Architecture

Meyocks & Priebe Advertising specializes in advertising for the agricultural and food industries. When the company decided to create new offices, it wanted to emphasize the rural bias in their work and so welcomed the architects' keenness to exploit appropriate elements from vernacular architecture. The architecture team not only studied many farms in Iowa for details of building materials, finishings, and technical solutions, it also compiled catalogs of agricultural installations and machinery.

With the support of this exhaustive research, the architects set about finding new interpretations and uses for many of the details they had recorded. Generally speaking, the idea was not to reproduce traditional building methods but simply to evoke the fields of Iowa and the people working in them by using elements proper to them: barns, granaries, and fences. Elements such as the translucent fiber-glass panels, solid concrete walls with accessories screwed straight into them, unvarnished wooden panels, and perforated metal panels were used to create the offices and work spaces for the company's creative staff.

The central conference room represents an attempt to re-create the atmosphere of a granary. Light seeps in from the outside through the gaps between the wooden boards, while the rafters suggest the form of a traditional roof.

Architects: Herbert Lewis Kruse Blunck Architecture
Location: Des Moines, Iowa, United States
Photographs: Farshid Assassi

Some elements, like these corrugated-metal grain silos, were put straight into the offices and recycled as meeting rooms or reception areas for clients.

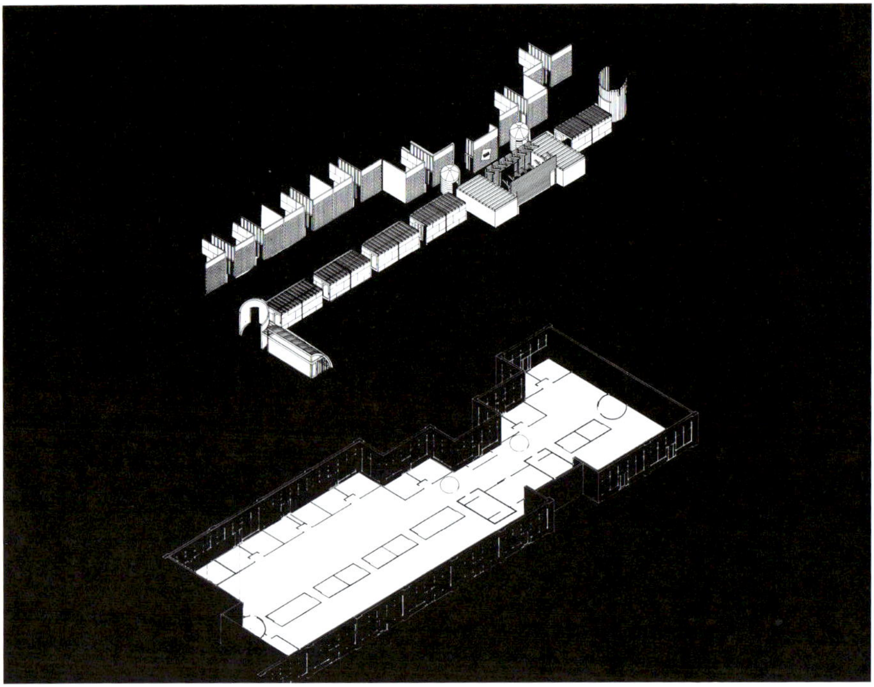

German Design Center

Norman Foster & Partners

Essen, in Germany's industrial heartland, is particularly noted for its mining, but these days heavy industry has given way to new technologies and many of its biggest factories have been closed. In order to preserve the city's industrial heritage, many of these buildings have been refurbished and converted to new uses. In this case, Norman Foster & Partners were faced with the challenge of transforming a mining complex into the new headquarters of the German Design Center.

The original factory had been built in the year 1927 by the architects Fritz Schupp and Martin Kremmer. It was closed down in 1986 when coal production ceased to be profitable.

Almost all the interior had to be fitted out as space for permanent and temporary exhibitions. One of the main aims of the project was to bring out the contrast between the monolithic industrial architecture and small-scale design, where the impact depends on subtle details of finishings and materials.

Architects: Norman Foster & Partners
Location: Essen, Germany
Photographs: Nigel Young

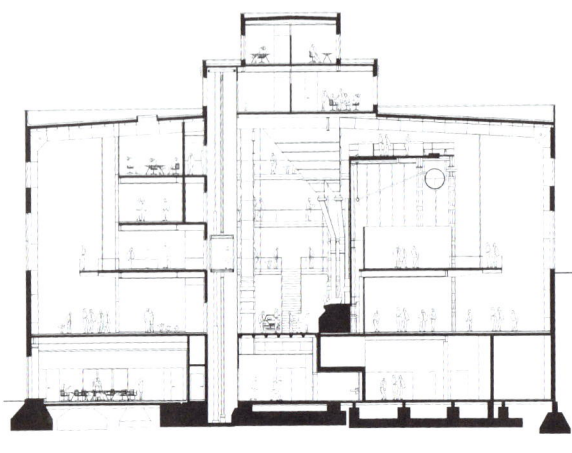

The façade was restored during the building work, and any elements alien to the compositional language of its original design were eliminated. The chimney had to be demolished as it was unstable.

Inside, the architects decided to accentuate the building's architectural past by brutally stripping bare the original structure and leaving it virtually free of any treatment or additions.

The layout of the building revolves around the central axis; perimeter spaces are open right up to the roof.

Nuremberg | Wirth

These offices are situated in a former industrial area on the outskirts of Nuremberg that has now been replanned, with special emphasis on the peripheral green spaces brightening up the neighborhood. The old factory that was refurbished for this project by the Wirth group nestles in the middle of one of these garden areas.

The client wanted a single space for all the work tables, in order to eliminate any sense of hierarchy, enhance teamwork, and facilitate communication between the different groups of workers. Following this brief, the architects did not put up any partitions but merely restored and fitted out the original space with great sensitivity and astuteness. In order not to mask the skylights typical of factories in this region – and obviously desirable for the natural light they allow in throughout the day – Wirth put all the service installations into a few tubes that unobtrusively criss-cross the ceiling without distracting from the overall view of the space. Stainless steel lamps evoke the building's industrial legacy.

Architects: Wirth
Location: Nuremberg, Germany
Photographs: Karin Hessman/Artur

The photo above shows the state of the building before the conversion.

Michaelides & Bednash | Buschow Henley

The architects Buschow Henley have created a space full of surprises, intrigue, charm, and suggestive movement by means of only a few, minimal interventions to this old Art Deco factory in the center of London.

The client, Michaelides & Bednash, is an innovative communications strategy company that demanded the conversion should be original, challenging and evocative, but in keeping with the building. After a lively debate, the architects decided to opt for functional simplicity and visual purity. It proved impossible to resolve the complex problems that emerged within the framework of a conventional office layout. The project came to life only after a thorough re-examination of the requirements of an office space.

The layout provides a series of interlinked "psychological" spaces that define potential work areas. One of the mechanisms created within the conversion's hierarchical system consists of tables where one person works on an individual basis, but has at his or her disposal all the facilities needed to make room for other collaborators. In contrast, other more secluded spaces provide a chance to escape from the background noise, work quietly on ideas, read, or make phone calls. A third "psychological" space comprises two sound-proofed rooms for more private meetings and work.

The architects responsible concluded: "We have deliberately gone against the typological metamorphosis of the office with its roots as a factory toward the more contemporary situation of a resource center. In this case, we believe that the typology has been supplanted by the universality."

Architects: Buschow Henley
Location: London, United Kingdom
Photographs: Nick Kane/Arcaid

The end result of the manipulation of space and psychological factors is an environment that is equally attractive and suitable as a home, office, or public meeting place.

Concrete, wood, glass, steel, plaster, and concrete are the traditional materials used for the walls, ceilings, floor, furniture, and doors.

The abstract simplicity of the conversion emphasizes the materials, proportions, natural colors, tones, and textures of the components.

Shepherd's Bush Studios

John McAslan & Partners

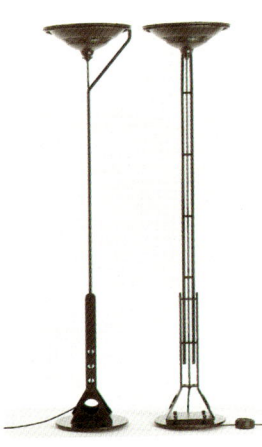

The conversion of this warehouse involved a total of 32,270 square feet (3,000 sq m) spread over three levels within a solid concrete structure. The rehabilitation of this old industrial space in London was made possible by the reforms introduced by Margaret Thatcher, which granted subsidies for the rehabilitation of old buildings of a certain architectural quality.

The work carried out by John McAslan had two main aims: on the one hand, the solution of functional problems relating to the organization of space and services; on the other, the creation of an appropriate setting for the building's new use as studios as well as offices in Shepherd's Bush. The interior was organized around a new vertical opening, spanning three floors, which opens up the central axis and provides a connection between the spaces on either side. All the communications within the building revolve around this central hub, which is crowned by a skylight on the roof that allows natural light to penetrate right to the bottom of the building. The installations and services are boldly displayed in a high-tech mannerist style, so that they become sculptural features in their own right. The brash robustness of these elements is balanced, however, by the delicacy of the new staircases, as well as the lamps and furniture that were specially designed for the building.

Architects: John McAslan & Partners
Location: London, United Kingdom
Photographs: Richard Bryant/Arcaid

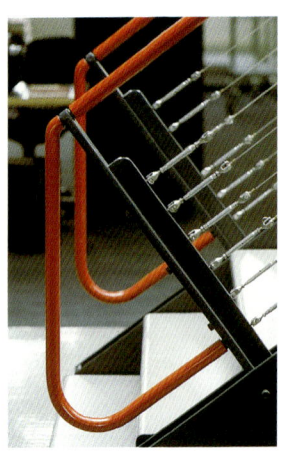

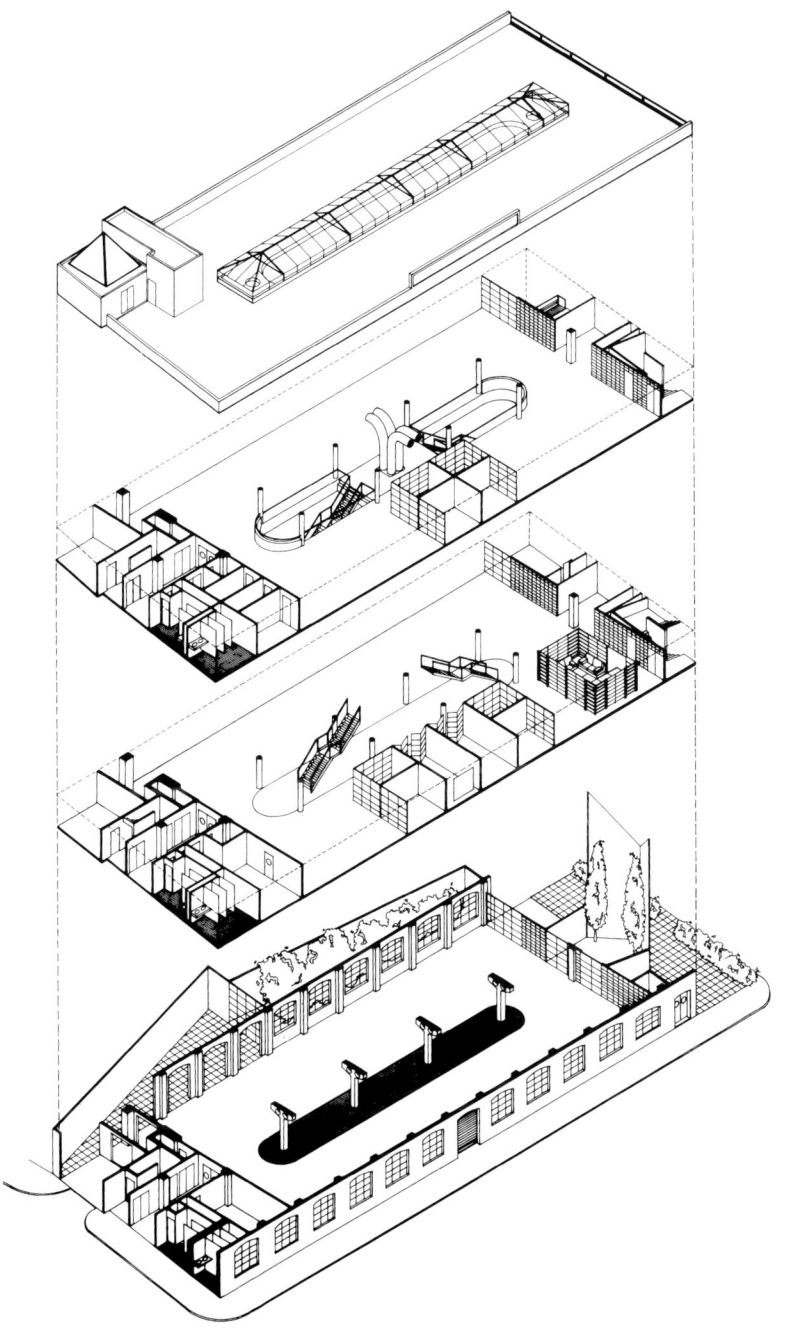

London Merchant Securities

John McAslan & Partners

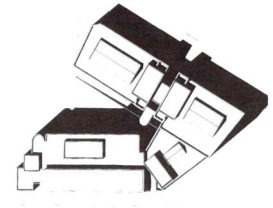

This project, which was completed in 1992, encapsulates the essential philosophy of McAslan and his team. It combined the overhaul of a major 1920s industrial building with the construction of a new office block, divided into administrative areas and design studios. The entire floor space of both sections amounted to 188,000 square feet (17,500 sq m).

Part of the old building had to be knocked down to make way for the new one, bordering on Rosebery Avenue in north London, which boasts a sophisticated, well-proportioned glass façade that follows the tradition established by the German architect Mies van der Rohe. As for the old building, the aim was to adapt the structure to its new functions, which resulted in daring contrasts between the modernity of the new installations and their more traditional setting. The circulation and service areas were concentrated in a new glass tower that forms the intersection between the two blocks. The completed buildings revel in the interplay between old and new, between the past and present, particularly in the choice of materials used in the design.

The work of McAslan and his team has always been defined by the imaginative and thoughtful use and combination of new materials coupled with innovative details employed in the construction work.

Architects: John McAslan & Partners
Location: London, United Kingdom
Photographs: Peter Cook/View

Cross-section

The transition between the old and new buildings is emphasized by the deliberate contrast between the finishings in both areas.

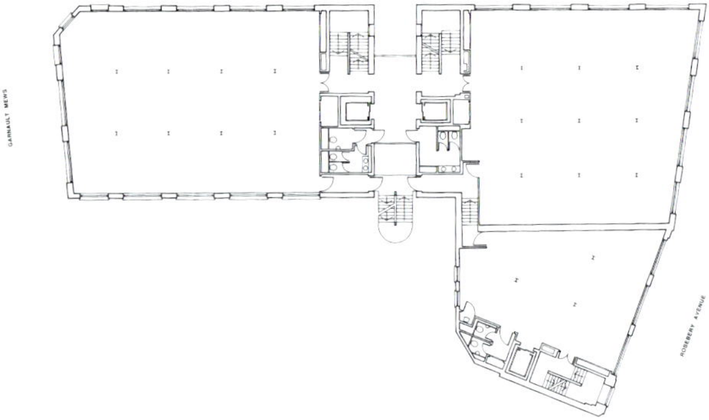

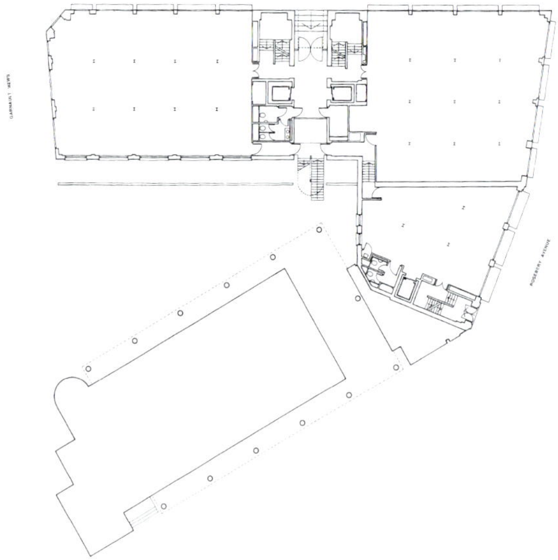

Advertising agency | John McAslan & Partners

This conversion in St. Peter's Street was one of the first projects carried out by John McAslan and his former partner Jamie Troughton. It involved turning a 8,600-square-foot (800 sq m) Victorian warehouse into studios for an advertising agency. It was undertaken in two phases, starting in 1988 and ending in 1991, and it is a model of low-cost refurbishing every bit as effective as McAslan's more famous later work.

One of the main aims was to maintain the original structure of the warehouse. The electrical wiring and other installations were left exposed, and any new additions were carefully integrated, down to the last detail. The new all-glass entrance in the façade gives onto a double-height space and an elegant staircase leading to the lower floor and the inner courtyard. The entrance to the courtyard echoes that of the main façade, with a glass door and a window above it re-creating the double-height effect; alongside, a wall made of translucent concrete bricks increases the substantial luminosity of the lower area. A large horizontal metal girder crosses the back wall and serves as a frame for the translucent wall, which is a reference to the *Maison de Verre* (Glass House) designed by the architect Pierre Charreau.

This conversion focused on enhancing the qualities intrinsic to the building: its structure and perimeter walls, and the incidence of sunlight.

Architects: John McAslan & Partners
Location: London, United Kingdom
Photographs: Peter Cook/View

Composition of the back wall that gives onto the rear courtyard.

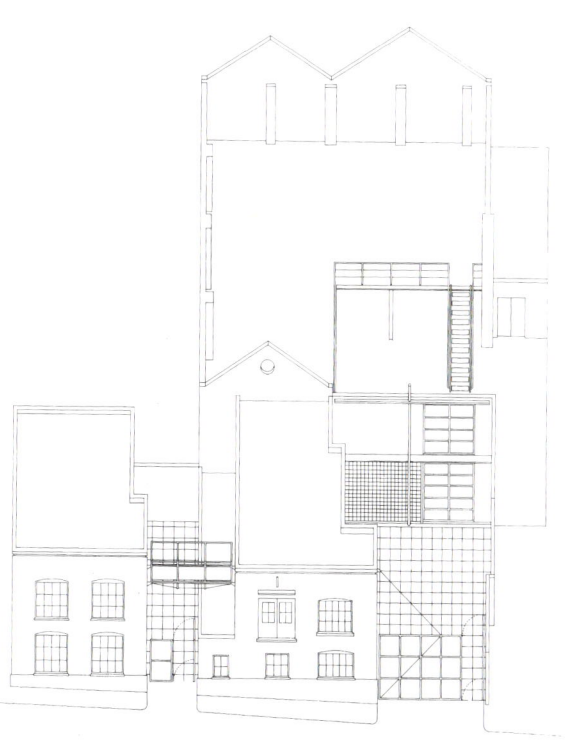

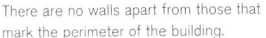

There are no walls apart from those that mark the perimeter of the building.

Derwent Valley Holding

John McAslan & Partners

The conversion of this building at numbers 1 and 3, Colebrooke Place, London, into offices for the Derwent Valley holding company was completed in 1990. It is a fine example of John McAslan's ability to convert buildings into spaces that are not only functional but also attractive, despite their unpromising original structure.

The starting point was a 6,500 square-foot (600 sq m) industrial building put up in 1950, of no architectural interest whatsoever in conventional terms; the roof, with its original if unexciting structure, was the most prominent feature, but even this was in a poor state.

The conversion turned the building into an inviting workplace by concentrating on a few simple parameters: special attention to the use of natural light, repairs to the original finishings, and the installation of a mezzanine running along the whole of one side.

This additional platform is supported by circular concrete pillars given a surprising beauty by their original and imaginative connection with the floor above them. This attention given to the use and combination of materials distinguishes every aspect of the project: the exposed brick walls have been given a coat of paint and the oak floor has been cleaned and varnished.

The whole project was extremely simple, with no superfluous details.

Architects: John McAslan & Partners
Location: London, United Kingdom
Photographs: Peter Cook/View

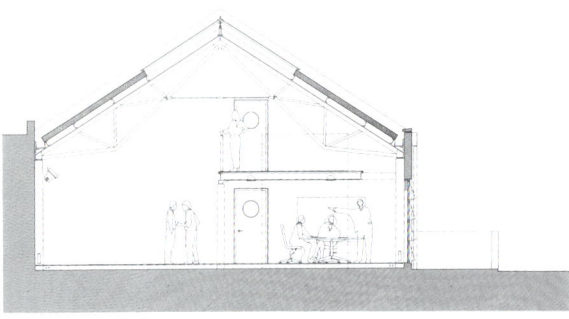

Cross-section

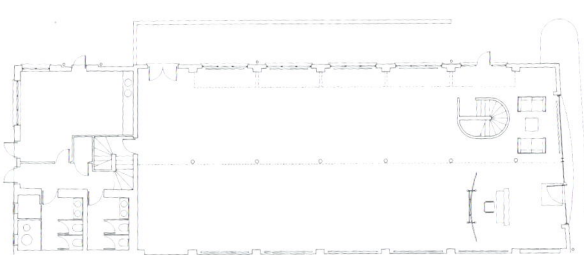

Ground plan

> The asymmetry created by the mezzanine gives variety to the space below through the addition of the balcony and lower ceiling.

Thames & Hudson | John McAslan & Partners

The architects John McAslan & Partners have worked on buildings for use in a wide variety of fields, including education, business, transport, and the art world.

The British publishing house Thames & Hudson commissioned McAslan and his team to restore an old 1930s warehouse in London's West End. The building, spread over 21,500 square feet (2,000 sq m), is the company's new headquarters and accommodates a staff of 120 people. The details of the furnishings for this large workforce were given the same attention as the overall layout.

The main focal point of the building is the atrium on the central axis, which was given over to a library containing 20,000 books (including, of course, those published by the company itself). The visual communication between each open-plan floor is provided by the unenclosed stairwell that rises from the same central axis. Further isolated nuclei, again on the central axis, contain the service and maintenance equipment. The offices and studios extend neatly along each floor and open onto the main communication atrium, and they are therefore visually connected with the rest of the building.

The scheme applied to this old warehouse greatly enhances the building's spatial continuity, its fluidity, and the internal communication between the building's horizontal and vertical planes.

Architects: John McAslan & Partners
Location: London, United Kingdom
Photographs: Peter Cook/View

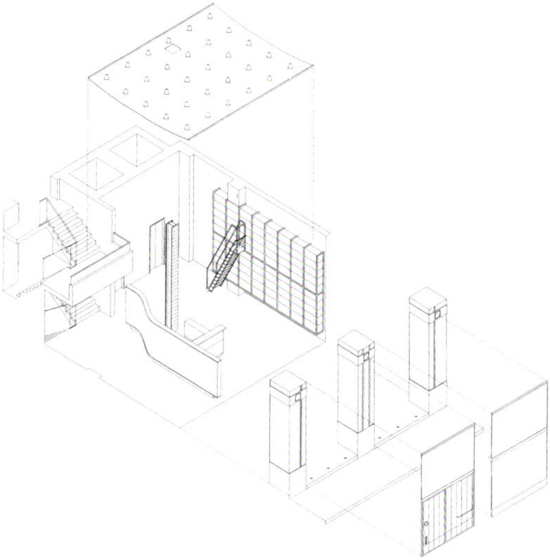

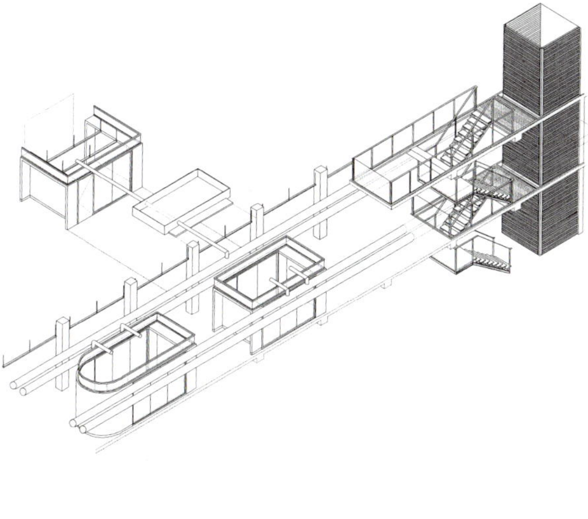

The layout of the air-conditioning system constitutes one of the main structural elements of this project and emphasizes the rational, linear distribution of the floors.

The layout of the staircase in the central atrium opens up a vertical line of visual communication between the floors.

All the elements on each floor are arranged lengthwise, following the line dictated by the rows of pillars.

Williams Murray Banks | Pierre d'Avoine Architect

Williams Murray Banks (WMB) is a recently formed company devoted to graphic design and packaging, whose headquarters are in Heal's Building in London's West End. The project by Pierre d'Avoine Architects involved refurbishing two areas in its interior: the main office (100 feet/30 m. long by 21 feet/6.5 m. wide by 8 feet/2.5 m. high) and a small conference room. WMB wanted the main office to be a flexible space, normally open on all sides but also capable of being converted into three independent offices when necessary.

Almost all the new elements are located on the central axis, which is covered by a false wooden ceiling. The tables, shelves, closets, and benches mark out a rhythm along this axis, which functions along the lines of a graphic scale. The existing structure (ceilings and perimeter walls) has been painted a pale, almost white color; the concrete floor has been lacquered with graphite.

The low budget did not permit the installation of any conventional office furniture. To make sure that the whole space could be furnished, any finishing that demanded the collaboration of outside companies was ruled out, and the decision was taken to use the same material for all the elements: ash plywood panels.

Architects: Pierre d'Avoine Architects
Location: London, United Kingdom
Photographs: David Grandgorge

The vertical slates constitute a mobile element which, like the sliding panels, gives a sense of scale and texture to the space.

The architects' idea was to emphasize the relationship between the exceptional length of the room and its low ceiling. The sliding panels serve as both walls and doors.

Metropolis Studios Ltd. | Powell-Tuck, Connor & Orefelt

The company Metropolis Studios Ltd. obtained the municipal building permit required to turn part of the old electricity plant in Chiswick, west London, into a recording studio. It held a competition, with restricted entry, and the team of Powell-Tuck, Connor, & Orefelt emerged as the winners.

The initial brief demanded total respect for the building's original 19th-century structure and a rigorous control of the acoustics, given its proximity to a residential area. It was decided to put a big box that would satisfy all the company's needs inside the walls of the old building, without ever actually touching them; made of reinforced concrete, it had its own separate foundations.

The design of the inner structures revolves around the central atrium, which defines the space as a series of asymmetrical prisms linked together by ramps and multidirectional staircases. This means that the reception area and the offices are interconnected and have access to the upper stories. The platform with the reception area and offices leads up to the bar and toilets; from there a suspended gangway provides access to the small studios on the third floor (there is more extensive, acoustically insulated studio space on the first floor). The top studios are isolated from the rest of the building by a slightly sloping wall.

This project is an outstanding exercise in architecture and design that finds the right balance between historical memory and the use of totally innovative idioms.

Architects: Powell-Tuck, Connor & Orefelt
Location: London, United Kingdom

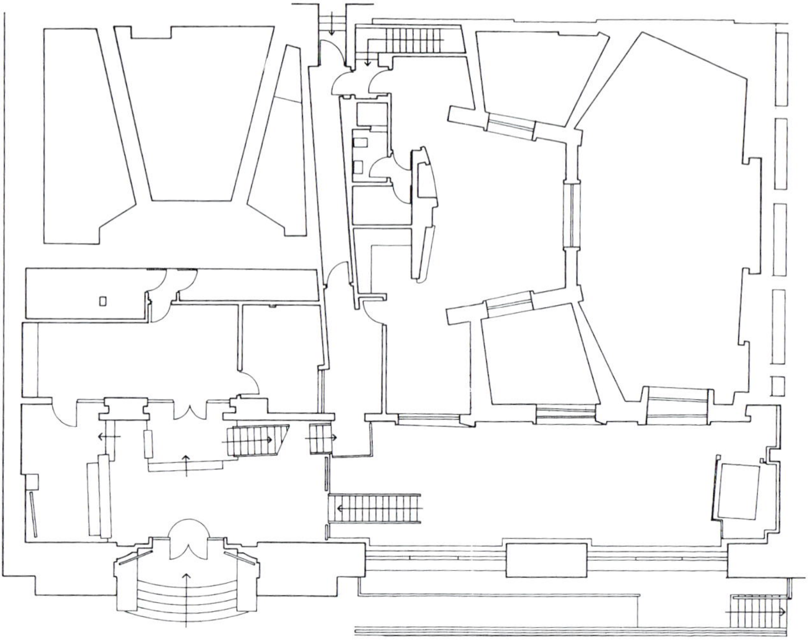

Ground plan of the first floor, with the reception areas and offices.

The top floor, with the smaller studios and mixing rooms.

Studio in Glasgow | Anderson Christie Architects

The premises inside which the architects Anderson and Christie decided to set up their office were formerly a bakery. Although the perimeter was very irregularly shaped, the interior had some distinctive features, such as the huge steel baking ovens, the exposed brick wall, and the metal structure. Anderson and Christie worked to an extremely tight budget, most of which went on fixing technical defects, such as damp patches on walls, and providing appropriate soundproofing too. They altered only those walls that were in vital need of repair; these were treated and painted in very intense colors to exaggerate the contrast with the untouched bricks and stones elsewhere, and to create chromatic focal points.

Due to the precarious condition of the original floors, new concrete ones were also put in. This material, like the exposed walls and other rough finishings, provides reminders of the building's original function. Nevertheless, the overall impression is one of sophistication, due to the main structural elements in the interior: the staircases, banisters, partitions, artificial lighting, doors, and the furniture contained in the different areas.

To sum up, although this type of conversion usually seeks to recover the original space, this bakery will certainly never be the same again.

Architects: Anderson Christie Architects
Location: Glasgow, United Kingdom
Photographs: Kevin McCourt

First floor

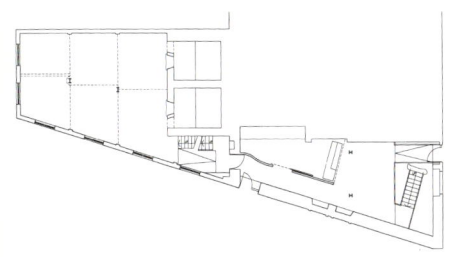

The studio is situated on a busy street in Glasgow's West End. The entrance is on the first floor of a Victorian residential building; the work area is at the rear, once occupied by the bakery's ovens.

Second floor

Third floor

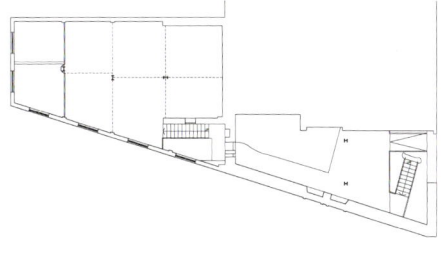

There are two meeting areas: one for internal meetings, next to the drawing studio; the other for clients, alongside the reception area. The incorporation of new inner views by removing some of the lower ceilings was one of the basic premises of the project, as it allowed the architects to dominate and enhance the connection and continuity of the entire space, even on the vertical plane.

Labotron.
Offices and workshops

Pep Zazurca i Codolà

This loft is situated on the first floor of a building in the Eixample neighborhood of Barcelona. Its shape is typical of the district – a rectangle with a narrow façade on the street, two long party walls, and a large area in the back courtyard with its own separate roof but no windows in the walls. The reception area is situated in the front, close to the street; beyond, two long corridors divide the space.

The aim of the project was to take as much advantage as possible of the natural light, which barely penetrates the big area in the back, either from the street or the big skylights cut into the roof.

On the basis of these criteria, it was decided to eliminate any intermediary partitions and thereby enhance both the physical and the visual continuity of the space.

The reception counter is situated behind the all-glass entrance door. One of the long corridors leads to the main area at the back, containing the administration area and the offices. The other corridor houses the workshop and receives sunlight from the street, although passers-by cannot see inside because it is visually protected by a mat glass window treated with acid. Finally, both corridors, running parallel with the party walls, open out onto the back area, where there are cubicles that are used for storage and service equipment.

The entire premises are fitted with a concrete floor. Laminated wood has been used for the furniture and sliding doors.

Architect: Pep Zazurca i Codolà
Location: Barcelona, Spain
Photographs: Eugeni Pons

The vertical separations consist of pale laminated wood panels topped with glass stretching up to the roof; these maintain the visual continuity and maximize the entrance of light.

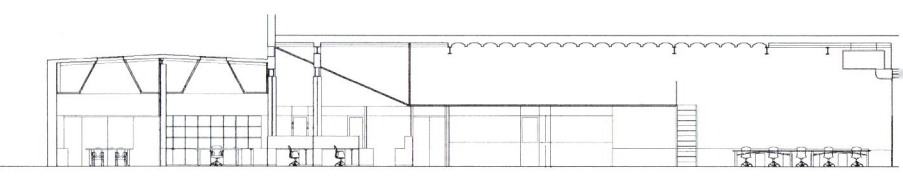

Longitudinal section

The side cubicles containing the toilets and bar unit are painted electric blue, so that there is an immediate visual impact when the door is opened.

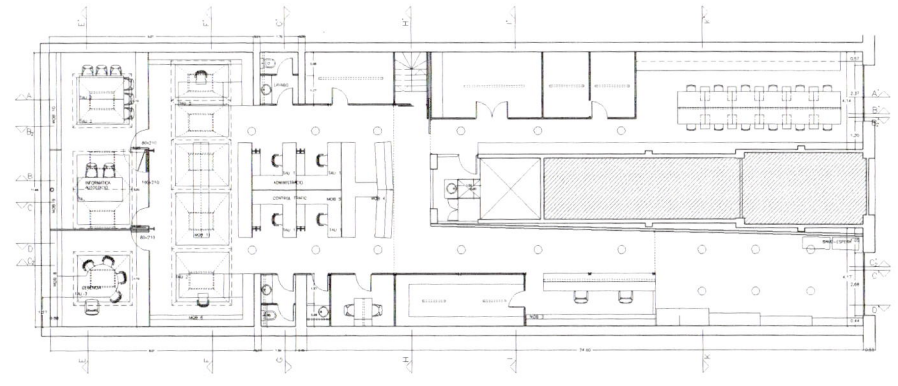

Ground plan

Double You | Marc Viader i Oliva

Double You is a company devoted to advertising and website design that has established its new headquarters in a 2,540-square-foot (236 sq m) industrial building in the heart of Barcelona's residential neighborhood of Gràcia. The entire block was once devoted to industrial activity, and it still proudly bears witness to its former life as a factory. Inside this loft, the original elements — staircases, patios, service elevators, and industrial materials — all take on a new life.

The project, designed by the architect Marc Viader, was organized around three axes that articulate the entire area: three double-sided rows of tables crossing the space, surrounded by the cables that feed each computer terminal. The tables do not stretch to the two walls lined with windows, however, and so the space in front of these walls is freed for other activities. The wall looking out on the church across the street, for example, is lined with work tables. The opposite wall, which gives onto the back patio, is broken by a unit containing the toilets, and another new element — a transparent cube for meetings — has been added near the entrance.

The modular form of the tables means that they can be regrouped if any of the teams need to work closely together at any given moment. All the furniture for the office has been designed with the same dynamism and versatility that has been applied to the overall use of the space.

Architect: Marc Viader i Oliva
Location: Barcelona, Spain
Photographs: Jordi Miralles

Papers, disks, monitors, keyboards, games, colored card, candies, posters, magazines, books, a TV set: the work tables had to cater for all these accessories – and more!

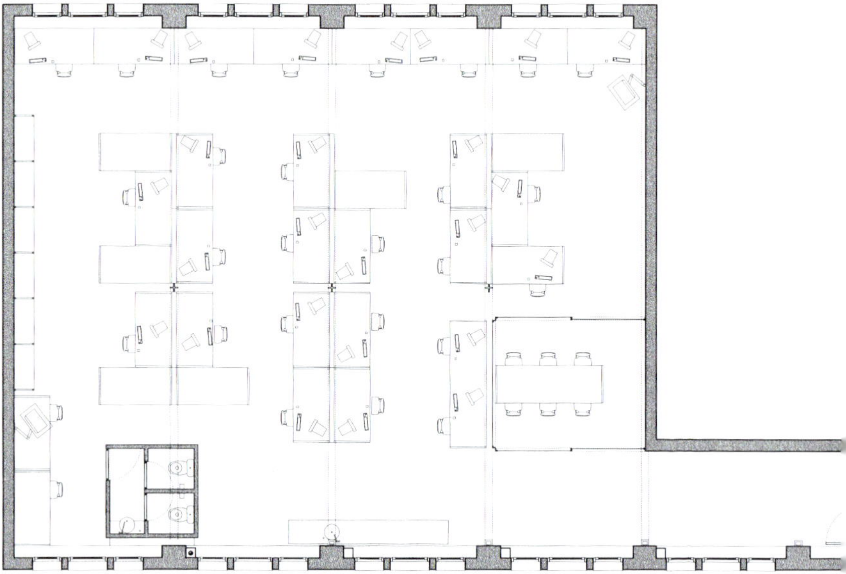

The stone wall, stained glass, and rose windows of the church across the street form part of the inner landscape of the office.

Hispano 20
José Ángel Rodrigo García

The main aim of this design for the Hispano 20 – a division of a major bank aimed at young people – was the creation of a distinctive corporate image with a youthful look that is capable of being adapted to any type of space. The architect came up with a series of formal and aesthetic ideas to differentiate the various areas.

Glass walls weave their way sinuously through the premises to create transparent compartments, banishing the traditional concept of closed offices and leaving the activities of the staff open to public view.

One prominent feature is the mezzanine, which contains an exhibition area with access to the front offices and a balcony overlooking the reception area. The first floor is spread over two levels; one near the façade, containing the cash machines, and the other below the mezzanine, with work desks, a meeting room, and a high-ceilinged space with the archives and change machines.

A diversity of materials has been used: bullet-proof glass lined with butiral for varying degrees of thickness on the façades and inner walls; Italian marble on the floor of the first story; laminated wood and Marmoleum on the mezzanine; black porcelain in the restrooms; and plaster and paint on a Veloglas cladding to finish the horizontal and vertical panels.

The lighting mainly comes from an array of dicroic lamps backed up by fluorescent tubes and, in the exhibition area, by wall projectors on an electrified rail in the ceiling.

The furniture flaunts postmodern and avant-garde details in a daring mixture of contrasts that perfectly reflects the image the company wants to project.

Architect: José Ángel Rodrigo García
Location: Barcelona, Spain

Montardit SA | Josep Juvé & Núria Jolis

This prestigious purveyor of fine high-class food products entrusted the design of its headquarters and storage space in Barcelona's Eixample neighborhood to the studio of Juvé & Jolis. The premises, which are situated on the first floor, were once divided into two, each with a façade on the street. Instead, one single space was created to cater for all the functional needs of the company's program.

The entrance in the glass front leads directly onto the reception area, which has a wooden floor and exposed brick walls. A wooden partition crosses this space to divide it into two; on the right, there is a waiting area and, on the left, a meeting room. The offices are reached through a glass door, emblazoned with the company's initials. The practical furnishings have been arranged in line with the structure of the space to create several work areas. Two rooms in the back are separate from the offices: a relaxation area and another meeting room.

Generally speaking, the furniture is classical, although it combines old pieces with works by contemporary designers, such as the armchairs and table by Nancy Robbins and the Colilla lamp by Ordeig.

The work of Juvé & Jolis in the Montardit offices is an example of a single space in which highly varied areas succeed one another without losing control of the multiple perspectives provided by the setting.

Architects: Josep Juvé & Núria Jolis
Location: Barcelona, Spain
Photographs: Eugeni Pons

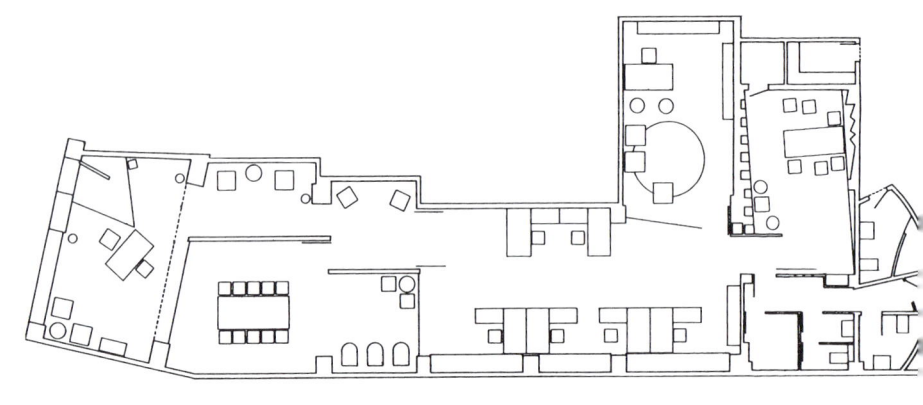

The space is not marked out by partitions – which would spoil the perspective – but by the particular design features in each individual area.

Those work areas that are not open are separated off only by glass panels. In this way they display the staff's activity and promote the company's image.

GCA | GCA Arquitectes Associats

The studio of the GCA architectural team in Barcelona occupies the site of former textile warehouses on the first floor of a building dating from 1946.

Such buildings were traditionally divided into parts: the offices in the front, incorporated into the rest of the block, and the storage area behind, stretching right to the back, with its own separate roof. This particular building had some enclosed offices near the entrance, complete with classical touches like cornices and moldings. Beyond lay a bare space, interrupted only by latticed metal girders and pillars.

The architects opted for a two-pronged approach: they sought to preserve the character of the existing offices, by restoring the woodwork and equipping them as reception and administration areas, but they bestowed an unequivocally modern look on the former warehouse, which was to be used for the design work. Although the project was based on a dialogue of opposites, the new design studio almost inevitably ended up attracting all the attention. It was conceived as a big white box, lit from above by two large skylights, and its layout is determined by the work process, from the projection and drawing area to the supervision of the building work. This sequence culminates in a large exterior patio.

Light is the primordial element. White walls, maple floors, and glass screens combine to create a minimalist space, in which spatial boundaries are eliminated in favor of multiple views and perspectives.

Architects: GCA Arquitectes Associats
Location: Barcelona, Spain
Photographs: Jordi Miralles

Over 200 people work in these offices, so the meeting areas acquired a special importance. The entrance hall, in particular, was conceived as a multi-purpose space where it is even possible to play ping-pong.

Casadesús studio | Antoni Casadesús

Many of the details are white, so they do not pass unnoticed when light is reflected off them.

Antoni Casadesús converted a space once used by a textile company into his own design studio and home.

The size of the house – around 1,600 square feet (148 sq m) – its great height, the rear patio facing toward the southeast and, above all, its excellent location, just a few yards from the Passeig de Gràcia, in the very center of Barcelona. convert it into the stuff of dreams.

A central strip, with a small garden and the kitchen, separates the most private area of the home – bedroom, bathroom, and mezzanine – from a big double-height sitting room that gives onto the back yard. This layout makes it possible to keep the various functions independent of each other and establish various degrees of privacy, whilst also maintaining visual connections between every part of the house. Even the entrance affords a view of both the intermediate garden and the back terrace.

It is immediately apparent that the exterior has been treated with the same scrupulous care as the interior, with its exquisite composition and the choice of furniture.

Despite the considerable dimensions of the home, there is a high incidence of natural light throughout the rooms. Almost all the surfaces, including the floor and various pieces of furniture – a couch, a bookcase, the piano, a table – are white or pale colored.

Architect: Antoni Casadesús
Location: Barcelona, Spain
Photographs: Eugeni Pons

The floor throughout the house is made of white marble, except in the mezzanine, where it is teak.

The work chairs were designed by Charles Eames; the table by Isern and Bernal.

The bathroom is dominated by polished, gleaming surfaces. The faucets are by Philippe Starck.

B&B studio-home | Sergi Bastidas

This old forge on the island of Mallorca was refurbished by the architect Sergi Bastidas in order to install his studio and home. To take full advantage of the ample space available, he put a lot of thought into the partitions needed for the new layout. The solutions he found were deliberately lacking in extravagant visual impact and were based on luminosity, not only from the windows but also from the dividing panels, pale walls, and sliding screens, which all serve to mark off areas for receiving guests, holding meetings, working, parking, and housing service installations.

From an architectural point of view, an effort has been made to respect industrial characteristics. Therefore Bastidas has chosen simple lines, exposed structures, and rough materials like polished concrete on the floors. He also retained much of the building's old machinery in the design.

The area on the second floor – given over to the home, two offices, and a meeting room – is designed to be more intimate, with the functional spaces, like the bedroom, bathroom, and dressing room, separate from each other.

The creation of such comfort in so large a space without renouncing the building's industrial past bears witness to the architect's spatial awareness and his control over materials.

Architect: Sergi Bastidas
Location: Molinar, Palma de Mallorca. Spain
Photographs: Pere Planells

The staircase facilitates vertical communication, but, in visual terms, it merges into the lower floor on account of the material chosen for its construction.

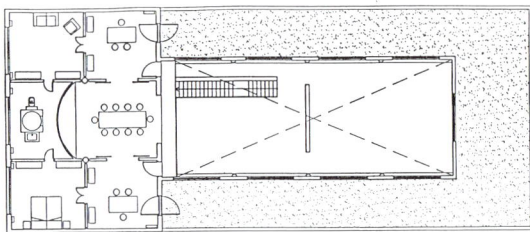

Top floor. Two offices and a meeting room have been attached to the domestic area.

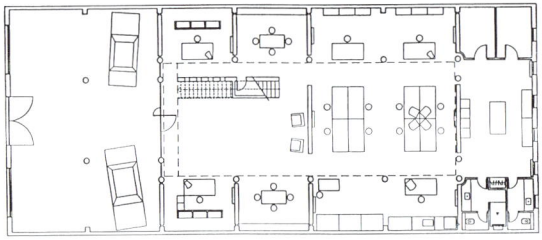

First floor

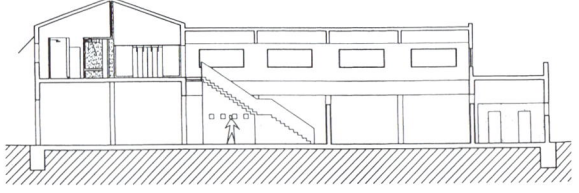

Longitudinal section

This kitchen area precedes the living area situated on the first floor.

Studio in Madrid | Enrique Bardají

Enrique Bardají's studio — which he designed himself — is located in a building that he also designed. So, Bardají was both client and architect, a coincidence reflected in the precision with which every element has been defined. The result is a bright expanse in which the studio functions extremely smoothly; this space, like the whole building, is distinguished by a series of deliberate industrial references.

One element that is fundamental to the project is luminosity. The central area is illuminated by a central skylight, covered by a canvas that filters the light. Three of the perimeter walls have windows stretching from floor to ceiling. Venetian blinds control the penetration of the sun into the building.

The general design work is carried out in the central area. The tables are fitted with big worktops that make it possible to draw by hand and refer to a computer at the same time. These tables are based on a design by the German architect Egor Eiermann.

Architect: Enrique Bardají
Location: Madrid, Spain
Photographs: Lionel Malka

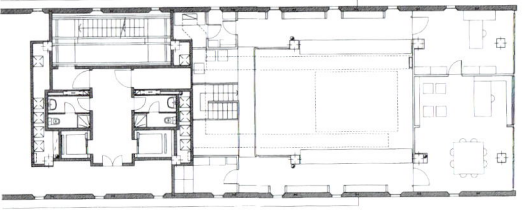

Mezzanine.
Enrique Bardají's office and the company records are situated in the mezzanine.

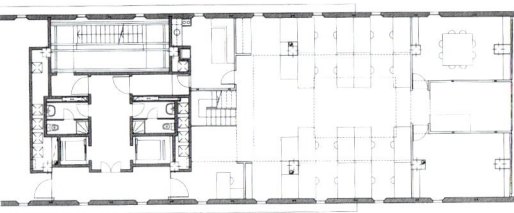

Lower floor.
The central area is surrounded by a library, conference room, machine room, and kitchen-dining room.

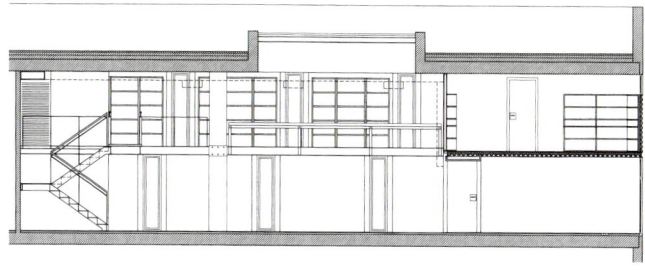

The air-conditioning ducts are covered with sheets of galvanized steel and left open to view throughout the studio.

The floor of the mezzanine is made of two DM sheets filled with soundproofing material and topped with linoleum. The sheets are supported by metal girders.

The floor is covered with thick blue linoleum, the walls and ceilings are painted white, and the exposed structure is pale gray.

Empty SA | Víctor López Cotelo

We should never cease to try to make our working life as enjoyable as possible. This premise was the basis of a complex but low-budget renovation project of a set of offices which had excellent interior architectural features. So many times these types of projects are left incomplete due to the unpromising characteristics of the original building and the limited financial resources available.

This particular project involved the conversion of commercial premises measuring 7,500 square feet (700 sq m) into offices for the company Empty SA; the work was completed in 1998. The architect, Víctor López, and his team decided right from the start to make their intervention as unobtrusive as possible. The basic strategy was to strip the interior of any superfluous trimmings and enhance the incidence of sunlight to compensate for the lack of views of the outside world.

After the demolition of all the extraneous building work that had been added over the years, the basic skeleton became visible again, and all the new office installations were accommodated to this stark, unadorned structure. Luminosity and spaces with the maximum of flexibility and versatility were considered indispensable for this office.

Architect: Víctor López Cotelo
Location: Madrid, Spain
Photographs: Luis Asín

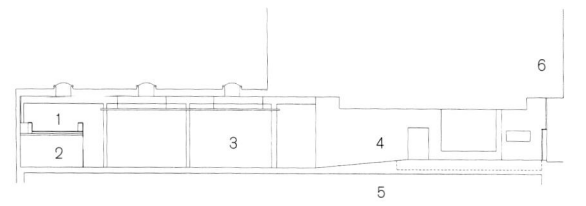

Longitudinal section
1. Administration
2. Conference room
3. Drawing studio
4. Ramp
5. Garages
6. Existing building

Longitudinal section

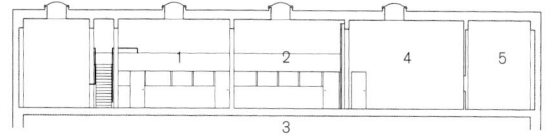

Cross-section
1. Administration
2. Office
3. Garages
4. Management
5. Store

Cross-section

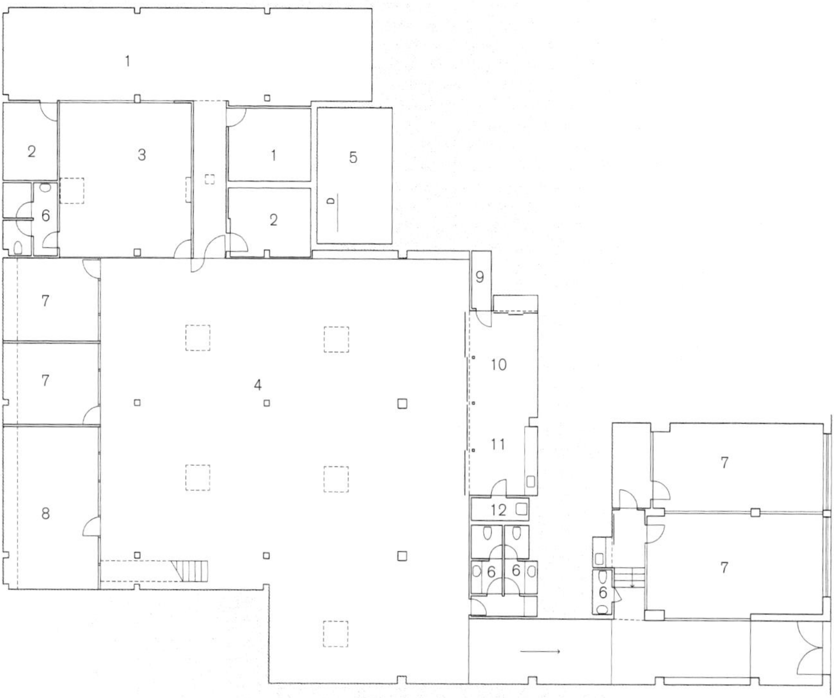

Ground plan
1. Store
2. Installations
3. Management
4. Drawing studio
5. Courtyard
6. Restroom
7. Office
8. Conference room
9. Clothes closet
10. Photocopy area
11. Kitchen
12. Garbage disposal

Ground plan

Large and small, far and near, open and closed; these dualities create interesting perspectives that make the new offices inviting spaces to work in.

The size of each area is determined by the pre-existing architectural elements, which give a precise sense of scale to the conversion.

Salamanca neighborhood

Manuel Serrano, Marta Rodríguez Ariño

These two architects fitted out an old industrial building in Madrid's Salamanca neighborhood to make a studio for themselves. Once the partitions that had been added to the original building were cleared away, there proved to be plenty of sources of natural light; nevertheless, the architects put skylights in the roof and extended the windows down to the floor, and they even dispensed entirely with the roof linking the offices with the conference room to create an interior garden.

The first floor houses the workspace, conference room, store, kitchen, restroom, and room for printing plans. The offices are situated on the mezzanine. The different spaces are divided by glass screens mounted on oxiron-painted metal frames, although the toilet and storage area are marked off by prefabricated panels. The room next to the garden — and indeed the garden itself — is used for informal meetings. The printing room is linked to the offices on the mezzanine by a service elevator. In the rear lie the storage area, a toilet finished with limestone, and a small kitchen with stainless-steel fittings and an industrial sink fitted into the counter.

The skylights in the roof are made of colorless cellular polycarbonate sheets with metal frames, which give way to reinforced glass in the lower parts.

Polished concrete treated with wax was chosen for the floor, and paving stones were used in the garden.

Architects: Manuel Serrano, Marta Rodríguez Ariño
Location: Madrid, Spain
Photographs: José Latova

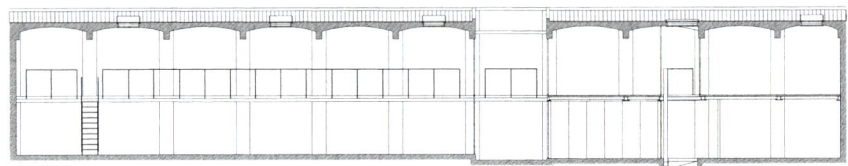

Longitudinal section

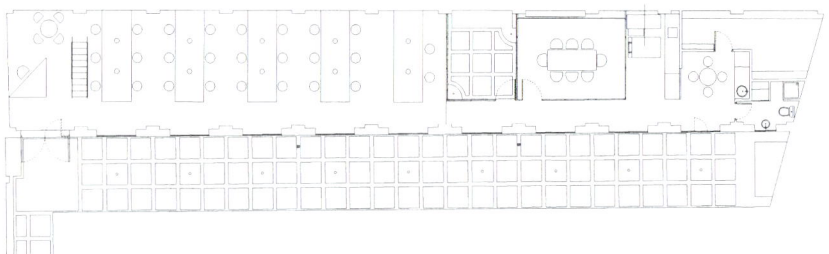

First floor

The workspace contains a library on a projecting metal gangway reached by a spiral staircase.

The mezzanine's structure is made of metal, and the floor is topped with insulating material and industrial parquet.

Cyclorama | Manuel Serrano, Marta Rodríguez Ariño

A cyclorama is a continuous backdrop. In theatrical terms, it is a physical or optical apparatus that makes it possible to portray a vast expanse of space in a confined area. It is an indispensable feature of photographic studios, where it provides a background for other smaller spaces or additional elements.

The principle of the cyclorama was applied when this 1930s industrial building, measuring around 3,200 square feet (300 sq m), was converted into a photographic studio. The building is typical of the blocks with patios built in Madrid in that period. It was originally spread over a single floor, but its interior has now been completely transformed. Two studios have been installed: one receives natural light; the other, smaller one is part of a light but sturdy platform that also houses some of the building's installations. To save space and avoid any unnecessary building work, this raised area is reached by two simple spiral staircases, one in the entrance, the other weaving its way through the mesh of cables and beams in the roof. The reception area is completely open to the large service and entrance corridor. The space opposite the reception area contains the toilets, bathroom, and kitchen, grouped together in a free-standing unit that has been oxidized and then varnished.

The reinforced concrete rafters of the original building have been left intact, and, as examples of industrial architecture, they blend effortlessly with the timeless eclecticism suggested by the cycloramas contained in the studios.

W

Architects: Manuel Serrano, Marta Rodríguez Ariño
Location: Madrid, Spain
Photographs: Julio Limia

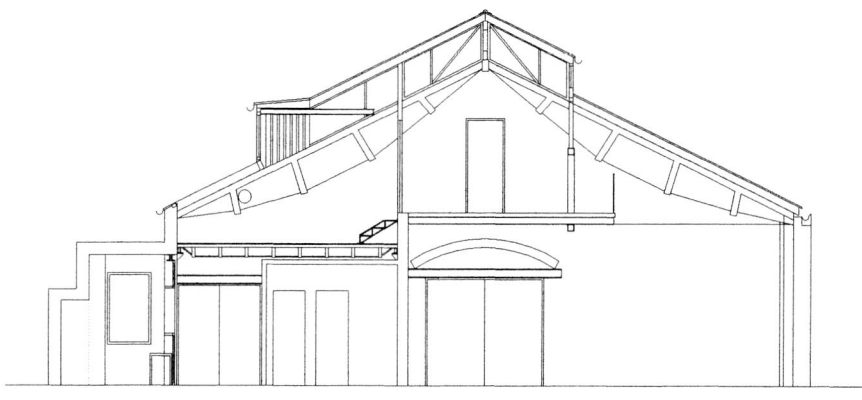

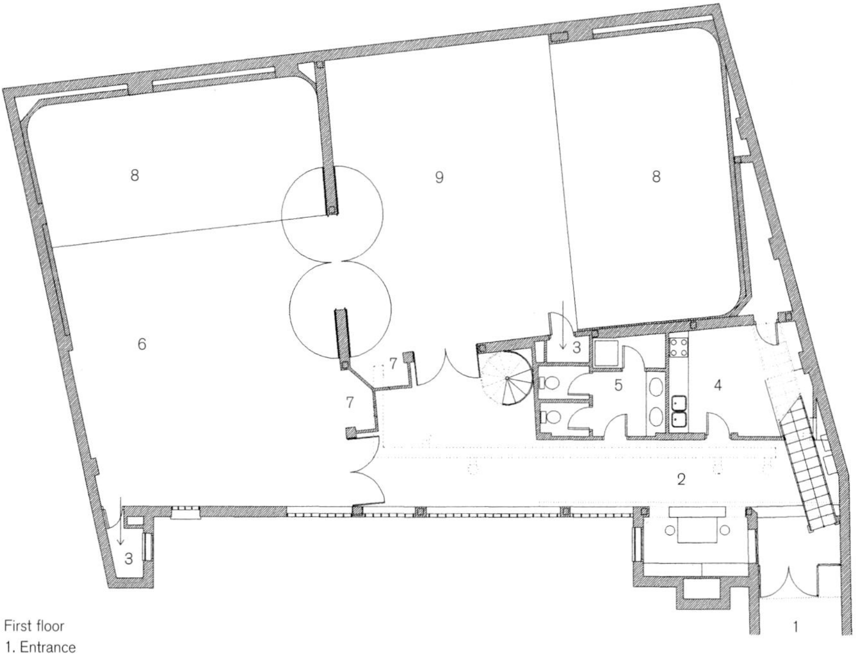

First floor
1. Entrance
2. Reception
3. Darkroom
4. Kitchen
5. Bathroom
6. Studio 1, with daylight
7. Make-up
8. Cyclorama
9. Studio 2

The roof, supported by a light metal structure, is made of lacquered metal sheets while the skylight in studio 1 is made of cellular metacrylate.

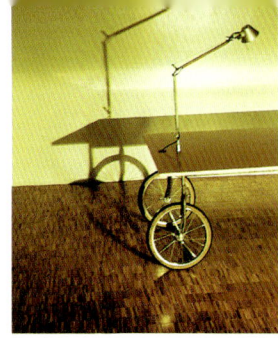

Architecture studio

José Miguel Usabiaga Bárcena

This building in San Sebastián was originally a warehouse belonging to the Spanish railroad company. It had been damaged and modified by a series of interventions that obscured the true nature of the building, so the architect in charge of its conversion decided to try to recover its rich historical legacy.

The project had a two-pronged approach: on the one hand, the restoration of the actual building, which demanded an almost archaeological concern for detail; on the other, the strictly new additions, where the meticulousness was just as evident, particularly in the use of transitions made with glass sheets – both transparent and translucent – whose delicacy did not overpower the building's historical character.

The new materials take an active part in this dialogue across time by creating a contrast with the aura of a long-lost industrial age that envelops the space. The new mezzanine, with its supporting structure made of solid steel, totally untreated and unprotected, is acquiring a tarnished coat of rust; it sits on the original beams, without damaging them in any way. The banister is made of the same steel, while the handrail has been assembled out of plumbing pipes. Most of the doors slide along steel structures, with the opening mechanism left visible, again evoking nostalgia for the huge industrial doors of old-fashioned warehouses.

Spaces, materials, trains, bicycles, metal: all play their part in recapturing the heroic age of the steam engine.

Architect: José Miguel Usabiaga Bárcena
Location: San Sebastián, Spain
Photographs: José Manuel Bielsa

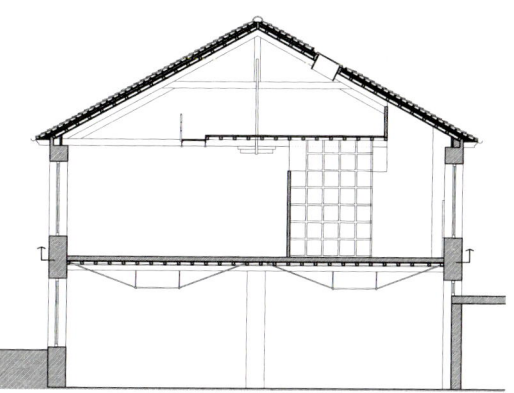

Cross-section

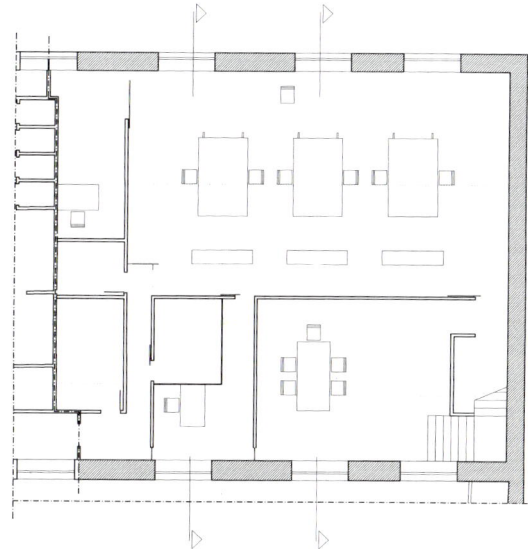

Ground plan

The thick, narrow floorboards are designed for industrial use; the entire perimeter is bordered with a metal rim that prevents contact between the wooden boards and the old walls.

The new partitions that divide the workshop and other areas are made of plaster, with a lacquered pale gray finish.

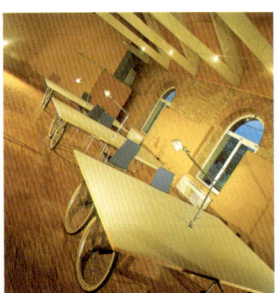

Before the conversion, there was a wooden floor covering the whole top space to create an attic. The partial removal of this barrier has opened up the area to reveal the intricacies of the rafters and the steel banister.

IU-EB headquarters

José Miguel Usabiaga Bárcena

This project involved the conversion of an old industrial space – situated in an inner courtyard in a block in the heart of Bilbao – into the Basque headquarters of the Izquierda Unida political party.

There were two main aspects of the conversion. The main spaces are intended for meetings; the open, sociable areas, the factory building, and the splashes of red all bear witness to the social history and ideals underlying this left-wing party. The other aspect concerns the day-to-day running of the organization, as reflected in the small meeting rooms and administrative offices.

The old factory is reached by following the red line painted on the wall of a gallery running through the first floor of a residential building. At the end of the gallery, a glass box marks the transition between the two spaces, like a prism. Once inside, the red of the baseboards provides an element of continuity, and this color reappears on the upper stories among the cellular polycarbonate and wooden cladding installed to make the building easier to heat. The wide, fluid corridor on the second floor – devoted to administration – hides a series of private, enclosed spaces that contrast with the geometrical forms of another glass box and a cylinder used for bigger meetings.

This project can be summed up as meditation in red on the historic soul of this old factory.

Architect: José Miguel Usabiaga Bárcena
Location: Bilbao, Spain
Photographs: José Manuel Bielsa

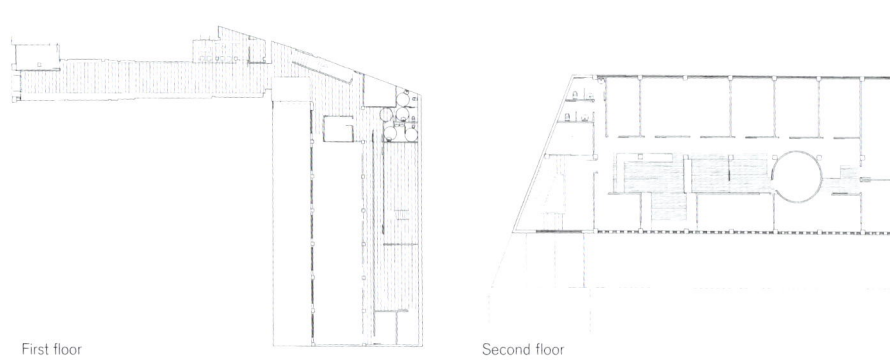

First floor

Second floor

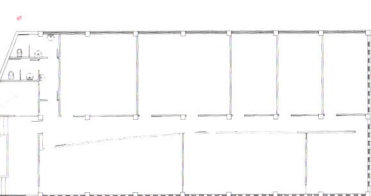

The lighting emphasizes the industrial atmosphere by means of a system of halogen lamps suspended from exposed, undisguised cabling.

d floor

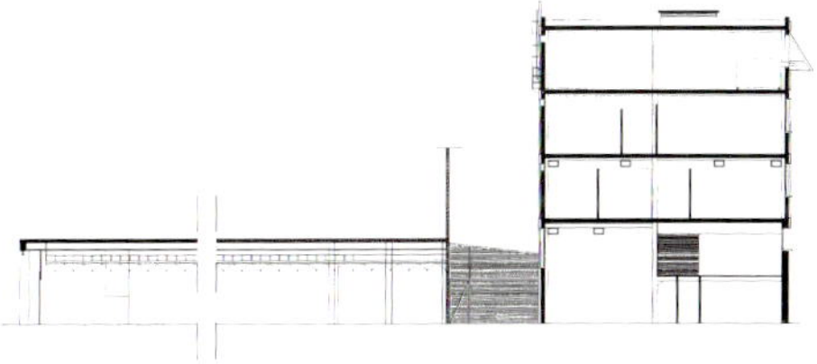

Longitudinal section

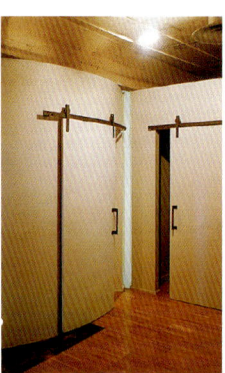

Sliding partitions with the closing mechanism left visible serve as doors in the simple office area.

The main hall is a double-height space with an upper section leading to the party's library and archives.

Studio Naço offices | Studio Naço

The offices of Studio Naço are situated in an old lumber yard which formerly lurked unnoticed inside a block in the Bastille neighborhood in Paris.

The architects comprising Studio Naço resolved to overhaul the old building and convert it into their workplace and headquarters. They pulled down a garage to leave the courtyard to the north as the point of access, as well as creating a distance from the street to allow the new façade to be seen in its entirety.

The façade was stripped of its old cladding of rotten timbers to reveal the spectacular wooden structure that had always held up the old building, as well as the forms that could be construed as symbols for the trees that provided this wood. The architects decided not only to restore this structure but also to put it on display; they made it transparent by covering it with a skin of glass. This glass front is supported by a metal substructure that controls the opening and closing of the windows electronically.

Architects: Studio Naço
Location: Paris, France
Photographs: Mario Pignata-Monti

The glass façade reveals the architects and designers at work, apparently in silence.

This cross-section shows the different work areas of the Studio Naço offices. The building emanates spaciousness, both horizontally and vertically. It is divided into three light-filled floors, each with an area of 1,300 square feet (120 sq m).

Each story has a single, enclosed cube – referred to as the "box" – that contains the services allocated to it: restrooms and closet on the first floor; photocopier and archives on the second; fax and store on the third. Partitions, doors, and false ceilings were completely ruled out.

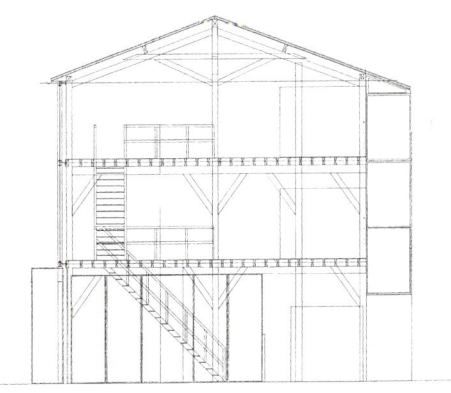

The structure and furnishings combine to create an interior full of contrasts. Studio Naço has balanced the inherent austerity of the building – rough stone walls and floors, bare wooden pillars and beams – with specially designed furniture, lamps, and radios to create a dynamic, colorful atmosphere that infuses the whole space with vitality and wit.

Silos in Amsterdam | Die architectengroep

The building that now contains the offices of Die architectengroep was once a silo that supplied flour for all the bakeries in Amsterdam. However, by the time the group decided to install their offices in the top five stories, the building had already undergone several modifications that had distorted its original appearance.

One basic premise of the conversion was the division of the building into a northern and a southern part. The latter contains the drawing studios, whereas the former holds the meeting rooms, administration, accounts, offices for the various partners, and the service staircase.

The space was divided by means of glass screens in sturdy wooden frames.

The installation of a skylight on the top story and the numerous perforations in the floors mean that sunshine can penetrate into every part of the building.

Brash, rough materials and finishings were chosen. This boldness shows that the architects were not overawed by the idiosyncrasies of this old flour warehouse. It also represents a reaction to the dominant aesthetic of contemporary Dutch architecture, which goes to almost obsessive lengths to achieve pristine perfection in building design.

Architects: Die architectengroep
Location: Amsterdam, Netherlands
Photographs: Christian Richters

The building's concrete porticos turn the bright drawing studio into a highly versatile space with access to the more private, compartmentalized offices set behind the glass screens along one side.

The visual and spatial continuity marked out by the structure of the porticos is maintained along both the transverse and the longitudinal axes.

Architecture office | Jacob Zeilon & Partners

In 1999 Jacob Zeilon & Partners installed their architecture office in a 1960s building that had first been the headquarters of a bank and then an advertising agency. The main purpose was to create a large, bright working space. The big arch that had once covered the bank was knocked down to make way for a free-standing mezzanine, which contains the customer service areas, stores, installations and two meeting rooms – one formal, the other more relaxed. There is also a cafeteria and a very spacious lounge area.

The first floor is a work area that is visually connected to the upper level from every point. The partitions have been finished with sturdy, functional materials, and their unobtrusive design reflects the subdued visual impact of this discreet, neutral setting. The lighting on the first floor, provided by low-voltage lamps set in the ceiling, contrasts with the warm lighting chosen for the upper level. The fluorescent tubes hidden in the printing room on the first story emphasize the apparent lightness of the floor above, which seems to float in mid-air, supported by a single pillar.

At night the striking interplay between the lights in the ceilings and the walls clad in Oregon pine is noticeable even from the street.

W

Architects: Jacob Zeilon & Partners
Location: Stockholm, Sweden
Photographs: Tomas Fälth

"A significant factor in the success of the alternative space – as in the success of the galleries that also set up shop there – is that it projects the image of artistic production"
Sharon Zukin, *Loft living: culture and capital in urban change*
(Baltimore, Md., The Johns Hopkins University Press, 1982)

trading

in a loft

R 20th Century | Mike Solis + Nick Dine. Dinersan Inc.

This company, which specializes in the sale of classics of modern design, has recently launched a new branch in the fashionable Tribeca neighborhood in Lower Manhattan. This opening signals the desire of the owners, Zesty Myers and Evan Snyderman, and their new European partner, Bjorn Stern, to expand the company's interests. The new premises boast a design gallery that presents an unrivaled collection of the work of the famous names of mid-20th-century design (as well as the not so famous, but equally representative of the era).

The space, measuring some 3,800 square feet (350 sq m), has been spread over various levels by the designers Mike Solis and Nick Dine. The space on the main floor, devoted to sales to the public, is characterized by the exposed brickwork, which contrasts sharply with the smoothness of the gray floor, treated with epoxy resin, and the high, white ceiling. A metal and glass staircase leads to a lower level, which includes an art gallery, a meeting room, and an exceptional library replete with books on design.

The overall effect of the new acquisition is one of light and continuity in a well-structured space, the ideal stage for displaying the work of great designers and for explaining the importance of their work.

Interior designers: Mike Solis + Nick Dine. Dinersan Inc.
Location: New York, United States
Photographs: Jordi Miralles

Sunlight pours into even the furthest recesses of the space.

Independent counters exhibit small collections of pottery or exquisite glassware.

Original designs by Arne Jacobsen, Edward Wormley, and Eero Saarinen do not overshadow those of the lesser-known, but equally accomplished, Cees Braakman, Kho Liang Le, and Tapio Wirkkala.

Spazionavigli | RBA. Roberto Brambilla & Associates

The well-known Spazionavigli by Cyrus Company made its mark on the American market with this showroom, which opened its doors to the public in December 1999 on Mercer Street, a busy shopping area in New York.

The atmosphere inside the showroom is unlike that of any other such establishment in Manhattan. Elegance, simplicity, and radiance are the watchwords here. The purity of the lines and forms, the soft whitish tones, and the pastel colors all contribute to bringing to life the company's philosophy on furnishings and interior design.

This company is highly renowned throughout Italy as a guarantor of high quality, matchless taste, and modern design in the field of interior decoration. It has three showrooms in Milan, strategically placed in prominent parts of the old city: the Via Borgospesso (Montenapoleone), the Via Alessandria (Naviglia district), and the Corso Garibaldi (Brera district). These centers offer designers, retailers, and style-conscious consumers the pick of the company's latest crop of domestic furniture, bed linen, decorative objects, and gift items.

The Cyrus Company has long recognized the importance of textile design in creating comfortable but elegant furniture. In 1971, for example, it pioneered the idea of an upholstered bed with removable covers. Since then, a restless quest for the most imaginative and practical answers to the demands of domestic interiors has resulted in trendsetting pieces at the cutting edge of contemporary Italian design.

Architects: RBA. Roberto Brambilla & Associates
Location: Manhattan, New York, United States
Photographs: Jordi Miralles

Cyrus Company produces beds – in both metal and wood – large and small armchairs, tables, chairs, and lamps.

The company has recently expanded its repertoire to enter the world of children's design.

Shin Choi in New York | Wormser + Associates

This simple but elegant store in Manhattan's SoHo district reflects the style and serenity characteristic of the clothes of the designer Shin Choi. Her retail store occupies a 2,700-square-foot (250 sq m) loft in a historic building dating from 1890 with several distinctive architectural features, including high ceilings, wooden floors, and skylights.

At the request of the designer herself, and in close collaboration with the artist Eric Anderson and the graphic designer Gamer Gutierrez, the architect Peter Wormser took on the task of refurbishing the space, as well as participating in the designs for the store's furniture. The conversion took barely two months, although it must be taken into account that the team of Wormser & Associates was also refurbishing the rest of the building at the time. They completely overhauled the façade and cleaned up the lofts, but they did leave some of the original elements intact.

The star of this particular show is the mobile changing room, with mirrors on the outer walls; this glides spectacularly in the sunlight that streams in through the skylight. This independent and practical unit, finished inside with birch plywood panels, adds versatility and flexibility to the layout of the display area. The birch furniture and minimalist inspiration provide the final, defining touches to the store's interior.

Brightly colored rice-paper panels set off perfectly the restrained tailoring of Choi's clothes, and also remind customers of her Korean origins.

W
Architects: Wormser + Associates
Location: New York, United States
Photographs: Jordi Miralles

The mobile changing room, complete with mirror, can be adapted to whatever spatial configuration is required by a new collection.

Rice-paper panels create evocative backgrounds that set off the clothes hung on them.

The birch-wood furniture is distinguished by its simple lines – in keeping with the spirit of Shin Choi's own designs.

Knitwear
Bailo + Rull
ADP. Arquitectes Associa[ts]

The old Esteve knitwear factory is situated in Igualada, a town near Barcelona. The basic architectural unit of this industrial building is a square measuring 20 x 20 feet (6 x 6 m), bounded by concrete pillars and arched summers and covered by a spherical cupola. These are ordered in a regular pattern, although this is broken by the crossroads next to the building. It was the former main entrance to the factory – which gives onto the crossroads – that the architects Manel Bailo and Rosa Rull, the founders of ADP, chose as a focal point for potential customers when they refurbished this part of the building to set up a store specializing in Esteve's products.

The square that defines this space was partially covered by a false ceiling, and the architects decided to open up not just the top, but also the sides of the entrance unit. They created a hard but elastic continuous surface, tensed against a wooden framework, running from the floor to the ceiling of the building. In this way, the store became completely separate from the rest of the factory, and the continuous, circular shape spreading out from the single entrance-exit stresses its self-contained nature. The surface of the concrete floor is dotted with encrusted colored buttons – a metaphor for the bustle and apparent disorder of the factory when it is fully operational.

W
Architects: Bailo + Rull ADP. Arquitectes Associats
Location: Barcelona, Spain
Photographs: Jordi Bernadó

The structure marking out the limits of the store is made of polycarbonate; its transparency offers glimpses of the factory and the activity within it.

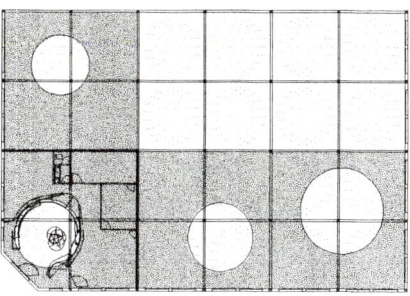

Ground plan of the entire premises.

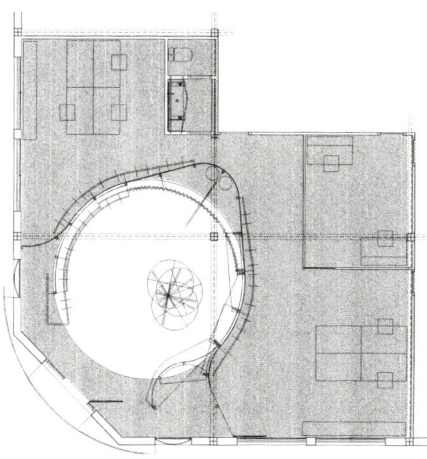

Ground plan of the store.

Round Store | Pep Zazurca i Codolà

Round Store is a clothes store in the basement of a protected building in Barcelona. It was in very bad condition, with cracks in the walls and improvised supports that had been added over the years to hold them up. The ceiling was supported by wood and metal beams. The space is 65 feet (20 m) long, with a width and height both of 15 feet (4.5 m).

Given the low budget available, it was decided to highlight some of the building's most distinctive features, such as the side walls, the ceiling, and the tube shape.

Zazurca installed a shelf unit made of sheets of glued wood shavings along the entire length of one side wall, from the floor to the ceiling. The top shelves are reached by a gangway with steps at both ends, to make the circulation more fluid and provide customers with the chance to peruse the store's entire stock by strolling in one direction below and doubling their tracks upstairs.

The shelves slope slightly to accommodate the irregularities of the wall behind it, thereby fortuitously providing more depth for storing the clothes. The changing rooms are at the far end of this wall, continuing the unbroken line of the shelves but masking its hidden depth. An illuminated rail set in the shelves creates not only a play of light but also a series of interesting perspectives.

The wall opposite the shelves is left unencumbered so it can be adorned with advertising for the various brands of clothing on sale in the store. The wall at the back is dominated by a large mirror, which makes the space seem much larger.

W

Architect: Pep Zazurca i Codolà
Location: Barcelona, Spain
Photographs: Eugeni Pons

The glass floor of the gangway seems like an inverted store window, displaying the clothes below.

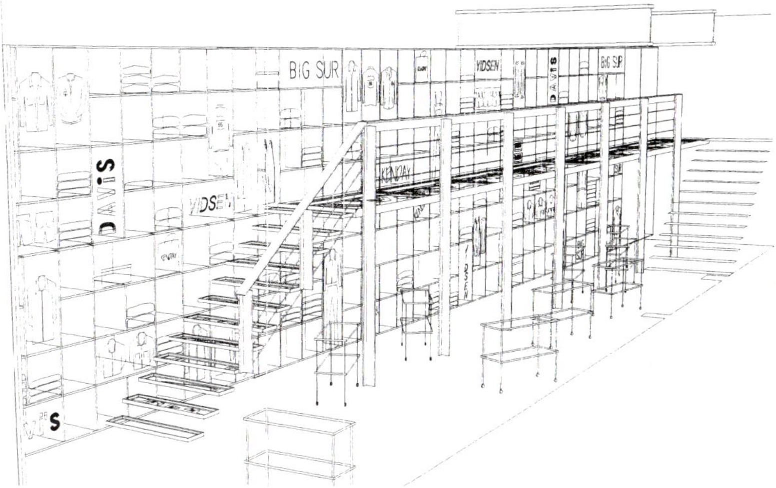

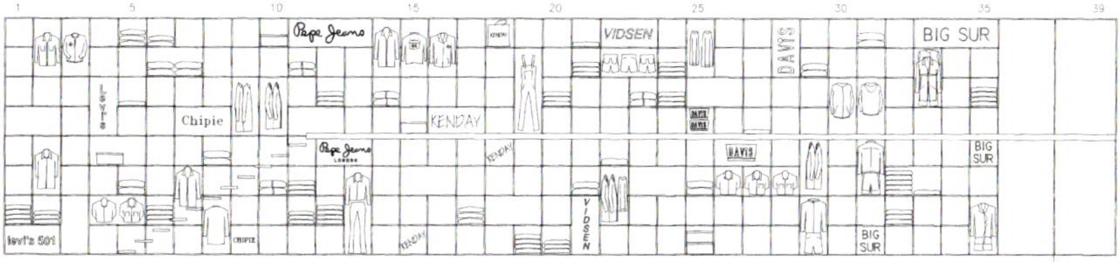

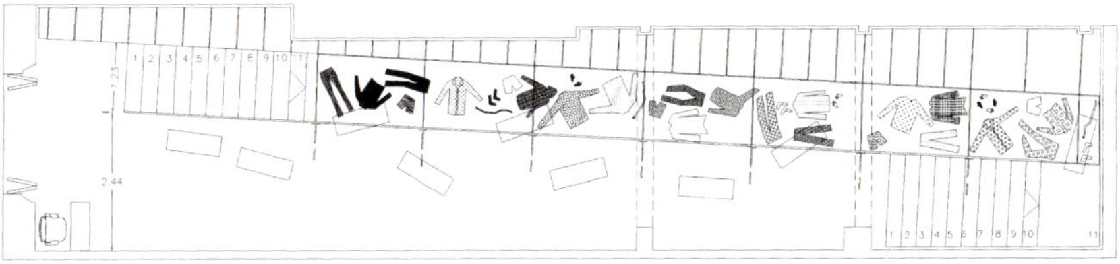

Joan Lao Mobiliario | Joan Lao

The sales point of Joan Lao's interior design company is situated in a huge space that once served as an automobile showroom. The premises follow a "U" shape, stretching from the exhibition area to the administration and sales section and then on to the design studio.

The first hall, containing a general display, is an open space completely covered by a wooden arch. Beyond this lies the sales department; the counter is integrated into the building's original structure, lodged in one of the pillars and supported by a series of wooden struts attached to a free-standing air-conditioning unit. Behind the sales area, the second exhibition space differs from the first in that only specific products are presented and the space is less open and flexible, with the dramatic architectural features coming into their own. The walls in this area are perforated by a row of openings, 8 feet (2.5 m) from the floor, each protected by a stainless-steel cylinder; these are designed to support any new cladding or possible additional structures.

The portico in the entrance marks the starting point of a compositional line leading to the shop, which will be repeated further on to instill in visitors the idea that they have crossed the threshold of a realm governed by a distinctive view of interior architecture, in which quality and professionalism are clearly the prime considerations.

Interior designer: Joan Lao
Location: Barcelona, Spain
Photographs: Joan Mundó

The rounded marble pebbles that cover the patio are extended into the interior to suggest an interaction between the two spaces.

The windows in the patio bear the same decorative motif as the portico marking the entrance from the street.

The steps of the staircase, covered with a layer of thin gravel, wind sinuously past the pillars.

The glass wall in the sales area extends up to the meeting room on the top floor, which is set apart by a wall clad with sheets of stone.

The vaults in the ceiling mark the rhythm of the beams of light.

Esprit | Citterio & Dwan

The Esprit loft in Antwerp is an example of hi-tech applied to interior design. The choice of this type of architectural language influenced the contrast that was set up between the exterior and interior. The building's external appearance is dominated by a regular, symmetrical brick façade, which bears absolutely no relationship to the array of glass and steel tubes within.

The basic structure of the interior is a maze of pillars and a kind of metal curtain masking the storage space. The total surface area amounts to 19,500 square feet (1,800 sq m), spread over several interconnected levels. The first floor contains the sales area, while the upper stories house the offices. These have been designed with the same materials as the rest of the interior: parquet floors and metal-framed structures that are both functional and futuristic. The difference between the offices and the sales area lies in the finishings: carpets and white walls in the former for greater comfort and luminosity, while the sales area is dominated by black, whose harshness is mitigated by the warmth of the sunlight that seeps through the large windows.

The originality of this project by Antonio Citterio and Terry Dwan is its use of technology, not just as a sop to modernity but as an artistic and symbolic language in its own right, perfectly expressing the public image that this company seeks to convey.

Architects: Citterio & Dwan
Location: Amberes, Belgium

863

Preu bo | Joan Lao

Joan Lao's design for Preu Bo created a light-filled space that brought out the timelessness and warmth of the original building and created a stunning showcase for clothes by the top names in fashion. The store covers two stories, each measuring 1,720 square feet (160 sq m). There is also a basement with offices and a storage area, which the conversion has linked to the front of the store by a staircase and service elevator. These create a large opening, some 23 feet (7 m) high, that provides glimpses of the activity below and transforms the spatial relationship between the two levels.

The store window regales potential customers with striking examples of the stock, with a clear view of the rest of the store receding into the distance behind. Those who cannot resist the temptation then enter via an oxidized-metal walkway that finishes with another display of clothes. One of the inside walls is lined with a series of long, continuous clothes rails, made of stainless-steel bars and with oxidized-iron supports topped by an *okume*-wood shelf for accessories. The floor is covered with typical Catalan paving stones.

The store is long and thin, although it widens at the back into an area dominated by three structural, wood-clad pillars; these mark out the changing rooms, the lounge, and the general display space. An elliptical mirror and three vertical lamps provide the finishing touches to this rear section.

Interior designer: Joan Lao
Location: Barcelona, Spain
Photographs: Eugeni Pons and Joan Mundó

One area has been set aside as a lounge, recalling the glamour of the sophisticated fashion houses of old.

The store's front and the metal staircase seem to merge into each other to create a single space in the entrance.

The conversion has retained the staircase going down into the back of the basement.

The floral decorations crowning the mirrors are an integral part of the store's design.

Becara

Emilio Tárraga + Pascua Ortega

The distinctive, luminous Becara furniture store, measuring 19,400 square feet (1,800 sq m) divided over two stories, was formerly a garage with a glass roof.

The owner and instigator of the conversion, Begoña Zunzunegui, collaborated closely on the new design with the architect and decorator.

Both levels of the store are open, with plenty of space to stroll about and examine everything on offer at leisure. Walkabouts are interrupted only by the various spaces that have been created: a charming greenhouse, a rest area where customers can have a coffee while they decide what color they want for the upholstery on their couch, a bookstore for consulting and purchasing publications imported from all over the world – not to mention the lounges, dining rooms, kitchens, and bedrooms assembled to demonstrate the Becara style.

The design in this wonderful setting has been considered down to the smallest detail: a warm pearl-gray color has been chosen for the walls to avoid distracting from the pieces on display; the floor alternates gray concrete, stripped teak, and rugs made of natural fibers.

Becara now designs and manufactures various ranges of furniture in both wrought iron and wood, as well as a host of decorative articles. It also sells reproductions of period furniture. The company has always managed to find innovative ways of presenting its collections and has established a position in the vanguard of European design.

Architects: Emilio Tárraga (architect) + Pascua Ortega (decorator)
Location: Madrid, Spain
Photographs: Pablo Zuloaga

La Farinera del Clot | Josie Abascal

La Farinera (flour mill) is an iron and adobe construction with ceramic decorations and Arabic-style roof tiles. It was built by the architect Josep Pericàs in the year 1898 in the *Modernista* style prevalent in Catalonia in that period. During the Spanish Civil War the building was used by the Generalitat (local government) of Catalonia; from 1942 it served as a warehouse for the wheat department of the Spanish Ministry of Agriculture; in 1970 it was again used for industrial purposes when it became a pasta factory. In 1991 it was closed down altogether, and only reopened after this conversion by Josie Abascal, which opened up new possibilities for this famous old factory by turning it into the Centre Cultural La Farinera del Clot, fully equipped to respond to the needs of the new millennium.

The building, with a total floor area of 28,400 square feet (2,635 sq m), is organized around a vertical communication nucleus on the southeast façade. This nucleus, running along a north-south axis, runs into the ground to permit access to all the stories, including the basement.

The various floors house a museum, an Internet café, a bar, an art gallery, meeting rooms, workshops, offices, a theater-lecture hall; the basement is devoted to the new information and communication technologies (Internet, multimedia, and music), as well as housing a local television and radio station. The Farinera has recovered its role as a factory, albeit of a very different kind – a factory of culture.

Architect: Josie Abascal
Location: Barcelona, Spain
Photographs: Zona 5. Boatella + Lloria

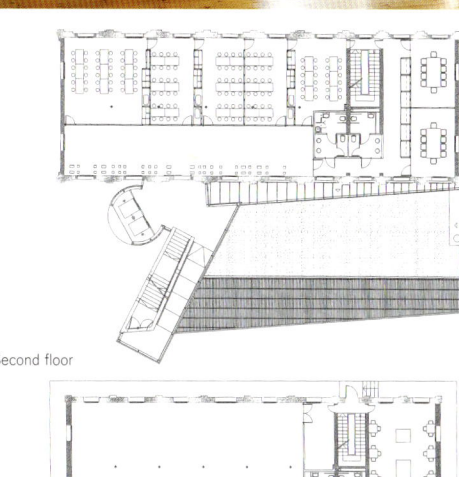

Second floor

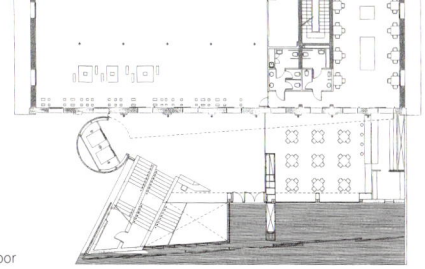

First floor

Cross-section

The interior has preserved some of the mill's original machinery, such as the mechanism for transporting flour and the pinewood ducts used to feed the various machines and mills.

The conversion has respected the building's original structure by refurbishing the most characteristic features and inserting transparent elements at the points where the old building meets the new additions.

ArtQuitect | Francesca Ricós Martí

In 1993 the ArtQuitect showroom was installed on the first floor of an early-20th-century building near the market of El Born in Barcelona. It had originally been used to store fruit and later became an art gallery. Now the existing structure has been adapted to another use: the exhibition and sale of domestic furnishings designed by renowned international architects.

The irregular floor space amounts to 2,800 square feet (260 sq m), spread over three levels and marked by the rhythm of the wrought-iron girders in the ceiling. Francesca Ricós left the wide open spaces largely unencumbered by putting display elements – made with sheets of perforated zinc and ash – against the walls; some of these hang directly from the walls, while others are free-standing, with industrial castors to make them more mobile.

The upper floor is a smaller area, measuring 775 square feet (72 sq m); it is divided by an exposed brick wall and dominated by a metal girder. This story, illuminated by halogen and fluorescent lighting, houses offices and a meeting room. The basement is used as a store.

Sunlight penetrates the façade through the windows set in the openings in the wall, which are a legacy of the original building.

Spatial continuity is guaranteed by the uniformity of the polished concrete floor and the plastic paint applied to the vaulted ceilings and the party walls. The intervention in this space has established a homogeneity that sets off the aesthetic qualities of the objects on display.

Interior designer: Francesca Ricós Martí
Location: Barcelona, Spain
Photographs: Eugeni Pons

The entrance is presided over by a fresco in a Neoclassical style, made with the sgraffito technique, that breaks with the overall color scheme.

White dominates all the surfaces, including the exposed brickwork of the walls.

889

In Mat. ArtQuitec | José Luis López Ibáñez

The ArtQuitec company, one of the foremost manufacturers of bathroom products, contributed to the annual Spring Design exhibitions when they were held in Barcelona in 1999. As the title ("Materials could never become objects without dreams") suggested, its show was intended to demonstrate that imagination is essential in all creative expression.

The 2,150-square-foot (200 sq m) space was located on the first floor of a building in Barcelona's old city. The irregular shape of the perimeter provided great spatial variety, although this was offset by the ever-present polished concrete floor, which helped unify all the different settings.

In the opening section, a jet-black screen served as a background for the white vinyl letters that form the title. Just in front of this stood the first of a series of translucent panels, made of polyester riveted to a light steel frame. The thin membrane of the panels provided the right degree of transparency for the creation of undefined shadows, enigmatic images, iridescent reflections – all powerful stimuli to the imagination.

To complement the running link of the panels, a group of four prismatic modules in the outer hall created mini-spaces that acted as settings for the company's new washbowls.

Discreet, highly controlled lighting, mounted on metal cables, and a repetitive soundtrack add to the evocative atmosphere, inviting visitors to dream with their eyes open.

Architect: José Luis López Ibáñez
Location: Barcelona, Spain
Photographs: Joan Mundó

The prismatic modules, which were designed to harmonize with the rest of the exhibition, measured 51 x 52 inches (1.3 x 1.33 m.). Their basic structure was of varnished steel and they were clad with polyester.

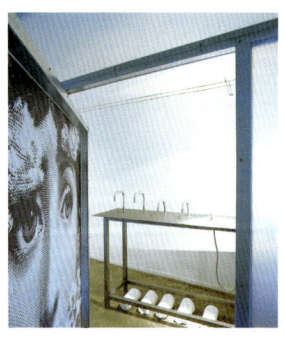

The graphic techniques used to create Fornasetti's enigmatic female faces helped to define the poetic atmosphere of the exhibition in visual terms.

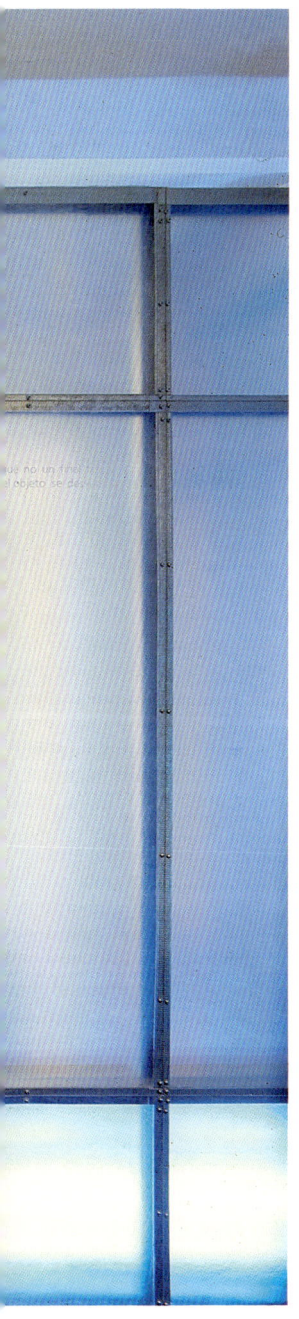

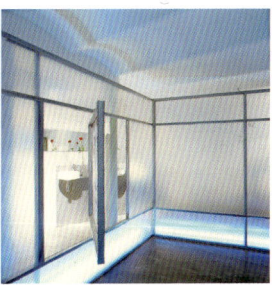

Light was the element that brought the show to life. A line of shaded neon lights was incorporated into the polyester panels to enhance the other-worldly effect.

Magna Pars | Luciano Maria Colombo

Magna Pars, on Milan's Via Tortona, is the multipurpose space that resulted from the complete overhaul of a 37,150-square-foot (3,450 sq m) building, formerly a cosmetics factory, and it bears all the hallmarks of the city's bourgeois architecture in the 1800s.

The conversion required a new functional restructuring, a revolutionary use of materials, and a definition of the main spaces of a building that was to be partially given over to offices but was also to serve as a venue for congresses. The central area, flanked by smaller spaces designed for a variety of activities, leads on to a restaurant near the smaller conference halls on the upper floors, which are reached by an elegant and practical gangway. The first floor contains halls for congresses and trade fairs.

The entire conversion is marked by the architect's respect for the original structure. The semi-covered spaces have been left unaltered and are now used for activities related to fashion, tourism, and advertising. Most of the settings in the building revolve around an interplay between transparent and opaque materials that establishes a series of fascinating and stimulating contrasts. The building's structural elements add unity to the new installations and largely determine their main characteristics.

The Radius hall is endowed with a mobile platform that can be installed to provide sloped seating for conferences, or removed to make room for exhibitions. All the halls are distinguished by equipment that enables them to be used in a variety of ways.

Architect: Luciano Maria Colombo
Location: Milan, Italy
Photographs: Matteo Piazza

Progetto Lodovico | Luciano Maria Colombo

Progetto Lodovico in Milan caters for people working in architecture, city planning, design, and communications; it serves them as both an operational center and a cultural reference point.

This initiative was the brainchild of young architects working under the guidance of Luciano Colombo; their conversion of one floor of the old Richard Ginori department store gave them the opportunity to revitalize a part of the city steeped in history and tradition.

The initial premise of the conversion was the expansion of the 32,250 square feet (3,000 sq m) originally exploited by taking in the adjoining areas, to create a usable space of 91,500 square feet (8,500 sq m). The laboratory is divided into workshops capable of receiving up to 80 professionals from all over Europe at any one time. Various installations provide a backup service: a conference room, two meeting halls, a legal department, administrative offices, and a secretariat. The whole setup is managed by a central governing body with its own public relations department.

The layout of Progetto Lodovico reflects the diversity of activities carried out in it, but, more than that, it also serves as a declaration of intent. The original structural elements enter into a dialogue with the imprints of the more recent interventions. The result is a neutral but flexible container with a precise formal and compositional identity. Progetto Lodovico is, above all else, a spur to collective reflection on potential new paths for architecture and city planning in Europe.

Architect: Luciano Maria Colombo
Location: Milan, Italy
Photographs: Matteo Piazza

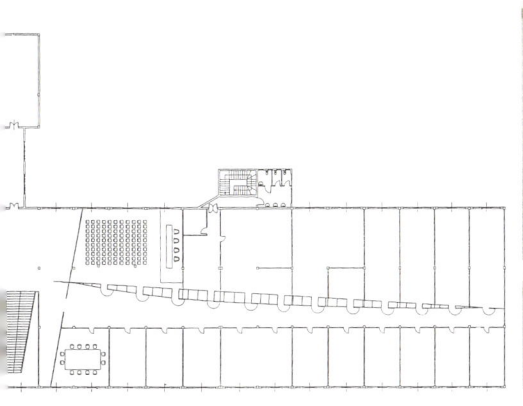

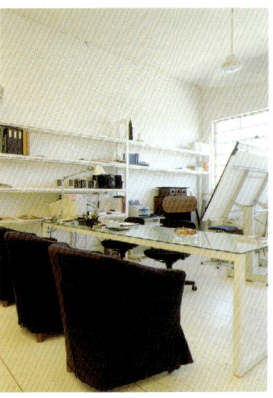

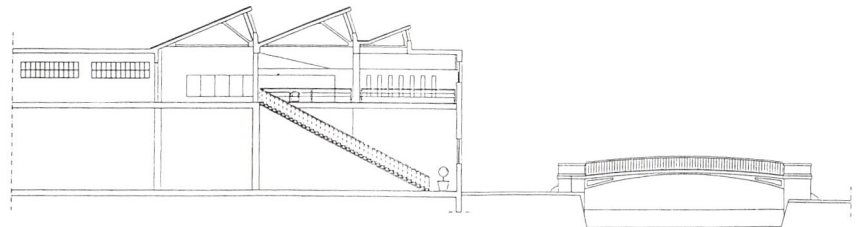
Cross-section

Nani Marquina showroom | Nani Marquina

The Nani Marquina company, founded in 1987, manufactures and distributes carpets for interior design; it has sought to project a strong commercial image by creating an instantly recognizable style.

The company's showroom is situated in an old industrial complex in the largely residential area of Gràcia in Barcelona; the building still has the typical layout of internal alleyways leading off a central courtyard. The complex comprises several buildings, interconnected by covered corridors and shared access points. It was once all used for industry but it has now been transformed into spacious premises for service companies or businesses involved in art and advertising. The façade is adorned with a fire escape and rows of large windows.

The conversion of this particular loft aimed to create an open space bathed in natural light, in the hope of providing a neutral background that shows off the designs and colors of the company's carpets to the best effect. For this reason, white was chosen for both the floor and the walls.

A transparent glass panel separates the office space from the showroom; this maintains the continuity of the space and sets up visual connections between the two areas. The constant presence of the company's carpets, on the walls and at a variety of angles on the floor, also unifies the space.

Carpets make their appearance in the office area too, but here the effect is more subdued and contemplative, in contrast to the exuberant showroom.

W
Interior designer: Nani Marquina
Location: Barcelona, Spain
Photographs: Jordi Miralles

1997 showcase | Estudi Metro

This space was created as a model for a home particularly suited to a photography buff. It was originally a factory but, despite its former industrial use, it is now a practical, comfortable (even luxurious) domestic space. The emphasis on photography is immediately apparent in the blowups of huge photos by William Klein and E. Gibson that preside over the bathroom and dressing room.

The effect of the sunlight pouring through the windows has been enhanced by the use of pale, neutral colors. Most of the artificial lighting is incandescent, with a few additional halogen lamps dotted about to create areas of greater intensity. More specific lighting is provided by auxiliary table lights and standard lamps.

The star of this show, however, is the furniture, which gives each different space a highly distinctive character – even though the pieces chosen all follow a common theme as regards the simplicity of line and the use of natural fibers. Wood is the dominant element: dyed and varnished DM for the tables, walnut-tinted cherry wood for the kitchen unit and tables in the dining room and office. A mirror has been fitted to the back of the dressing room to enlarge the space visually by providing new and surprising perspectives; it also adds warmth by bouncing off the reflections of the sunlight.

Interior designers: Estudi Metro
Location: Barcelona, Spain
Photographs: Zona 5. Boadella + Lloria

The furniture marks out the limits of each space just as effectively as the screens finished with stucco and mirrors.

1996 showcase | Francesc Rifé & Associats

The exhibition *Casa Decor '96* was put on in an old industrial building in the center of Barcelona to display independent modules intended as prototypes for different living spaces.

Francesc Rifé, the interior designer, presented a module of an experimental home. He created a split-level loft in a rectangular, 600-square-foot (56 sq m) area with a height of 16 feet (5.4 m.), in which the usable space is exploited to the maximum. It has openings along both sides of the structural perimeter to allow the penetration of sunlight.

The project revolves around the bathroom, which connects with all the other spaces. The bathtub is in the middle of the central block; the shower is to the rear, and the restroom is separated off by a sliding door. The injected-glass washbowl is placed directly under the opening in the ceiling.

A staircase integrated into the module provides access to the bedroom on the top level, complete with its own reading area. The kitchen acts as a continuation of the central module, as well as hiding the electrical and water installations. The stove is set in a huge block of granite that also serves as a dining table.

The audiovisual relaxation area is furnished with armchairs to take advantage of the empty space near the staircase.

The lighting and the color scheme play a vital role in highlighting the central block; this is clad with a pale-colored wood that contrasts with the dark tones of the outer walls and ceiling, which are little more than a backdrop to set off this ingenious showcase.

Interior designer: Francesc Rifé & Associats
Location: Barcelona, Spain
Photographs: Zona 5. Jaume Boadella. Toni Lloria

There is a circular window in the floor to provide a visual connection between the upper level and the bathroom.

The extractor is suspended from the upper structure to serve the electric cooker. A double-height glass panel set in one of the screens provides the finishing touch to this area.

The module is flanked by the kitchen-dining room and the small lounge area.

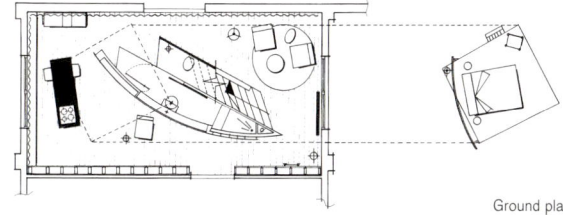

Ground plan

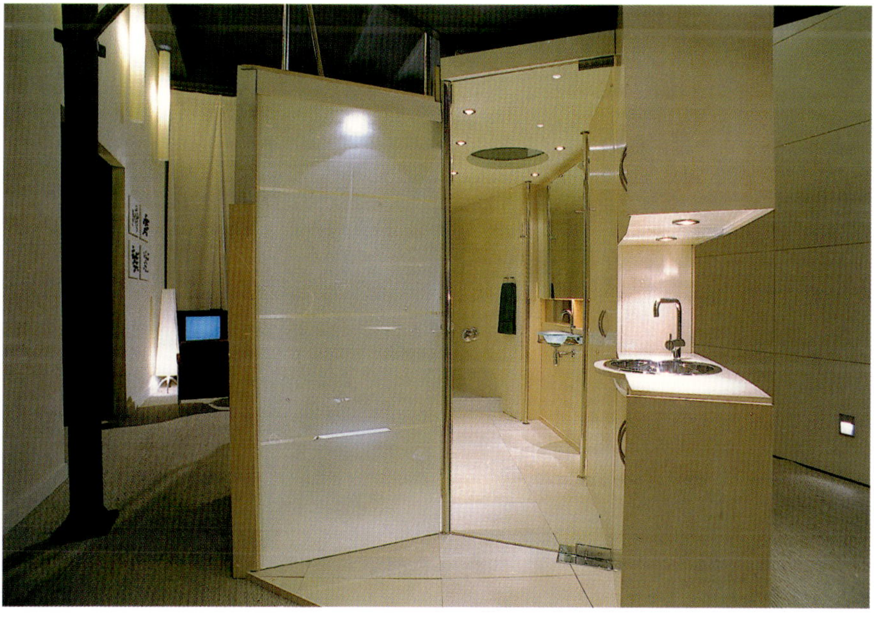

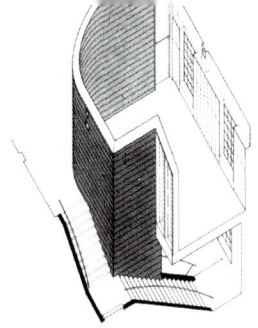

Two Italian showrooms | King-Miranda Associati

The Rossa building was constructed from brick at the beginning of the 20th century. For years it served as a factory, but it now houses some of the facilities of the company Aplicacioni SRL, which makes partitions for Palo Alto offices. The main building has two stories, and a lower, more recent extension; the total floor space amounts to 10,750 square feet (1,000 sq m).

The company's brief demanded three clearly defined areas: offices, a showroom, and storage space. The architects decided to put the store on the first floor, next to the service areas and the offices and showroom above.

The second project, for the manufacturers of air-conditioning equipment Olimpia Splendid SpA, required not only a showroom, but also the main entrance for the offices, the reception, and three meeting rooms, involving a total space of 2,045 square feet (190 sq m).

Here, the irregular form of the perimeter was determined by the fan-shaped roof: the beams incorporate a series of circular lamps and spotlights. These beams are painted blue, as are the walls, window frames, and baseboards; while the slightly sloping false ceiling is painted white to emphasize the play of lights and reflections.

Architects: King-Miranda Associati
Location: Treviso, Italy
Photographs: Andrea Zanzi

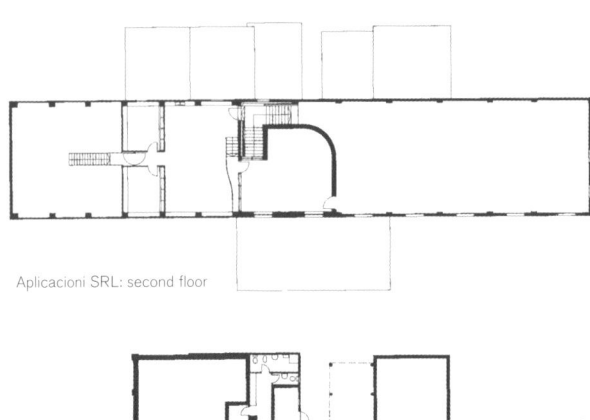

Aplicacioni SRL: second floor

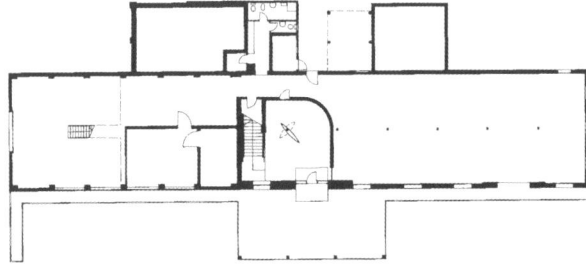

Aplicacioni SRL: first floor

A canopy separates the entrance from the parking lot. The reception area marks the boundary between the new and old buildings. The staircase, the walls, a pillar clad with steel and tin, and even the artificial lighting are all conceived as sculptural elements in their own right.

The offices in the extension are reached via the landing on the staircase; there are more stairs leading up to the second floor of the main building. There, the rough bronze finish of the curved wall in the reception area marks off the president's office. The rest of the floor is an open space used to mount exhibitions. The entire top floor is covered by a dark carpet specially designed for this project by King and Miranda.

A counter in one of the corners of the space in front of the entrance marks off the reception area. The rest of the space is used for exhibitions; these can be freely adapted, according to the needs of a particular season or the launching of new products.

General axonometric perspective of the Olimpia Splendid showroom.

P.S.1 Museum

Frederick Fisher, David Ross, Joseph Coriaty

The career of Frederick Fisher is closely linked to the world of art. Even before he started working as an architect, he had studied art in Oberlin College in Ohio and worked as an intern in the Metropolitan Museum of Art in New York, an experience that sets him apart from most architects. Much of his work has involved the conversion of pre-existing buildings – warehouses and abandoned factories – into spaces devoted to art.

Such is the case with the P.S.1 Museum, which for many years has been considered one of the flagships of the "found space" movement. This proposes radical new ways to exhibit art, by taking it out of the predetermined settings of traditional museums and stuffy institutions and bringing it back into the community.

This old school, situated in an industrial area near Queen's district in New York, offers 84,000 square feet (7,800 sq m) of floor space, with a huge variety of exhibition settings, including outdoor courtyards. The first decision was to transfer the entrance to the "U" shape at the back of the building, which has been transformed by erecting concrete walls. These enclose spaces designed to exhibit art in the open air. The central tower in the courtyard now provides the point of access, thereby focusing special attention on the imposing staircase in front.

The second floor contains the famous classroom galleries, which preserve the tradition of the P.S.1 as an alternative exhibition space. Other innovations include the artists in residence – who live and work in the museum – educational rooms, and spaces specially designed for the publications team.

W Architects: Frederick Fisher, David Ross, Joseph Coriaty
Location: New York, United States
Photographs: Michael Moran

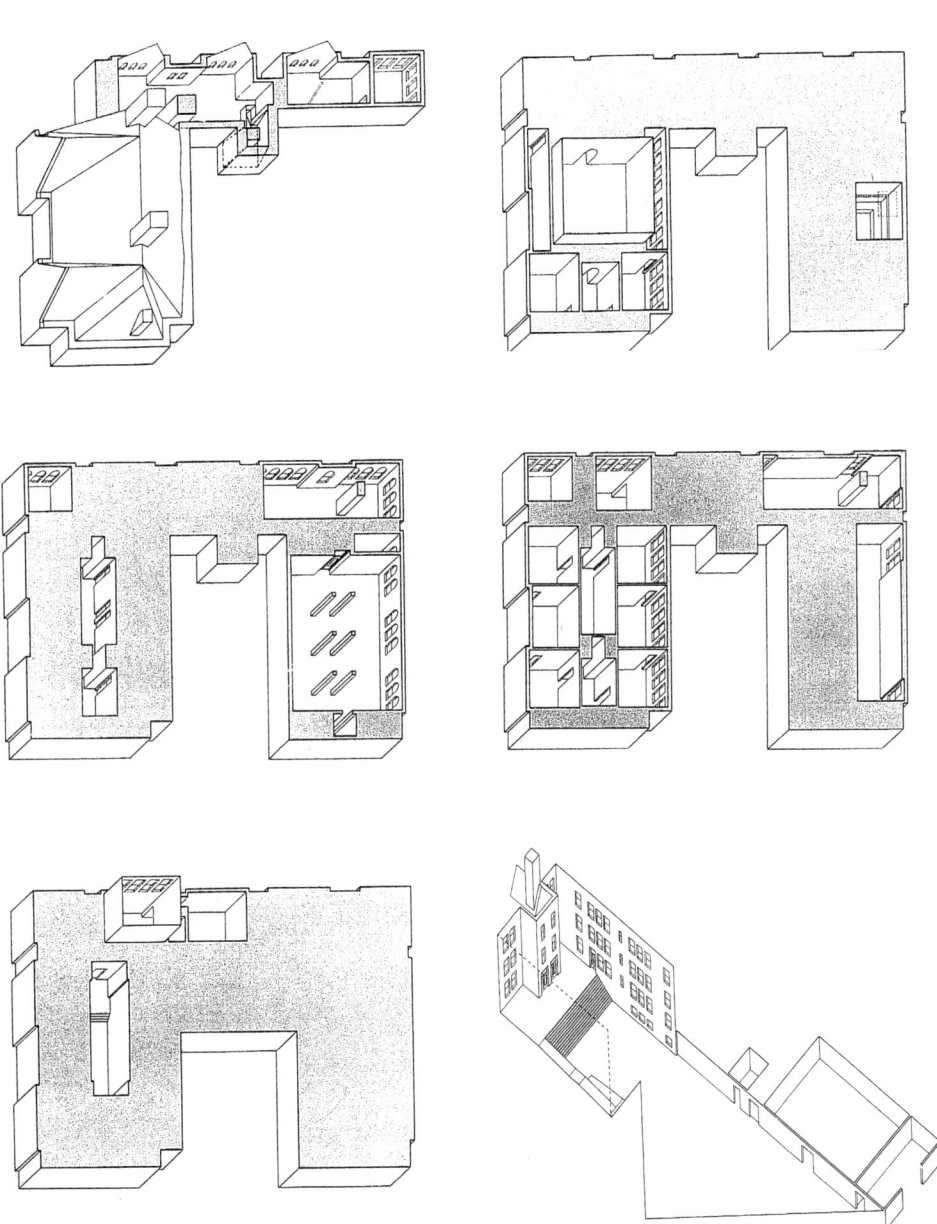

Dromokart | Florencia Costa Architecture

Dromokart is situated in a former industrial area near the Naviglio Pavese canal in Milan. The building, measuring 65,000 square feet (6,000 sq m), was formerly used to make wrought-iron propellers for boats but it has now been transformed into an ingenious, high-quality go-kart rink.

The project of the architect Florencia Costa's involved the creation of a circuit for the go-karts, along with meeting areas, a medical department, and a bar and restaurant with views of the track. The circuit is designed to cater for both the leisure activities of casual visitors and the training requirements of professional drivers.

The go-karts run on electric batteries that enable them to reach speeds of up to 45 miles (70 km) per hour. The building may have a long industrial history but its new installations belong squarely to the present. The tracks are computerized and there is no accumulation of smoke or toxic gases inside the building as the vehicles do not use any fuel. Moreover, undesirable noise is minimized by the use of absorbent rubber on the floor, reducing the friction of the tires on the track.

"The ecological approach to go-karting and the silence accompanying such speed inspired this dreamlike conception of space. The industrial setting helped me to imagine a neutral box with hardly any visible joins that could accentuate its repetition and rigor. Unlike other installations of this type, Dromokart has no colors, allowing natural light to be the main player on the stage. The same is true of the other special effects." states Florencia Costa.

Architects: Florencia Costa Architecture
Location: Milan, Italy
Photographs: Pino Guidolotti

MIGLIOR TEMPO
DEL MESE
CONCORRENTE KART TEMPO
CONCORRENTE KART TEMPO

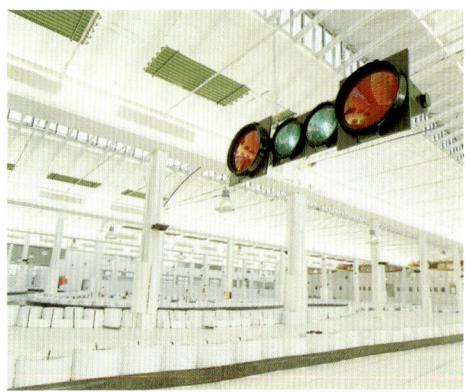

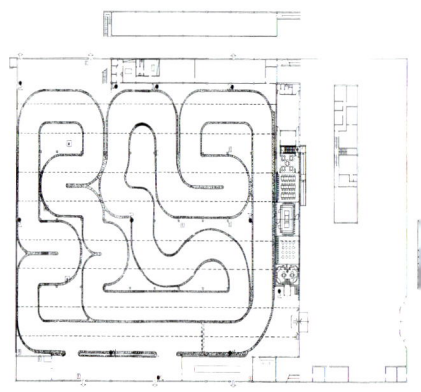

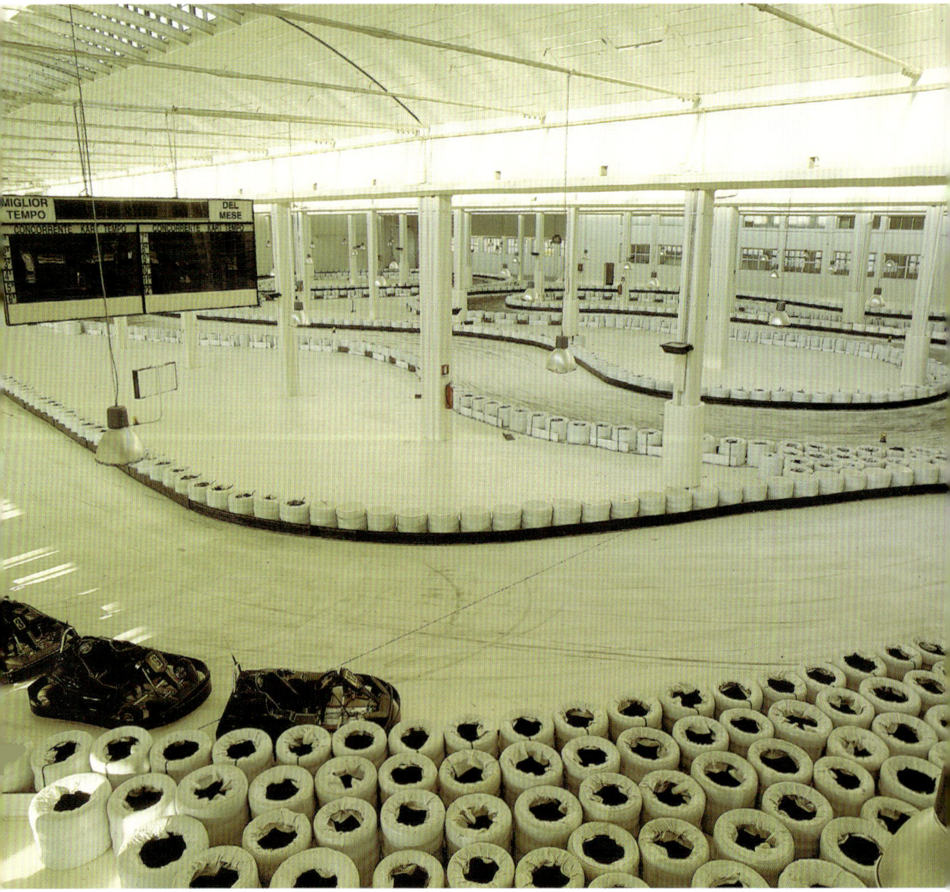

The main unit in the kitchen is clad with Carrara marble 2 inches (5 cm.) thick, while the counters in the bar and the hood over the stove are both made of birch wood.

The 46-foot-high (14 m) bar contrasts with the lower, more intimate space in the restaurant, which is only 11 feet (3.5 m) high.

The bar and restaurant area are dominated by the enormous hood over the kitchen, which supports the two symmetrical bar counters.

Talls Tallats

Eugeni Boldú, Orlando González

These premises in Barcelona's Sants neighborhood were originally a workshop producing copper pots and pans. They now house a hairdresser's/cafeteria, an example of the kind of single-setting commercial mixture that is forging a new conception of leisure activities.

The architects had only a small trapezoidal area to play with, and this had to remain open to keep the two separate operations side by side. The same consideration led them to treat the walls, floor, and ceiling in the same way throughout, thereby unifying the two spaces even further. No major building work was required, as it was decided to retain the floor tiles, leave the mesh of beams on view, and keep the cladding on two of the walls. The layout was primarily determined by the geometry of the space, which is longer than it is wide; the cafeteria was put in the front, while the hairdresser's was set up in the most private area, away from the street. Similarly, the entrance and the restroom mark a longitudinal access to one side of the two main areas.

The owners, Maite Calvo and Maria Àngels Pol, have added personal touches by juxtaposing original decorative elements with the equipment required to carry out their everyday activities in the cafeteria and hairdresser's. The Pop Art atmosphere springs from the desire to make every piece of furniture complementary to the setting and its owners.

Architects: Eugeni Boldú, Orlando González
Location: Barcelona, Spain
Photographs: Zona 5. Boadella + Lloria

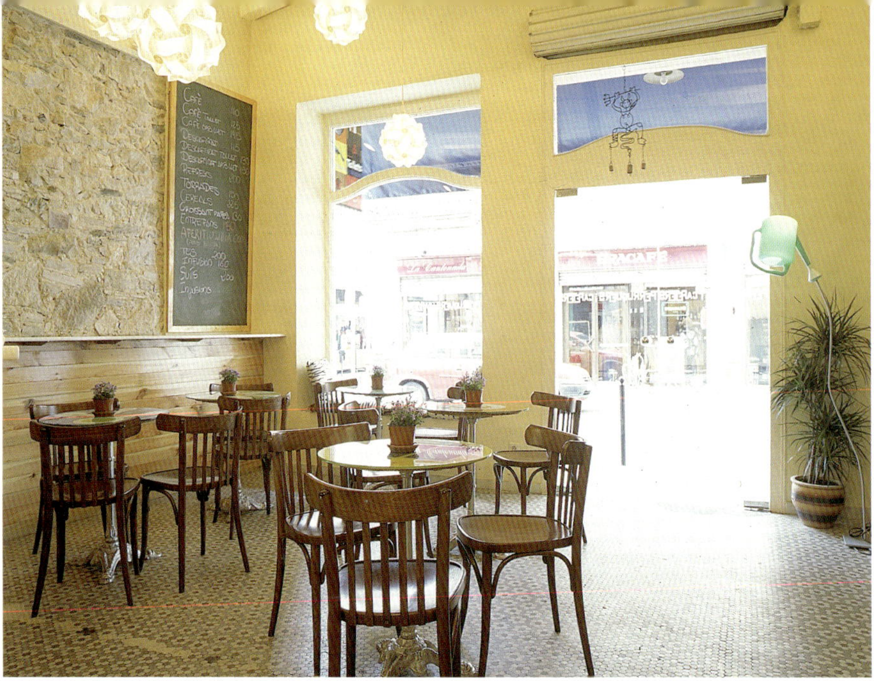
Cafè
Torrades
Entrepans
Tes 200

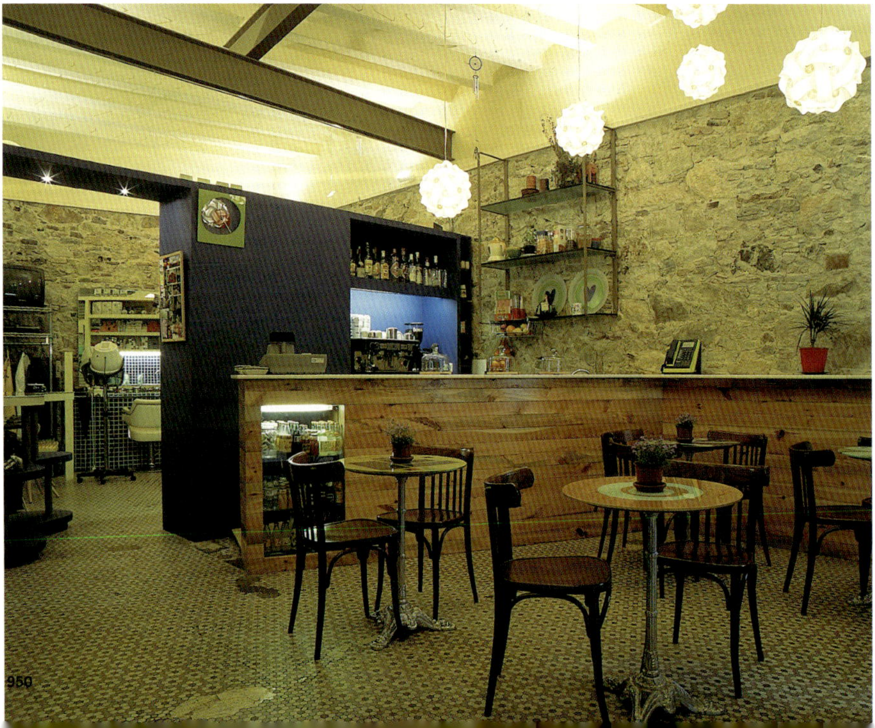

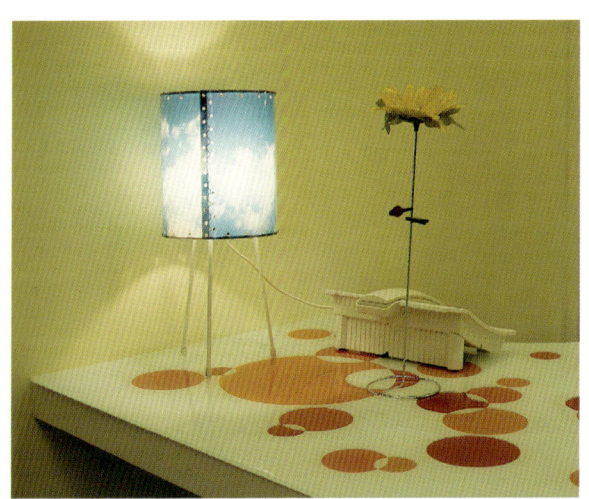

In the hairdresser's, the ameba-shaped counter, bookshelves, and wood stains were all custom-made to the owners' requirements.

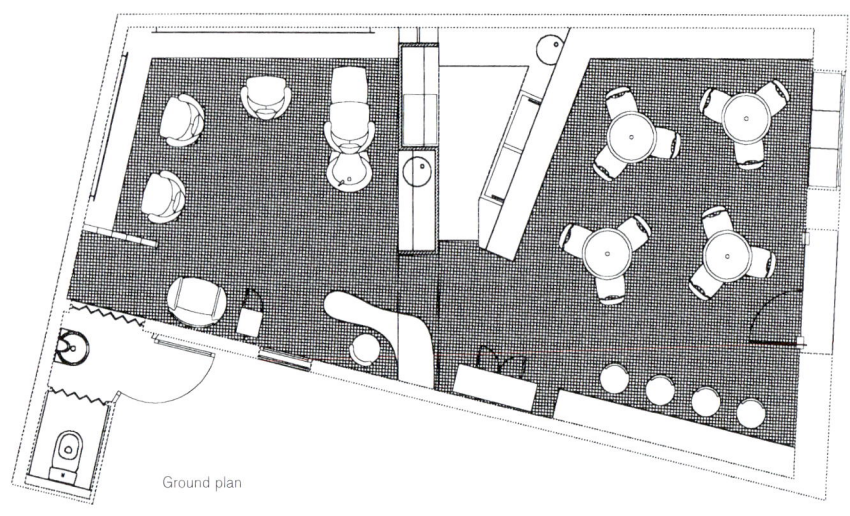

Ground plan

Bar Zoom | Pau Disseny Associats

The creation of this bar on the famous Spanish Costa Brava required the overhaul and decoration of a basement area that once served as a kitchen. The 10-foot-high (3 m) rectangular area, measuring 62 x 31 feet (19 x 9.5 m), is crossed by a row of four columns embedded in cubes 3 feet (1 m) high.

These cubes were the result of structural necessities; as the old building was in poor condition, the pillars were reinforced, and the work was disguised by surrounding them with large boxes made of rustic Galician pinewood sheets.

Soundproofing requirements created the need for two consecutive entrance doors, and the intermediary space in the hall was treated as a box replete with openings that allow newcomers to assess what is happening in the bar and soak up its atmosphere even before entering. The bar is strategically placed to avoid any architectural obstacles, like the cube elements, or any variations in the floor level. Behind it, a grid of shelves serves as a frame for the translucent parchment that acts as a screen for psychedelic images, which are distorted by the refraction of the liquor bottles on the shelves. The floor is covered with a layer of black-painted, polished concrete.

Interior designers: Pau Disseny Associats
Location: Lloret de Mar, Spain
Photographs: Eugeni Pons

The bar is fitted out with a mesh of lights made up of 475 low-energy bulbs and a couch that reproduces the charming shoreline of Lloret's beaches.

Ground plan

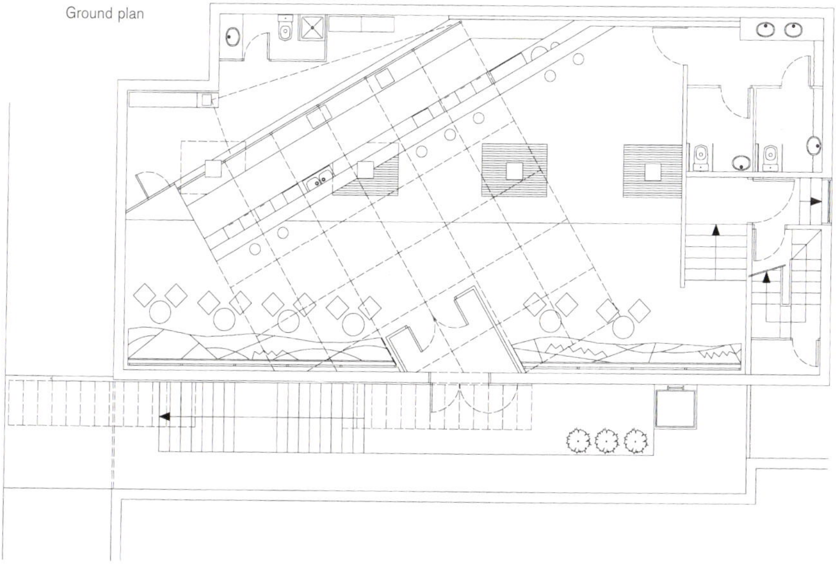

The cabin at the entrance to the bar offers glimpses of the space within through the incisions in its panels.

The lights behind the couch are shaded with glass and an added sheet of parchment. The fake-fur upholstered couch, which is the focal point of the whole bar, re-creates the beaches of Lloret with a combination of colored patches.

Club Caboool | Lorens Holm, Ray Simon

Paul Guzzardo is the owner of the Club Caboool, as well as the driving force behind its entry into cyberspace and the main collaborator of the architects responsible for the club's interior decoration. The project involved the conversion of part of an old shoe factory, dating from 1917, into a nightclub. The removal of extraneous building work from the main façade revealed two deteriorated twin arches, which the architects decided to restore and preserve. The front of the building was clad with concrete – a material that had already been used in a previous conversion.

The first story is a deep space divided by five columns along its central axis. The concrete floor slopes gently down toward the street. Three architectural elements have been added to the interior: a glass wall with metal frames parallel to the façade; a metal wall that winds through the pillars; and a huge mirror angled toward the entrance, the visual depth of its reflection seeming to recover the dead space of the bathroom hidden behind it.

An adaptable seating area lies opposite the main area; at the back there is a small stage and sound system, which can be isolated from the rest by closing the large drapes. There is also a video booth. The bar runs along one side and behind it a staircase leads to the privacy of the apartment on the first floor (see page 266).

The main aim of the conversion was to take advantage of the pre-existing forms and materials and respect the history of the building, rather than attempting to disguise it.

W

Architects: Lorens Holm, Ray Simon
Location: St. Louis, Missouri, United States
Photographs: Hedrich Blessing

Club Cabool has its own website, and the images from the eight video cameras are broadcast live on the Internet.

The monitors, mixed by a video-jockey, broadcast musical images with others found on the Internet, to reflect the confluence of the real and virtual worlds inside the club.

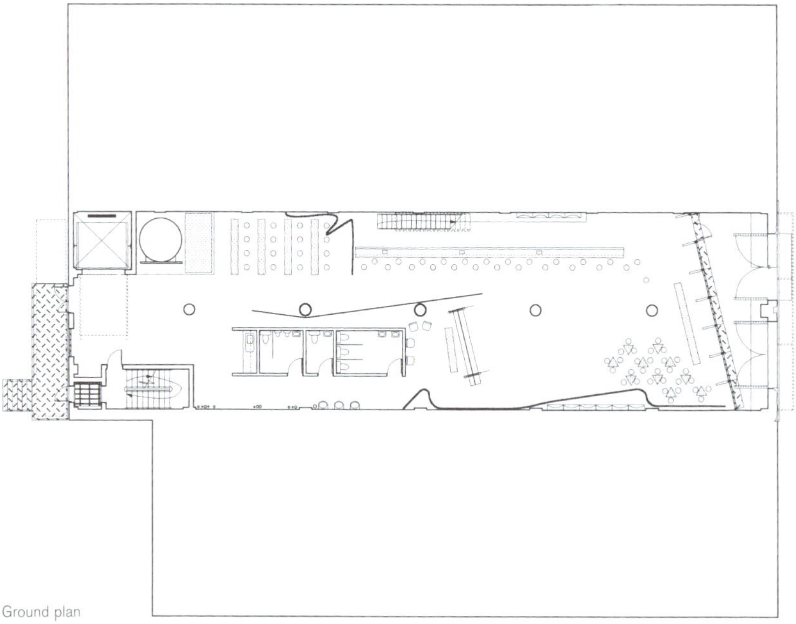

Ground plan

Taxim Nightpark | Branson Coates

The Taxim Nightpark in Istanbul sprung from a desire to transform an old factory into a multi-space leisure center similar to ones in Western Europe, Japan, and the United States. The idea was to create a modern complex with an elegant restaurant, a big discothèque, and various bars and dance floors, in an attempt to bring the latest trends in nightlife to the city.

The team formed by the British architects Nigel Coates and Doug Branson was confronted with an unequivocally industrial environment, comprising a long, thin entrance area that opens out onto a much wider space with very high ceilings.

The connecting elements, such as the gangway linking the restaurant to the discothèque, become symbolic reference points, like other idioms used by Branson and Coates, such as the aeronautical imagery and the repeated allusions to Turkish decorative traditions.

The two outstanding features of the double-height entrance hall are the metal gangway with glass sides that links the long, thin space with the main area, and a big vertical painting by Mark Prizeman. A complicated network of staircases connects the different levels. The restaurant is situated to the right of the entrance hall, which is conceived as an upmarket version of the local bazaars, with, it is claimed, the longest leather couch and the biggest bead curtain in the world. The stunningly lit bar space is designed to evoke a runway; Turkish Airlines has donated some pieces to enhance the effect, such as the freight containers, which have been recycled as video control booths.

Architects: Branson Coates
Location: Istanbul, Turkey
Photographs: Valerie Bennet

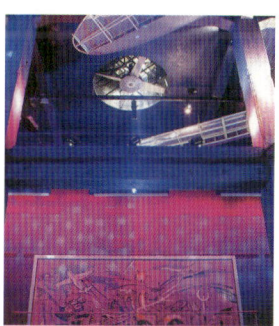

The creation of this night-time funfair drew on a masterly combination of local traditions and state-of-the-art design, all within a setting marked by a degree of physical deterioration.

Paci Restaurant

Roger Ferris + Partners Llc.

In its glory days, the American railroad system gave rise to some impressive buildings in important destinations like Washington, Philadelphia, and New York. The train stations tried to outdo each other in terms of opulence, and even modest ones indulged in a meticulous concern for decorative detail. When the railroad system was reformed, many of these buildings were left to waste. This old station in Southport, Connecticut, has been used for a variety of purposes, and it has undergone several transformations over the last 40 years.

The team of architects made up of Roger Ferris and his collaborator Robert Parisot considered that the building could become a focal point for the city once again if its architectural qualities were emphasized and if it were given a suitable function, such as that of a restaurant. The first task was to strip away any extraneous elements that had been added over the years; this process revealed an interesting wooden structure supporting the roof, which had to be reinforced. The brick perimeter walls were left exposed. A container made of maplewood panels was set in the interior, like a wagon robbed from an old train. This unit contains a bar and toilets, with a dining area on top.

Another eye-catching feature is the kitchen, installed behind a hanging screen that serves as a wall. The independence of this screen with respect to its surroundings is emphasized by projecting a big clock face onto it – a witty touch that recalls the charm of the station clocks of yesteryear.

W **Architects:** Roger Ferris + Partners Llc.
Location: Southport, Connecticut, United States
Photographs: Michael Moran

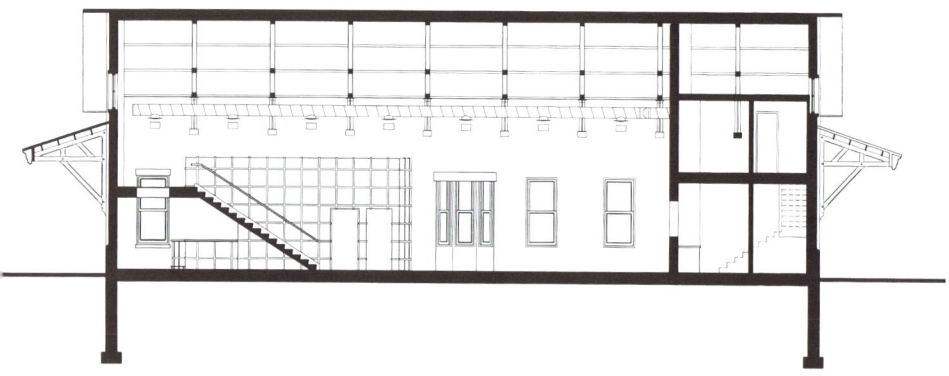

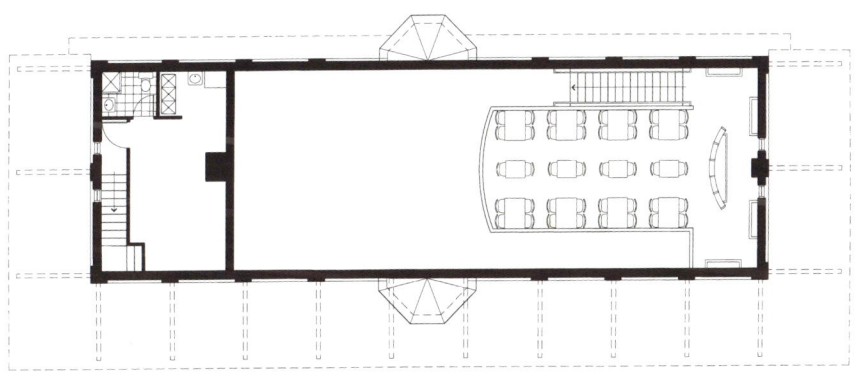
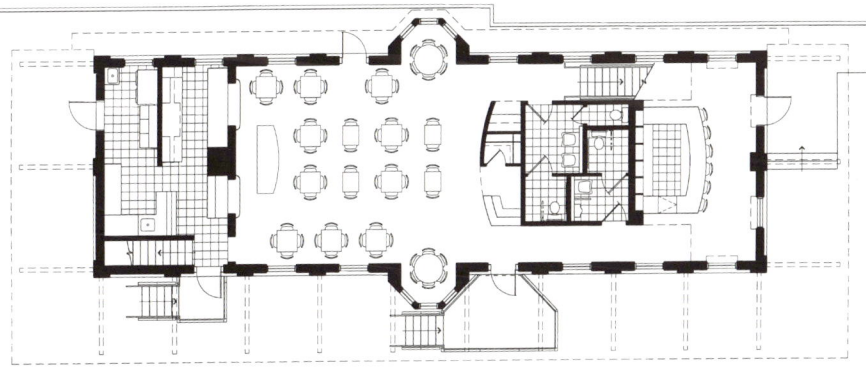

Restaurante Porto Colom

B&B Estudio de arquitectura

This old warehouse overlooking the sea in Porto Colom, on the island of Mallorca, provided the perfect raw material for a restaurant and bar. Furthermore, it offers some wonderful views, which can now be enjoyed from the adjacent terrace.

Architecturally speaking, the building has characteristics typical of the island – walls made of ashlar and wooden beams supported by iron summers – and the conversion sought to preserve all of these. It also respected the simple lines of the original façade and the interior layout. The first floor contains the kitchen area and a dining room; this offers typical local dishes, more expensive and substantial than the snacks available on the terrace. A more intimate space has been set apart from the dining room to allow for the bathrooms.

The interior decoration creates an environment that is both welcoming and highly sophisticated; the dominant elements – wood and leather – have been chosen for the warmth they bring to the setting. The lighting scheme has also been planned with meticulous care; it couples soft overhead lights with small, low lamps fixed to the walls at strategic points near the tables.

W
Architects: B&B Estudio de arquitectura
Location: Mallorca, Spain
Photographs: Pere Planells

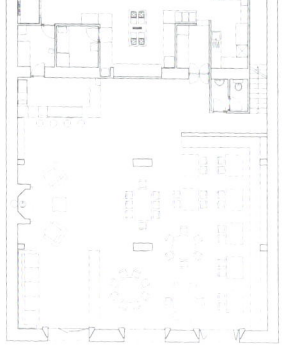

Ground plan

The atmosphere created in this space
has made it an ideal setting for
exhibitions of small paintings.

Restaurante Thèatron | Philippe Starck

The Restaurante Thèatron in the National Theatre in Mexico City is more than a place to eat, it is a stage set in its own right. Its customers do not go there just to have a drink or a meal, but to revel in its extravagant theatricality, like players on its stage. The Thèatron is the brainchild of the French designer Philippe Starck, who worked closely with the local architect Baltasar Vez to bring it to life.

The setting seeks the complicity of its audience. The various spaces abound in humorous contrasts – it is the muse of comedy that is being celebrated here. The entrance comprises an absurdly monumental staircase, leading directly onto a dark, thin corridor. One room is lit by an old-fashioned standard lamp, the next by a bare light bulb hanging from the ceiling on a cable. The restaurant itself seems to be submerged in mist, with ethereal white drapes winding through it, hanging from the ceiling down to the height of the chairs.

The enormous entrance hall, measuring over 3,000 square feet (300 sq m), is organized around three decorative elements: a huge blowup of a photo by Richard Avedon, around 30 feet (9 m) high and 20 feet (6 m) wide; a big staircase; and a gray velvet stage curtain with scarlet silk lining, over 40 feet (12 m) high and 50 feet (15 m) wide.

Starck's designs draw in the restaurant's guests, making them actors in a show and unleashing their imaginations.

Architect: Philippe Starck
Location: Mexico City, Mexico
Photographs: Alfredo Jacob Vilalta

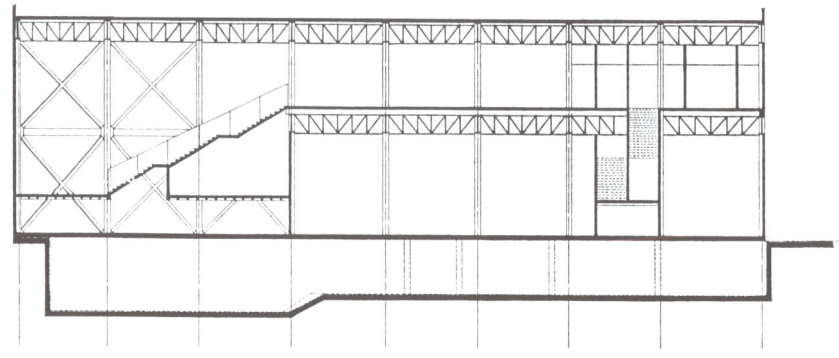

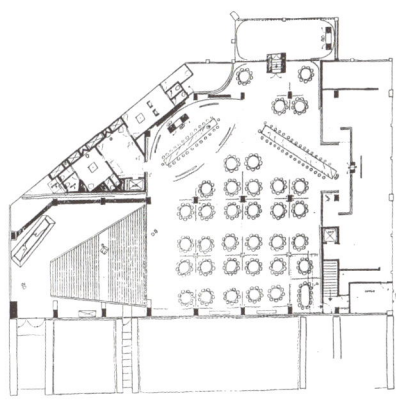
Ground plan of the restaurant.

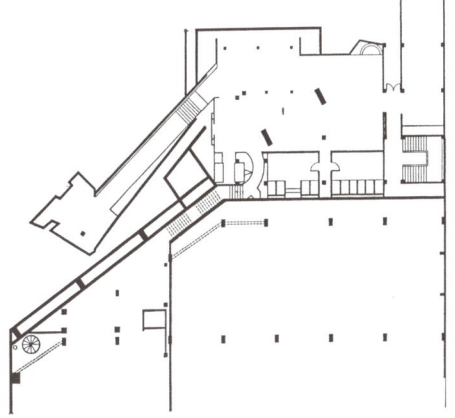
Ground plan of the basement.

The Thèatron is divided into three basic spaces: the hall, the restaurant, and the bar. The restaurant has seating for 280 diners, while the bar can hold 250 people. Most of the furniture is designed by Starck himself, although it is combined with period furniture and standard lamps over 8 feet (2.5 m) high.

The lighting in the pool room consists of a light bulb hanging from a cable. Starck's designs look for a dramatic effect, and to do this a simple light bulb can serve just as well as a standard lamp. In many cases the effect is achieved through distortion or caricature. The restrooms, for example, are exaggeratedly narrow and high; they are only 3 feet (0.9 m) wide and 5 feet (1.5 m) deep, but they are 12 feet (3.5 m) high. The walls are clad with riveted metal sheets.

Belgo Centraal | Ron Arad, Alison Brooks

The work of Ron Arad is characterized by his constant search for the hidden beauty of a space and the dignity of mundane reality.

The Belgian restaurant concept that was pioneered in the Chalk Farm Belgo Noord in north London was extended to this former warehouse in the West End, this time with three added functions of offices, a beer store, and a sidewalk café.

The experience begins on the street. The kitchen – where everything is cooked by steaming – is open to view through the 21-foot-high (6 m) windows of the façade. There are two entrances to the restaurant, connected by a pedestrian walkway sheltered from the bustling streets outside.

The resolution of the restaurant's roof is particularly striking. The basic structure is a sloping sheet of glass, supported, and partially obscured, by a series of molded panels. Other similarly eye-catching features are the outer walls, painted bright red up to the height of the entrance; the specially designed chairs and tables; the steel accessories that recur throughout the space; and the unusual shapes of the decorative elements. All these bear witness to Ron Arad's cheeky, provocative style.

This project is typical of Arad's work as it springs from his distinctive view of the creative process, which abhors all stereotypical trends whilst always operating on the cutting edge of modern design. Arad flies above conventions; his use of new forms of expression to search for beauty is coupled with an uncommon elegance.

Architects: Ron Arad, Alison Brooks
Location: London, United Kingdom
Photographs: F. Busam/Architekturphoto

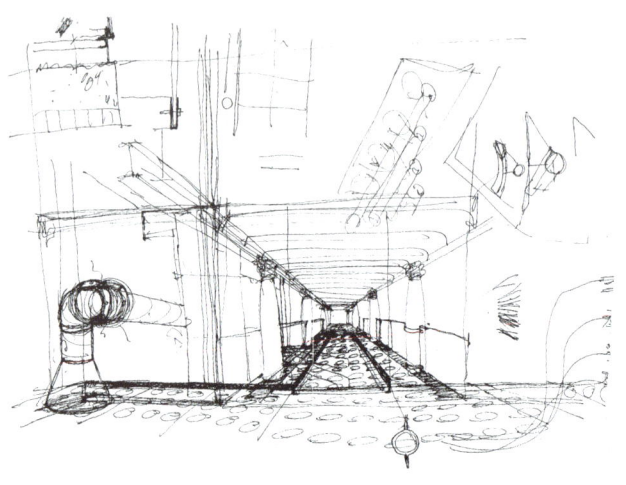

It was decided to introduce daylight through the ceiling, while respecting the original curved shapes of the roof.

The treated-glass window has a full view of the kitchen counter, 70 feet (22 m) long, and the enormous reserves of plates and pans. The way to the two dining rooms is indicated by the beam of light on the floor.

Belgo Zuid | FOA. Foreign Office Architects

Belgo is an international restaurant chain that serves typical Belgian food – mussels, fries, and beer – and exploits Belgian idiosyncrasies as a marketing device. The brief for the architects of the FOA team, Farshid Moussavi and Alejandro Zaera, was to revitalize the architectural surroundings of this new branch, although the furnishings had to conform to the standard models used in all the company's restaurants.

Belgo Zuid is located in an old dance theater in the Notting Hill Gate neighborhood of London. The underlying strategy of the conversion consisted of playing with all the elements by exploiting both the building's layout and its formal and structural qualities, as well as indulging in a taste for *kitsch*.

The original building was in such a parlous state that much of it had to be demolished to fulfill the requirements of its new function. Both the walls and the roof of the main dining area were rebuilt; they were clad with sheets of stainless steel on the outside, while on the inside they are lined with oak boards.

The building's façade is only 10 feet (3 m) wide, but it does have four stories. A 40-foot-high (12 m) rotating sign looms over the entrance; this opens onto a corridor 10 feet (3 m) wide and 65 feet (20 m) long that leads onto the surprisingly spacious restaurant area.

Architects: FOA. Foreign Office Architects
Location: London, United Kingdom
Photographs: Valerie Bennett